ARAB INDUSTRIALISATION AND ECONOMIC INTEGRATION

EDITED BY ROBERTO ALIBONI

ST. MARTIN'S PRESS NEW YORK

For information write:
St. Martin's Press Inc., 175 Fifth Avenue, New York, N.Y. 10010
Printed in Great Britain
Library of Congress Catalog Card Number: 78–10632
ISBN 0–312–04702–9
First published in the United States of America in 1979

Library of Congress Cataloging in Publication Data

Main entry under title:
Arab industrialization and economic integration.

Includes index.
CONTENTS: Hershlag, Z.T. Industrialisation in Arab countries. – Makdisi, S.A. Arab economic co-operation. – Bouhdiba, A. Arab migrations.
1. Arab countries – Industries. 2. Arab countries – Economic integration. 3. Labor mobility – Arab countries. I. Aliboni, Roberto. II. Hershlag, Zvi Yehuda. Industrialisation in Arab countries. 1979. III. Makdisi, Samir A. Arab economic co-operation. 1979. IV. Bouhdiba, Abdelwahab. Arab migrations. 1979.
HC498.A714 1979 330.9'17'4927 78–10632
ISBN 0–312–04702–9

CONTENTS

Preface 9

1. Industrialisation in Arab Countries: Patterns, Options and Strategies *Z.Y. Hershlag* 13

2. Arab Economic Co-operation *Samir A. Makdisi* 90

3. Arab Migrations *Abdelwahab Bouhdiba* 134

Notes on Contributors 189

Index 191

PREFACE

This book is a result of a research project on 'Development and Stability in the Mediterranean' which the Istituto Affari Internazionali started in December 1973. It follows an earlier work which I edited in the same series: *L'Industrializzazione del Mediterranea: movimenti di manodopera e capitali.* The book will thus conclude the examination of the economic questions which it was decided to investigate during the project.

In the earlier volume an important dynamic factor in the industrialisation of the less developed countries in the Mediterranean was taken into account, namely the relationship between Western direct investment and migratory flows from the south to the north of the area. In this volume, the contributors examine three different aspects of an equally important factor – inter-Arab co-operation. The three studies which it comprises were independently commissioned by the IAI from the scholars concerned. Their inclusion together in one volume was decided upon by the IAI in accordance with the overall conception of its research programme in this area. Their publication in one volume does not therefore, reflect joint research or team work as in the earlier volume where the research was organised directly within the Institute.

Although this second book, like the first, deals with international questions, these are examined at a regional level; the analysis is concentrated in the Arab world; less emphasis is given to the Southern European countries. The reason for this is that in the years between the beginning and the conclusion of the project, the changes which occurred in Southern Europe rendered the area's role far more complicated than it had been a few years earlier. Portugal, Spain and Greece's applications to become members of the EEC made it necessary to research these questions in greater detail. The IAI thus decided to do this in a separate research project, specifically centred around Southern Europe and Southern European relations with the EEC. This work, which is still in progress, is being carried out in collaboration with the Centre for Contemporary European Studies at the University of Sussex.

As we stated in the introduction to the earlier volume, this decision does not mean that the Institute considers external factors to be more important than internal ones in industrialisation. It is evident that internal accumulation, the mobilisation of national resources and the economic policies adopted by individual countries play a determining role in the process. What it does mean is that faced with the need to make a choice, we have decided to concentrate on certain external factors, just as we decided to examine industrial rather than agricultural problems, despite the fact that the latter are no less important than the former in determining development. When we made this choice we were guided by the impression that, in comparison with detailed studies of endogenous factors affecting development, there had been fewer analyses of international and regional factors. The preference given to industrialisation was due to the political and economic importance which this is given by the countries concerned, as Professor Hershlag pointed out at the beginning of his study, as well as to the urgency with which they seem to be approaching the problem (which is obliging the industrialised countries to restructure their economies and to reopen the discussion over the management of the international economy, a theme which has always interested the Institute).

Given all this, what are the main questions which the book examines? In the first contribution, Professor Zvi Y. Hershlag, Director of the David Horowitz Institute for the Study of Developing Countries at Tel Aviv University has analysed the industrial strategies, sectorial options, economic policies and attempts at harmonisation and co-operation of the Arab countries. He thus supplies a detailed picture of their convergences and divergences, their potential, the difficulties they face, their successes and their mistakes. His paper emphasises how certain sectorial and technical options are likely to be unsuccessful without the opening of a wider market than those at present available.

In the second contribution, Professor Samir Makdisi, Chairman of the Economics Department at the American University in Beirut, analyses a key element in any conceivable industrialisation process, namely co-operation and economic integration. He pays special attention to trade in manufactures and prospects for the future in this field, which he considers of vital importance if there is to be a positive interreaction between economic growth and integration. His paper underscores the importance of co-ordinating economic policies if economic integration is to be sustained and considers some implications to the world economy from closer Arab economic co-operation.

In the third contribution, Professor Abdelwahab Boudhiba, who teaches sociology at Tunis University and is Director of the CERES

(Centre d'Etudes et de Recherches Economiques et Sociales) examines Arab labour flows. This is an extremely important question and one which poses significant problems for the development of the Arab countries. These suffer from serious imbalances in factor distribution. Potentially countries with differing factor endowments could prove to be complementary. In practice, however, there are many forces hindering this, from the slowness with which potential host countries have proceeded in transforming their financial resources into fixed capital, to the political obstacles which have been placed in the way of immigration by foreign workers. It is well known, for example, that the criteria used by Saudi Arabia to balance inflows of different nationalities, encourage immigration by Pakistanis and Koreans and limit opportunities for Arabs. Boudhiba gives a picture, on the one hand, of Arab emigration towards Europe and, on the other, of inter-Arab migration (which is of especial interest as a practically unexplored field). He then tries to identify the relationship between the two flows and their general significance for Arab development prospects.

Roberto Aliboni
Istituto Affari Internazionali
Rome

1 INDUSTRIALISATION IN ARAB COUNTRIES: PATTERNS, OPTIONS AND STRATEGIES

Z.Y. Hershlag

Introduction

The Arab countries present a wide and diversified spectrum, both geographically and economically, apart from political, institutional and social aspects. They are not synonymous with the standard concept of the Middle East, in which a number of important economies are non-Arab; while on the other hand a substantial number of Arab countries are part of the African continent. Also the concept of Mediterranean does not apply exactly to this case, in view of countries such as Iraq, Sudan or the Arab Peninsula.

Consequently, the concept of industrial scenarios, in the positive as well as in the normative sense, significantly differs in its contents and targets, for instance, in the (oil) 'haves' versus the 'have-nots'; or, in the Arab 'confrontation (largely poor) countries' (Egypt, Syria and Jordan), with poor resources but burdened with an immense defence load and opting for a war-oriented industry, versus the rest of the Arab countries, many of them actually or potentially rich, with a much freer choice of options, though not necessarily leading to modern, efficient industrialisation.

These dichotomies give rise to different scenarios, not only with regard to internal industrial development, but also to intra-regional relationships – an interaction of unequals – and to extra-regional association with non-Mediterranean industrial economies, and regional economic groupings and communities.

In this context, wishful thinking must not be confused with realistic extrapolated trends and feasible targets, envisaging available human and capital factor endowments, complementarity and competitiveness within and outside the region, as well as considerations of static and dynamic comparative advantages and economies of scale, which come to the fore in different scenarios of integration.

This study will discuss the overall regional and individual national industrial structures and activities; analyse prevailing and potential industrial trends, and set the stage for the investigation of optional concepts and strategies of industrialisation and integration, with due attention to national targets, on the one hand, and comparative advantage, economies of scale and international economic relations, on the other hand.

The very definition of industry presents a number of substantive and statistical problems. Industrialisation, either as an aim in itself or as a major strategic variable in overall development, is explicitly related to the Clark-Kuznets model of growth through transition from primary low-level to secondary high-level processing sectors. Occasionally, mining activities, though primary by definition, are included in industrial output and employment. However, in the pre-processing stage, mining, as well as agriculture, constitutes the backbone of primary production and exports, and consequently, of the overall primary structure of the national product and employment. At its relatively low productivity level and without the aggregate values-added derived in various stages of processing, it therefore perpetuates low-level stagnation, non-industrial structure, long-term adverse terms of trade (if the disputed Prebisch model is accepted) and semi-colonial dependence of underdeveloped countries on industrialised countries.[1]

In developing countries, a negative correlation was found between the share and growth of extractive industries, and the level and growth of per capita income. In any case, a growth of the mining sector is not a sufficient stimulus and cause of the development of manufacturing industry, and it may even deepen the primary structure of the economy. A too rapid increase in extractive ('destructible' or 'exhaustible') industries may lead to a prospective lack of opportunities in ten to twenty years' time.

With some hesitation, we shall adopt here the three-sectors classification and include in industry only processing and manufacturing in the widest sense, which covers *inter alia* the industrial processing of agricultural and of mineral raw materials, but excludes the primary commodities themselves. One of the hardly surmountable difficulties lies in the deficiencies of statistics, which, apart from overall shortcomings, often refer to industry as including mining as well, while sometimes excluding agricultural processed commodities (then to be found among the agricultural data). Whenever possible, this statistical confusing procedure will be eliminated or, if unavoidable, at least indicated.

The Philosophy and Strategy of Industrialisation – General

A close examination of past industrial history and performance shows that even during the 'indigenous' industrial revolutions in England,

Germany, France and the United States of America, imported technology, skills and capital significantly contributed to domestic industrialisation. Political, fiscal and other measures were employed to accelerate and protect the process of industrialisation, with theoretical and empirical justification largely supplied by Friedrich List, as early as 130 years ago.

Recently, in less developed countries, including some in the Middle East, the aftermath of the First World War, and then the Second World War, again placed industry in the focus of accelerated planned development, designed to increase living standards rapidly and reduce dependence on domestic primary output, on the one hand, and on developed industrialised powers, on the other. However, while poor and retarded physical and human domestic infrastructure have contradicted fundamental conditions of industrial development, the industrialisation requirements and the availability of international capital, technology and know-how, well over and above those offered to the industrialising West two hundred years ago, have prompted an invitation of foreign entrepreneurship and resources and new forms of domination, *inter alia,* by multinational companies. The rather unsuccessful encounter between the hesitant external commitments and the fragile indigenous socio-economic structure resulted in a great deal of frustration and gave rise to second thoughts on the relative strategic importance of industry and agriculture, at least in the short run. The issue was amplified and complicated by international fluctuations in commodity prices, an upsurge in oil prices, the growing pressure of population growth and a menacing food shortage.

Under the inspiration of the emerging concept of new international order, the revival of industry-oriented development is no more viewed as a universal panacea for all ills of the less developed countries (LDCs), but rather as part and parcel of the new trend of self-reliance, cohesion and integration, combined with growing pressures on the North (and partly on OPEC) for more assistance, concessional funds and more international equity through commodities price stabilisation, buffer stocks of food and other produce, and easier marketing conditions.

Since the early days of modern economic theory, industry has appeared, under different names and definitions, as the leading sector in the growth process. From Smith's 'roundabout methods of production', through List's north-south differentiations in climatic conditions, factor endowments and economic potentials, Schumpeter's 'innovation' and entrepreneurship, and Myrdal's, Rostow's and Hirschman's linkages and spread-effects – the present concept of industrialisation largely came round to Rosenstein-Rodan's view of industry as a major strategy for both development *and* greater equality of income distribution. The equality-oriented concept of industrialisation has two aspects – a domestic one and an international one, both fraught with dangers of contradictions and dichotomies.

Internally, while industrialisation is expected to increase the aggregate value-added, and attract and employ the surplus rural labour, it can also widen the income inequality gap between the modern industrial sector and the traditional agricultural sector.[2] Moreover, a real danger arises that capital-intensive industry, largely favoured in developing economies and competing with traditional labour-intensive manufacture, may even reduce industrial employment – a Myrdalian 'backwash effect' – thus exposing open and disguised rural and urban employment to an even greater shortage of employment opportunities.[3] Even where industrial employment did increase, it grew less rapidly than urban labour supply, due to capital-intensive methods as well as to under-utilisation of capacity.[4]

It is the contention of some, mainly Marxist economists, that the poor performance of manufacture in LDCs per head of *total* population, should be attributed to the foreign-induced, capital-intensive industrialisation, which does not permit labour absorption to keep pace with the dynamic growth of the industrial sector. Consequently, while nations as such *are* developing, the majority of people are not, and inequality is growing.[5]

Combined agricultural-industrial development efforts and planning, focusing on labour-intensive agro-industry on the one hand, and on a growing domestic market and effective demand resulting from a more efficient and higher-income agriculture on the other, are expected to avoid the dangers referred to. Still, the menace of unequal growth poles is real.

The international aspect of the dichotomy is largely reflected in the 'centre-periphery' concept of Raoul Prebisch, pointing to the LDCs' disadvantage in international trade, with industrial economies at the 'centre' and primary producing economies at the 'periphery'. The LDCs' disadvantage results from their adverse terms of trade and limitations in exports in general, as well as in restraints in investment, modern services and modern mentality and attitudes. Accelerated industrialisation of primary economies is expected gradually to bridge over the centre-periphery gap and thus reduce international inequality. This approach is strengthened by some more optimistic concepts of growth poles, such as that of François Perroux, indicating that urban industrial growth poles, or centres, are bound to diffuse development to the periphery.

This optimism has not been borne out, so far at least, by international economic realities. The LDCs' share in world manufacturing and world trade has still remained very poor. If confronted with the industrial Western developed area of OECD, total imports of manufactured goods from *all* LDCs constituted in 1975 only 7.4 per cent of OECD's imports, while Japan and USA supplied 18 per cent each, United Kingdom 8 per cent, West Germany 7.8 per cent, and France 5.7 per cent.[6]

The concept of 'industry-first strategy' derives from the assumption, partly *ex ante* and partly *ex post,* that modern industry is able to raise per capita income, accumulate capital resources for investment, and improve the balance of payments (either by import-substitution, or by export-drive, or by both) at a much more rapid rate than any other strategy.[7]

This assumption also believes in the competitiveness of LDCs' industrial exports due to lower production costs, and frequently Hong Kong and Singapore are quoted as cases in point. This latter assumption implies labour-intensive industrialisation, with labour relatively cheap under surplus conditions. Thus increase in output is to be accompanied by an increase in employment.

In principle, industrial strategies, as economic strategies at large, are designed to maximise and reap the benefits of international specialisation resulting from comparative advantages. However, the strategies of less developed countries, in the words of the RIO report, 'in formulating their industrialization policies will, with due consideration to differences in factor endowment and stages of development, need to give priority to the creation of employment and to the production of goods required to satisfy basic human needs, the processing of local raw materials and the expansion of exports of manufactured goods'.[8] Both models, that of comparative advantage and specialisation and that of RIO, are heavily interfered with and even adversely affected by hectic international business fluctuations, e.g. the upsurge in oil prices and instability of commodity prices, recession in demand in developed markets, monetary upheavals in inflationary spirals. Furthermore, comparative advantage, economies of scale and optimal size of production units – are all bound to a definite prevailing technology. A different technology may radically change the parameters of these concepts and influence the patterns of industrialisation, employment opportunities, trade creation and diversion, competitiveness, integration and liberalisation.

However, even in developed countries it proves difficult to dismantle or readjust ensconced technologies, and Great Britain became for a time a deplorable case in point. The LDCs' rigidities are much less liable to be overcome and streamlined by market forces alone. The control of the market mechanism, which became indispensable also in industrialised economies, seems to be imperative within the framework of, preferably, indicative planning. At the same time, disregard for the market mechanism, at the domestic and even more on the international level, can be fatal, particularly for an industrialising economy, which may easily fall prey to the trap of 'almighty' planning and control. Careful and unbiased collection of basic and relevant data, study of their significance and interrelationship, examination of the power and limitations of international market forces, scrutiny of the industrial linkages inside industry and with other sectors, and adaptation of technology to the prevailing domestic production factors, consumption patterns and feasible export prospects – possibly with the aid of adequate domestic R & D – belong to the fundamental requirements of reasonable industrial planning. The latter's efficient and flexible execution is decisively dependent on the quality, integrity and competence of the government and its agencies, a major development issue *per se* in the LDCs.

Long-term targets of a developing economy, notwithstanding numberless collisions of differing views and models, will nearly always remain: population growth control, increase in per capita income through modernisation of agriculture, industry and services, efficient management and greater domestic and international equality. A relatively recent addition is the quality of life, in the north as well as in the south, implying a healthier environment even at the expense of rapid technological and economic progress, and particularly industrialisation. The now plausibly pictured image of the year 2000 assumes various, sometimes diametrically opposed, apocalyptic Orwellian (adapted from 1984 to 2000), or optimistic Kahnian dimensions.

The real work starts with short-term targets and planning, which have to measure up to real situations, obstacles and needs; their success or failure can be checked, with the effect of early warning but also of early frustration. The attempts to translate long-term into short-term programming usually lead to the stages-approach. With regard to industrial development, Hoffman suggests four historical stages, in the *first* of which, schematically, the output of consumer goods is five times larger than the net output of capital and production goods, while in the fourth stage the latter output is five times greater than the output of consumer goods.[9] Empirically, this scheme seems on the whole to suit historical industrial patterns, although with changes in consumption patterns following higher living standards and greater demand for durable consumer goods the scenarios may be different, as a result of either an autonomous process or central guidance of the economy. In particular the latter is able to change the sequence of stages, e.g. in socialist and some developing countries with – let us put it again schematically – an interchange between the second and the fourth stage, following a politically predetermined stress on an earlier development of the capital goods sector.

The whole issue of industrial structure and the aligned industrial strategy must be viewed in dynamic terms and against a background of empirical experience. For instance, technical progress rendered possible larger yields of energy, iron and steel from less raw material. Consequently, in the developed industrial countries, manufacture increased more rapidly than extractive industries – 6 per cent versus 2.7 per cent on an annual average – in the period 1958-60 till 1968-70. In the developing countries just the opposite occurred with unfavourable structural consequences.[10] This differential growth was also reflected in changes in labour productivity in manufacturing industry, which in the period 1955-70 grew annually by 6 per cent in Communist developed countries, 4 per cent in Western developed countries and 3 per cent in the LDCs.[11]

The growing demand for oil and other raw materials (despite their progressively more efficient and economical utilisation) on the international market for refining and processing, as well as permanently improving transportation facilities, sped up the output of extractive industries in the less developed countries. Table 1.1 presents Bairoch's changes in non-Communist LDCs.[12] Although mineral output experienced many fluctuations, its long-term growth is evident, even if outstripped by the increase in the fuel index.

The recent 'openness' and liberalisation in some LDCs do attract more foreign investment, although there are divergent opinions on the causal relationship of industrialisation and liberalisation, with strong indications that the second follows the first, rather than the other way round. In addition, concern is expressed by some observers that industrial sectors in LDCs are increasingly controlled by foreign firms and multinationals, with production and sales exceeding those of national industries, leading to resulting income-effects favourable to foreign investors rather than to the host countries.[13]

Table 1.1 Index of Output in Extractive Industries of Non-Communist LDCs (1963 = 100)

Period	Fuel	Minerals	Total
1900	0.9	9.1	1.8
1913	3.3	17.9	4.8
1936–8	12.4	37.8	15.1
1958–60	69.8	79.3	70.8
1968–70	173.0	128.0	162.3

This leads to the issue of global industrial division of labour, via production and trade channels. The rather widely accepted Heckscher-Ohlin theory attributes the trade effect, by comparative advantage, to the relative factor proportions; or, in Tinbergen's wording, each country should and will have the industries 'requiring the same factor mix as the country is endowed with'.[14] Manufactured exports increase more easily and rapidly as a result of a 'more rapid growth of capital and human skills relative to unskilled labour'.[15] However, with regard to the international division of labour – not only from the trade aspect – these cannot serve as the only criteria. Also other factor endowments and considerations deeply affect industrial options and strategies, such as satisfaction of basic needs of the majority, considerations of energy and raw materials, environmental constraints, and adjustments with other economies, in particular with industrial countries, to avoid as far as possible, clashes, adverse effects and damage.

In the process of international re-division of labour, a transfer of technology, or sometimes of a whole industry, takes place from the 'innovation country' elsewhere, due to the attraction of low wages, a main reason for R. Vernon's product cycle theory.[16] But low wages are not necessarily identical with low costs;[17] according to Johnson,[18] other factors may affect competitiveness, labour division and international trade, e.g. low capital costs or access to a large protected market for the product. Moreover, the opening of Western Europe for labour from some LDCs has also detracted investors from the readiness to invest in the countries of immigrant labour's origin (although recently, political and economic issues have prompted a reversal in this attitude). This (except, in principle rather than in fact, for the oil *nouveaux riches* on account of abundant capital) lends support to the thesis that industrial investments are attracted mainly to already developed areas, where adequate infrastructure offers better prospects of efficiency and profits. Consequently, the rich become richer and the poor poorer.

In passing to industrial options and strategies, a number of popular alternatives need be examined. Countries facing development targets, policies and planning are almost automatically confronted with three sets of alternatives:

a. Industrial versus agricultural development;
b. Capital-intensive versus labour-intensive investment strategies;
c. Import-substitutes versus export-oriented policies.

These alternatives may also be referred to as the differential options or scenarios in the developmental process. The very term 'alternatives' implies free policy choices, while both theoretical assumptions and empirical evidence restrict the degree of freedom of planners and policy-makers in selecting preferable scenarios and targets. A seemingly easy answer of 'balanced' strategies – even though plausible in view of undesirable imbalances and disequilibria in the development processes – is hardly applicable under conditions of scarcity and asymmetry of prevailing factor endowments in the LDCs on the one hand, and of socio-political requirements and targets on the other hand.

Although the three sets of alternatives mentioned are interlocked, largely via the comparative-advantage effect, a few specific comments can be made on each one.

a. Decisions on an industrial versus agricultural development strategy depend on the factor endowment, on the one hand, and on the expected income results on the other. Both – similar to the other alternative of capital- versus labour-intensity – are tied to the comparative-advantage principle. The latter, as already mentioned, should be dealt with on a flexible, dynamic basis. In the short run at least, the factor endowments in developing countries – land, raw materials, manpower and skills – point to a desirable preference for agriculture (or primary production) rather than for modern industry. Even the expected income (and income equality) results are in favour of agricultural development, promising quicker returns to a majority of manpower and population. Preference, if accorded to industry, involves not only priorities in capital investments, but also more comprehensive priorities in location, education and training, social amenities, etc., which may adversely influence agriculture, infrastructure and welfare of the majority of population.

However, in the longer run, and according to the experience of industrialised economies, greater job opportunities, an accumulation of value-added and larger real income, industrial outlets for agricultural produce, urban demand and markets for agricultural commodities, structural diversification of production, labour and trade, and, consequently, greater balance and flexibility of the economy – all support the case of industrialisation, at least as a long-term strategy. For developing, still primary producing countries, the particular aspect of equilibrated sustained growth is important. Also industry, and consequently the whole national product, suffer setbacks due to cyclical economic fluctuations. However, agricultural primary producers are also affected, on top of economic cycles, by natural seasonal fluctuations, droughts, floods and diseases, all frequently causing a fall in, or even a negative rate of, growth, despite significant investments and industrial success. An increase in industry's weight should, therefore, equilibrate the rate of growth.

b. The dilemma of capital- versus labour-intensive investment faces both agriculture and industry. It is frequently wrongly assumed that modernisation of agriculture necessarily results in diminishing demand for labour and, consequently, in unemployment. In principle, substituting mechanisation for labour does lead to a smaller demand for labour; but since modernisation of agriculture also means additional land improvement, crop diversification, fertilisation, irrigation, storage facilities, etc., the employment effect may also be favourable. Still, overall empirical evidence shows that modernised agriculture is able to dispense with large amounts of labour and, at the same time, significantly increase most efficient agricultural production.

The same is true, to a large extent, with regard to industry. On the one hand, modern industrial growth encouraged new methods and patterns of industrial production and created an immense amount of new job opportunities all over the world. On the other hand, in particular in developing countries, modern mechanisation, technology and large-scale enterprises brought about a significant absolute and relative increase in industrial production, but a much smaller increase in industrial employment, and in many instances even a fall in the latter. In the short run at least, from the viewpoint of factor endowments and overall national targets, labour-intensive industrial investments seem to be preferable in developing economies, particularly if the social – rather than private – benefit/cost criteria (or social marginal productivity) serve as a major yardstick in decision-making.

c. In practice even more than in theory, import-substitution rather than export-drive got the upper hand in the LDCs. A number of reasons is given to justify the case of import-substitution:

Domestically processed goods, based on agriculture and/or mineral raw materials, facilitate the absorption of agricultural produce, raise agricultural income, increase domestic value-added resulting from processing, fully utilise the advantage of the domestic, existing, secure and well-known local market, render protection of developing industry feasible, and save foreign exchange. The avoidance of, sometimes, cut-throat competition abroad (in the export-oriented case), on the one hand, and lower opportunity costs at home under conditions of the prevailing supply of domestic resources, on the other hand, strengthen the case of import-substitution.[19]

However, already this latter argument of opportunity costs, in combination with a number of other factors, lends support to the opposite, export-drive orientation.

First, there is a limit to import-substitution. Certain goods and services cannot be produced at home, must be imported and paid for by exports, either primary or secondary. Following a relative saturation of the domestic demand by import-substituting industries, export outlets must be found to render the continued existence of those industries economically viable, i.e. to avoid fragmentation and diseconomies of scale, even though a progressive change in consumer tastes and baskets may further encourage import-substituting industries.

Recently a shift has taken place to an outward-oriented policy of industrialisation. Protection of import substitutes has proved no cheaper than export subsidies. In the longer run, the exposure of domestic industry to international competition in prices and quality proves a better incentive to efficient industrialisation and development than protracted support to inefficient, often monopolistic and price-arbitrary enterprises, protected by the often defunct and unsustainable 'infant-industry' argument. Continued tariff or administrative barriers result in counter-measures, while reciprocal tariff cutting – though a menace in the shorter run – improves competitiveness, at least in more advantageous export-oriented industries of developing countries. Limited exports from LDCs need not be necessarily a result of handicapped or faulty industry, but of tariff and other barriers in industrial countries even in sectors with LDCs' comparative advantage.[20]

A number of measures have been employed to encourage export-oriented strategy, such as: legislation to promote foreign investment, joint ventures, including those with transnationals (in refining, petrochemicals, iron and steel, fertiliser, aluminium), and creation of free zones. Two major dangers may emerge in this respect; one, that the multinationals will leave to the LDCs – as they have done in the past – only a single-technology process with little value-added, while shifting more complex and sophisticated processes to other areas, chiefly their own metropolitan regions. Second, closely linked to the first, the advanced export-oriented industrial sector may become – again as it has done in the past – a non-integrated enclave, with little impact on the LDCs' own production structure.[21]

It transpires that there is no easy choice between the various alternatives and no escape from each one's complications. It seems that in the shorter run – under prevailing conditions in the LDCs, their factor endowments, and socio-cultural structure – agro-industry, labour-intensive methods and import-substitution, in combination, constitute the backbone of an industrialisation strategy which has fairly good chances of success. In concrete regional or national strategy, however, in view of the particular conditions and requirements, a different choice or combination, free from rigid principles, may be desired and selected, on the merit of the case.

A Global View of Arab Industry

Industrial development, as reflected in its share in national product, employment, investment and exports, as well as in productivity, in comparison with developed economies, is still in its infancy in the Arab countries. This rather blunt statement can be supported by adequate evidence,[22] notwithstanding the fact that some Arab countries have registered significant success in domestic handicrafts and some of them even in scattered modern industrial attempts. The only important qualification is that generalisations may conceal a degree of inaccuracy, while a closer observation of specific national economies will reveal differential states and patterns of industrial growth.

By the mid-1970s, total Arab population constituted about 3.5 per cent of world population, while the Arab contribution to total world industrial output has been estimated at 0.4-0.5 per cent only. Even in foodstuffs, textiles and clothing, the Arab share in world production does not exceed 1 per cent. While per capita industrial output in West Germany was $1,249, and in the USA $1,054, it matched only some

Table 1.2 Select Economic Indicators of Arab Countries and Israel

Item	Algeria	Egypt	Iraq	Israel	Jordan	Kuwait	Lebanon	Libya	Morocco	Oman	Saudi Arabia	Sudan	Syria	Tunisia
Average annual growth rate of population (%) 1960–73	3.2	2.5	3.2	3.1	3.3	9.4	2.6	3.7	2.6	2.1	1.7	2.8	3.3	2.1
Average annual growth rate of GNP (%) 1960–73	4.8	4.0	6.6	8.9	4.6	7.0	5.6	14.8	4.2	13.9	10.4	1.9	5.8[b]	6.3
Ditto, 1965–73	8.1	3.3	7.1	9.7	0.7	5.1	6.2	10.1	5.4	15.9	11.6	2.2	6.6	8.0
% of urban population 1970	39.0	38.0	51.0	82.0	44.0 (1960)	22.0	58.0	28.0	35.0	5.0		22.0	44.0	44.0
% of labour force in industry, 1970	13.0	16.0	10.0	28.0	10.0	34.0	17.0	16.0 (1960)	15.0	37.0 (1960)	10.0 (1960)		20.0	19.0
% of mining in GDP, 1960–73	14.2		33.1			–		57.3	5.3	59.3	54.0[b]	0.3		5.0
1965–73	16.2		32.5			61.0		58.3	5.1	54.4	54.9	0.3		5.7
% of manufacturing in GDP 1960–73	11.9	21.5[a]	9.5	24.2[a]	10.4[a]	2.5	13.4[a]	2.2	12.5	0.2	7.8[b]	7.3	17.7[a]	9.3
1965–73	12.5	21.6[a]	9.5	24.1[a]	12.0[a]	3.2	13.6[a]	2.1	12.4	0.1	7.8	8.2	18.4[a]	9.8
Average annual growth in manufacturing 1965–73	6.0	5.5	7.0	12.2[c]	3.6	–	6.0	10.1	6.1	–	–	–	5.3[c]	6.1
KwH per capita 1970/1	148.0	244.0	224.0	2,550.0	78.0	3,487.0	747.0	220.0	125.0	160.0	143.0	25.0	162.0	155.0
Defence expenditure as % of general government revenue (1973)	4.9[e]	52.0	28.5	49.9[d]	101.5[e]	7.0	18.2[e]	4.1[f]	16.2[e]	17.9[d]	25.0	13.9	62.5[f]	4.4
% of total goods exports, 1973-minerals	84.5	11.2	95.2[d]	2.4[d]	24.5	94.2	6.7[d]	98.4	30.1[d]	–	99.7	1.1[d]	18.6[d]	46.7
manufactures	1.6	21.3	1.7[d]	74.8[d]	41.5	4.1	63.4[d]	1.4	14.3[d]	–	0.3	0.1[d]	13.4[d]	17.8
% of total goods imports, 1973 machinery & equipment	40.9	24.8	34.6	30.5[d]	15.9	32.6[d]	24.2[d]	34.3[d]	26.3[d]	24.2[d]	35.8[d]	22.1[d]	22.5[d]	32.4
other manufacture	25.8	26.0	30.9	38.6[d]	40.7	44.4[d]	36.2[d]	35.8	26.6[d]	–	34.9[d]	42.0	32.3[d]	26.8
Terms of trade, 1973 (1967–8 = 100)	164.5	150.7[g]	129.4	92.6	82.4	152.1	116.3	189.9	98.6	–	122.3	87.5	123.1	118.7
Commodity concentration in exports (3 major commodities) 1972	71.9	57.6	94.7	1.7	21.5	70.2	4.6	99.6	26.2	100.0	93.6	68.0	60.2	35.3

a. Including mining
b. 1963–73
c. 1965–72
d. 1972
e. Central government
f. 1971
g. Strong deviation from adverse trend
Source: World Bank, ***World Tables 1976,*** and complementary sources.

$30 in the Arab countries. Since Arab industrial consumption per capita reached about $52, the excess demand of over $20 per capita had to be supplied by imports, thus presenting a *prima facie* case for a strategy of import-substitution. These data alone explain the poor contribution of manufactures to total exports – ranging from 0.1 per cent to 20 per cent in Arab countries, with the exception of Lebanon and Jordan, although other factors, such as low competitiveness or tariff and non-tariff barriers, are also responsible for this state of affairs. Domestically, industry's share in national product falls below 18 per cent on the average, but it varies from 2-3 per cent in Libya and Kuwait, 8-12 per cent in Saudi Arabia, Sudan, Tunisia, Jordan, Iraq, Algeria and Morocco, and 14-21 per cent in Lebanon, Syria and Egypt – compared with about 24-25 per cent in Israel.[23]

Arab industry cannot as yet be considered a catalyst of the 'push-pull' effect or a supplier of extensive employment opportunities, due to its limited scope and the tendency to capital- rather than labour-intensive technology. In comprehensive terms, industrial employment including mining and other non-manufacturing sectors ranges from 10-25 per cent of total employment, but in more exacting terms of truly industrial employment, only 10 per cent and even less.

According to minimum criteria of an industrialised country suggested by Sutcliffe,[24] at least 25 per cent of national product should be derived from industrial output, 60 per cent of which is to be produced by factories (thus to exclude primary mineral production and handicraft), with no less than 10 per cent of manpower in the industrial sector. Only 30 countries meet all three criteria and Sutcliffe himself admits a certain arbitrariness of his model, particularly for small economies, where the relative share of industry may be high and still the economy and society do not have an industrial character.

Most Arab countries do not meet the criteria required, and only some fetch the employment target, which by the way, Sutcliffe puts at a very low level, much below that existing in developed economies. Also the criterion of mainly factory-derived output does not apply to Arab industry, which in spite of the much disputed inclination to mammoth industries, consists predominantly of small enterprises, particularly in densely populated areas. In many industries, 90 per cent of workers are employed in small firms, e.g. in food, wood, footwear, clothing or furniture.[25]

More sophisticated criteria suggested by the United Nations, though also arguable, use complementary indicators of industrial levels, such as energy consumption per capita, steel output per capita, cotton consumption by industry per capita, and transportation of goods moved by railway, in terms of t/kms per capita. Findings show that the presently prevailing indicators in Arab countries resemble those in the pre-industrial stage in England (around the year 1800) and in France (around 1840). However, when compared to present-day industrial economies, a tremendous gap comes to the fore, as reflected in Table 1.3.[26]

Table 1.3 Indicators of Industrial Development, 1970

Country	Energy consumption per capita in kg of coal equivalent	Steel output per capita in kg	Cotton consumption by industry per capita in kg	Transportation of goods per capita moved by railway in t/km
Algeria	462	2	0.2	98
Egypt	268	7	0.6	100
Iraq	597	3	0.1	241
Morocco	194		0.5	171
Syria	483	2	0.3	16
Tunisia	247	38	0.6	258
Great Britain	5,360	500	3	480
Japan	3,210	900	7	610
United States	11,140	580	8	5,440
USSR	4,450	480	7	10,270

As mentioned, these indicators also suffer from shortcomings. A particular case in point is energy. The latter is almost unanimously acclaimed as the symbol of modern industry and economic progress. However, apart from the persisting argument on intermediate technology, investigations have proved a significant under-utilisation of installed electricity capacity, ranging from 16 to 37 per cent.[27] This raises two serious problems: one, inadequate opportunities for absorbing all capacity available; second, misallocation of resources sometimes unnecessarily channelled to new instalments instead of to other lines of investment activity, particularly in areas of comparative advantage. For instance, in Egypt, the textile industry increased its demand to reach 40 per cent of total cotton output, with significant exports, and is in dire need of replacements and rehabilitation to remain competitive, but it is adversely affected by diversion of capital to other, possibly less promising uses.[28]

The infancy of industry in the Arab countries is also highlighted by its asymmetric location, with 70 per cent concentrated in four countries – Egypt, Lebanon, Morocco and Algeria (accounting between them for about 50 per cent of Arab population) – and 30 per cent only in more than ten other countries. Moreover, structural concentration is also evident: 53 per cent of manufacturing in Arab countries consists of food, textiles and clothing, with the consumer goods share in Arab manufacturing estimated at 61 per cent; in developed countries it is set at 30-32 per cent. Heavier industry, though a symbol of industrial standards in the LDCs and in the Arab countries, is still in its initial stages, either due to limited domestic demand, e.g. refined petroleum products which are only some 13 per cent of locally refined products, or due to a number of more complex reasons, such as the steel industry, for which the present demand is optimistically estimated at some 7 million tons – planned short-term consumption for 1985, 25 million tons, and projected consumption in the year 2000, 100 million tons.[29] Further potential exists in the paper industry, which in the early 1970s supplied only 38.5 per cent of Arab consumption, and in cement, with a consumption of 13 million to 15 million tons, and an expected demand of 33 million tons by 1980.[30]

Most food is processed in Morocco, Egypt, Algeria and Tunisia; most textiles (plus leather) in Egypt, Syria, Algeria and Morocco; wood and furniture in Lebanon, Algeria, Morocco and Syria; paper in Egypt, Morocco and Iraq; metals in Algeria, Egypt and Morocco.[31] Algeria excels in liquified natural gas, produced entirely for exports, with a present processing capacity of over 5 billion cubic metres of natural gas (and current gas output of 8 billion cubic metres).

In the Gulf area, industry is so far poor, except the oil sector, although potential exists for a large-scale industry, if the idea of a Gulf common market materialises.[32] In this area particular stress is put on chemicals and petrochemicals, which, for instance, in Kuwait contribute 62 per cent to its industrial production, as compared with 32 per cent in Iraq, 15-18 per cent in Egypt, Morocco and Jordan, and 4 per cent in Syria. So far, OPEC (and the Arabs) have concentrated on the acquisition of tankers for transportation of crude oil, while refining was located close to the markets rather than to the resources. Recently, greater attention has been paid to refining, possibly non-conventional, with an increase in the number of chemical and even food by-products.[33]

The trade structure of most Arab countries reflects the still pre-industrial stage of their economies, with primary produce dominating exports and industrial goods getting the upper hand in imports, with a quite important share of machinery and equipment, required by national economies which opted for a development drive. While the share of industrial goods in total imports of goods fluctuates around 50 to 70 per cent, their ratios in goods exports range from 0.1 per cent (for Sudan) and 0.3 per cent (for Saudi Arabia) to an exceptional 63.0 per cent (for Lebanon). Countries such as Syria, Tunisia and Morocco are in the middle range of 13 to 21 per cent, Egypt is recently accorded as much as more than 30 per cent, and Jordan about 40 per cent.[34] All the figures exclude minerals and oil, as far as statistics can be considered more or less reliable, but they present both industrial manufacture and handicraft. If oil, other goods and commodities as well as services were accounted for on the exports bill, the average share of industrial manufactured exports in total Arab exports on current accounts would fall perhaps below 1 per cent.[35]

In the last decade, from the mid-1960s to mid-1970s, annual growth of manufacturing averaged about 6 per cent in major Arab countries, as compared with over 10 per cent in Israel. In individual countries, the annual rates of growth ranged from 3.6 per cent in Jordan, to 5.3 per cent in Syria, 5.5 per cent in Egypt, 6.0 per cent in Algeria and Lebanon, 6.1 per cent in Morocco and Tunisia, 7.0 per cent in Iraq, and 10.1 per cent in Libya. These averages fell below those of the preceding decade, in particular in Syria and Egypt (in which it admittedly fell to 3 per cent in 1973, to less than 0 in 1974, until it picked up again later), and may partly be attributed to the two wars of 1967[36] and 1973.[37] However, the main reason for this unsatisfactory growth, which did not match the planned development targets to offset the secularly lower rate of agricultural growth,[38] should be sought in low effective demand and Engel-curve-like patterns of consumption[39] and in industrial performance itself, as reflected in its structure, investment patterns and productivity. A number of bottle-necks retard industrial growth, some material – such as shortages in raw material, spare parts and foreign exchange, some human – such as red tape and obstinate bureaucracy. Blame must be put on deficient industrial management in the wider sense, which includes programming, attitudes and entrepreneurship.

With regard to the structure of industry, public entrepreneurship and ownership, which gathered momentum since the early 1960s, have become a major factor in the main Arab economies, such as Egypt,

Syria, Algeria and Iraq. All large industries, with 75-80 per cent of output value, became public; planned public investment in industry has reached 80-90 per cent of total industrial investment – and 50 per cent of government investment has been directed to industry, largely heavy and large-scale. This has bearing on the distribution of industrial activity between the private and public sectors and on the overall industrial strategy. Public entrepreneurship concentrates on mineral extraction, gas, oil and iron and steel processing, mechanical, electrical and power industry; while food, textiles, leather and shoes industries are largely left to smaller private entrepreneurship and handicraft. Large-scale public enterprises are mainly capital-intensive and require skilled manpower, which is in short supply; they can hardly offer massive adequate job opportunities, and encounter numerous technical, managerial and efficiency problems, adversely affecting profitability.[40] True, small entrepreneurs can also make mistakes and fail. But major mistakes and mismanagement in large ventures must result in greater failures and heavy costs.

Since the early 1970s, some sort of 'new economic policy' opened up new vistas to foreign and domestic private entrepreneurship, which may improve – though probably not regain – its status in future, along with small-scale enterprise. Recent liberalism can be explained, in its economic aspect, by a simple comparison of investment targets and implementation rates. In Egypt, the latter reached only 35 per cent during the period 1966-75, due to the military burden and shortage of funds.[41] The new economic policies are expected to produce better results.

Traditional handicrafts and small-scale industry, which, at least in some Arab countries, still constitute the backbone of the industrial sector, are unable to reach modern productivity standards, except for specialised branches which enjoy traditional comparative advantage and international reputation. Moreover, the often political pressures in favour of super-modern technology and large-scale industrial projects, characteristic of development plans in many developing countries, including the Middle East, have frequently had a double-edged adverse impact: 1. Misallocation of investment, handicapping the smaller or even larger existing industries, such as textiles or cement, in dire need of capital for renewal and modernisation of equipment, and replacements, stocks and current transaction – thus perpetuating low productivity; 2. Plunging into grandiose, expensive, large-scale Western-style projects (such as iron and steel mills, or car assembly plants), which, under prevailing economic and social conditions of scarce capital and skilled human resources (both labour and management), low effective demand in non-integrated domestic markets, and limited access to the highly competitive international market, suffer from under-utilisation of productive capacity and low productivity,[42] which are reflected in a very high capital-output ratio. Some Arab sources complain that frequently 'a small error in a mammoth project may turn out to be very expensive indeed . . .' and 'given this stage of Middle East development, it is advisable to forego measures of scale and prestige – in favour of projects whose scale and technology can be absorbed'.[43]

In the final analysis, what results from the two adverse aspects mentioned, is overall unsatisfactory industrial productivity, which in the production function $Y = f(K, L, R)$ [or, as a growth function, $\Delta Y - f\Delta(K, L, R)$] is presented by R as a residual production factor. Economic growth largely depends on the relative contribution of this R, i.e. productivity or quality of the production factors capital and labour, whose quantitative inputs alone do not explain fully the rapid or slow growth of the economy, or, in our case, of industry. It may easily happen, as shown by empirical evidence, that even a substantial influx of capital and labour inputs may not lead to proportionate increase in product, if the residual, namely productivity, is not growing at a sufficient rate. This will keep the per capita (or per employee) output stagnant, sometimes even regressive, sometimes only slowly improving.

Data for combined industrial productivity of capital and labour are not generally available for Arab countries, but an indication can be found in macro-data, which show that during the 1960s the increase in productivity contributed only 0.5 to 2 per cent to average annual per capita growth of 4 to 5 per cent in non-oil countries. Thus, main reasons for the not impressively high per capita growth have been relatively massive capital inputs. On the other hand, the residual R, namely productivity or quality of production factors, has remained sluggish due to a number of serious drawbacks, characteristic in particular of the industrial sector: malinvestment, under-utilisation of capacity, an excessively large, partly parasitic, bureaucracy,[44] and inadequate and ill-conceived education and professional training, sometimes handicapped in budgetary terms, and even more often in terms of quality and adjustment to true economic and social requirements, thus leading to disguised or open unemployment and brain drain.[45] This latter phenomenon is of a much greater weight and importance than is usually realised. Apart from the brain drain resulting from ill-adjusted education and training, frequently well-adjusted and skilled manpower leaves for more attractive jobs outside their own countries and often outside the area. This exodus of professional and skilled labour deprives countries, such as Syria or Jordan, of valuable assets, which prove to become an abortive investment.[46]

If we try to identify the chief characteristics and drawbacks of Arab industry, in order to analyse and project its strategy and options, the following issues should be underscored:[47]

a. The prevailing dispersal of industry between various countries is completely incidental, unco-ordinated and hardly serving the purposes of employment and income level in both the individual national economics and the total Arab community, without serious attention to the various aspects of economies of scale and comparative advantage.

b. Within this dispersal, 70 per cent of total manufacturing industry is concentrated in four countries only. This is accompanied by deficient location and distribution of industries within the economies themselves.

c. Light industry, mainly foodstuffs and textiles, constitute nearly two-thirds of the total sector.

d. Arab national economies favour, each separately, the import-substitution approach, without major efforts at co-operation in this field.

e. Small domestic markets, with concentration of effective demand in narrow risk strata, render difficult large-scale modern production, while at the same time encouraging substantial luxury imports.

f. Idle productive capacity is one of the important reasons of low productivity, apart from other factors adversely affecting the low R (residual).

g. Inadequacy of indigenous R & D makes industry almost totally dependent on foreign know-how and imported technology (not necessarily adjusted to domestic needs and conditions), and, *inter alia,* perpetuates the lack of surveys and research of natural resources, beyond the known and popular ones, such as oil or phosphates.

A Concise Survey of Select National Industries

The Arab industrial scenarios and industrial integration are being discussed here from a global Arab angle, although the disparities of individual economies in problems and prospects have been indicated. A detailed analysis of each economy's industrial state and options might bring out the particular features and potentials of every country but, perhaps, create a lack of perspective on the overall problems of the area, their interrelations and their confrontation with the outside world. Instead, in order not to fall prey to the wrong idea that the area is one more or less monolithic unit, it may be useful to point out in a concise form the characteristic individual traits and industrial issues in a number of Arab countries, particularly those bordering on the Mediterranean, and for this purpose four Middle Eastern countries – Egypt, Syria, Jordan and Iraq – and three Maghreb countries – Algeria, Morocco and Tunisia – have been selected.

Egypt

Egypt's main socio-economic preoccupation has been for a long time the disproportionate growth of its population and of real national product, accompanied by deep social inequality; in the past, because of the polarised distribution of wealth (chiefly land), and since the new regime, largely due to the large and ever-growing gap between the new governmental, administrative and military élite and the vast poor majority. The heavy burden of military expenses,[48] though substantially financed from abroad, has rendered difficult diversion of scarce resources to productive investment, and the intermittent wars caused material losses, lack of security essential for investment activities, and recurring breaks in industrialisation and development attempts. The socialisation of the economic system, though formally conducive to central economic planning, with stress on industry, has not been efficient enough to bring about the expected results. It is difficult to imagine how the Arab confrontation countries and Israel can make a real and sustained breakthrough without a true and lasting peace. Even if some military investments and economic linkages do generate certain industrial and technological achievements, secure certain external funds and offer some employment outlets, it transpires, in the not too long run, that disequilibrium, internal and external deficits, accumulating national debt, accelerated inflation, and insecure and unfavourable conditions for industrial entrepreneurship prove stronger than temporary booms and upward trends.

However, in our context, the political situation may be considered as one of the prevailing, though disagreeable, factors, with the only proviso that peace in the area should significantly enforce a favourable industrial scenario.

Egypt's industrial growth has been uneven in the last 25 years; since the revolution, and also in the last decade, it has registered ups and downs, the latter particularly in the war years, 1967 and 1973. Nevertheless, the average annual growth of 5.5-6.0 per cent exceeded that of agriculture and set in motion a structural change, more evident in the product than in employment. At present, industry already contributes over 20 per cent to Egypt's GNP, derived by only 12-13 per cent of industrial employees, and about one-third of total exports.[49] Even though this is still a low-level sector in comparison with developed economies, the country need not start from scratch in its industrialisation efforts. Instead, it must streamline the current industrial policies and integrate them with a long-term strategy, if industry, as planned, is to overtake agriculture in its contribution to GDP and if Egypt is thus to become an industrial-agricultural economy. In 1977, industry's share in national product was expected to exceed marginally the share of agriculture.

Some of the problems of Egyptian industry are reflected in its very structure, with 450,000 employees in over 150,000 private establishments (with only 2-3 per cent factory-type), and 500,000 employees in only 200 publicly owned plants. The contribution of the public sector to the industrial product has been even higher than to employment. Another structural feature is the position of textiles, with 52 per cent of all industrial output value and 50 per cent of all industrial employment, and, together with raw cotton, 70 per cent of all exports. Also food processing, whose relative share in industrial production fell by one-third, still contributes about 25 per cent to the industrial product. This presents the diversification issue, which the leaders of the country are aware of, but which must be carefully dealt with to avoid waste of resources. This process of diversification has been set in motion to a certain degree, following the already mentioned reduced share of foodstuffs, and substantial increases in the shares of oil refining, chemicals, engineering and electrical products, building materials, tyres and tubes. The particular importance of this gradual change is in the backward and forward linkages of the main developing sectors. What remains a source of concern is insufficient employment absorption and diversification of its structure, largely due to the capital-intensive character of industrial investments, but also due to more complex reasons, referred to below.[50]

The current priorities aim at the reconstruction of the Suez Canal area (planned as a major industrial, possibly free-zone centre), better utilisation of idle industrial capacity (mainly evident in the food industry, but also in chemicals, construction materials, metal and engineering – and less so in textiles), and preference for the completion of ongoing projects (accorded two-thirds of investments). All this is within the framework of the industrial plan, which for 1976-80 envisages capital investment of £E 2.4 billion, with the aid of private, chiefly foreign capital (an additional 25 per cent on top of domestic resources), and concentration on steel and other metals, petrochemicals, nitrogen fertiliser, cement and electric power.[51]

The ten-year development programme, 1973-82, has aimed at producing, by the end of the period, 60 million tons crude oil, 16 million tons oil products, 5.5 million tons of fertiliser, 6 million tons cement, 2 million tons steel – some responding to growing domestic demand, some depending partly on the external market.[52]

The main obstacles of Egypt's industrial development can be indicated as follows: shortages in finance and foreign exchange; competition between industry and agriculture for scarce resources (if one disregards current excessive governmental spending); poor standards of production and productivity;[53] under-utilisation of capacity by at least 25 per cent on average (with some even higher estimates), due to bad management, shortage of raw materials and spare parts, and other drawbacks;[54] partly extra-economic considerations, e.g. in the iron and steel industry and even in car assembly (and of course military industry projects); abortive investments, e.g. in jet fighters; errors in location, e.g. of dairy factory products; too much protection,[55] *inter alia,* through a cost-*plus* method; excessive control and the recurring threat of nationalisation; and, last but not least, devastating bureaucracy, on which the 'new economic policy' shed even more light.[56]

The industry's advantages, opening up brighter prospects, may outweigh the drawbacks. Egypt has a large potential market, which may expand from the present low effective demand of a largely rural population to the growing demand of an industrialising society; its agricultural supply offers opportunities for successful agro-industry; its low wages may, for some time at least, add an element of comparative advantage and competitiveness, although it is partly offset by illiteracy, ill health and low efficiency;[57] it disposes of non-negligible skills, and enjoys an excellent geographical location, easily accessible both to a regional and an international market.

Industry is likely to be Egypt's key and leading growth sector in the development plans for the coming years. The solution of the current problems mentioned is of importance, but no less essential is a restructuring of its economic policies in the longer run, administrative and institutional reform, expansion and redirection of exports, and integration with the rest of the area.[58] The latter is perhaps of greater importance to Egypt than to some other Arab countries, in view of its relative shortage in raw materials, the need for financial co-operation, and the population pressure, which requires an answer to the classical dilemma: export of people or of goods, to secure jobs and adequate standards of living.

An intricate dilemma has been presented by the strategy of the recent plan which has envisaged a shift to a strong emphasis on growth rather than on the previous drive to expand social services and redistribute incomes. This trend has been supported by the IMF, whose assistance Egypt was seeking, but following the riots against the radical cuts in subsidies, both Egypt and IMF had second thoughts on the subject and the dilemma of maximisation of two functions at once (product and equity) will inescapably continue to occupy Egypt as it does with regard to all LDCs. The only alternative in a low-income economy is to mobilise resources from all extra-income, extra-profits, under-utilised capacities and distorted uses, plus available capital from abroad without infringing upon the subsistence income of the masses, falling into the trap of short-term liabilities, or undermining the balance of the resources equation. In looking for investment and growth criteria, social marginal profit rather than direct business profit must be employed, even if it threatens and blurs the efficiency considerations of individual ventures.

Syria

Syria followed Egypt, with a certain time-lag, both in the socialisation process and in the more recent liberalisation and openness of the economy. The first adversely affected private investment, and in actual fact industrial growth, while the second encouraged business confidence and an upsurge in industrial activities in the course of the 1970s.

The share of industry in national product increased from about 15 per cent by the mid-1960s to over 20 per cent by the mid-1970s.[59] This, however, includes mining, electricity, gas and water, and while some sources consider both figures over-estimated, the order of magnitude and change roughly remains true. Other sources indicate about 15 per cent for manufacturing alone, but a growing share of total industry in GDP, in excess of that of agriculture. In fact, the relative share of industry in GNP largely results from the hectic fluctuations in agriculture, as in other similar economies, rather than from industrial changes themselves.

Despite liberalisation, particularly since 1974, the share of public industrial investment increased from 65 per cent in 1970 to 75 per cent in 1975.[60] This can be explained by Syria's emphasis on chemical, mechanical and heavy industry, within the general priority accorded in the plan to industry. Public entrepreneurship under Syrian (and socialist Arab) conditions is so far supposed to be the chief agent in this field. This may change if the liberalisation trend is sustained, if political safeguards prevail in the area, and also if, eventually, the order of priorities and strategic targets change.

As indicated elsewhere, it is unsafe to follow annual growth changes in industry, but *average* annual changes over longer periods may be instructive. In the 1964-72 period, average industrial growth per annum was 5.8 per cent; it fell to 1.9 per cent in 1973 (the October War), and picked up again in 1974, with 12.8 per cent. On the basis of the 1965 index (= 100), in the mid-1970s total industrial production reached 175, of which manufacturing 160, electricity and water 175, and extractive industry 2,284 (but with a relatively small weighted impact).

In manufacturing, the fastest progress was made in paper and printing, cement and electricity, followed by the food industry; the much slower progress occurred in the cotton and silk textile industries, hides and chemicals;[61] but productivity per labour unit was the highest in the capital-intensive, public basic metal industries, and the lowest in food, beer and tobacco. In the 1970s, productivity has not changed,[62] and industrial growth must be attributed mainly to an increase in employment, which stood at 100 (index basis) in 1970 and rose to 135 by the mid-1970s. Even so, overall employment in manufacturing did not exceed 11 per cent (and another 0.8 per cent in mining and quarrying, 7 per cent in construction, and 0.5 per cent in electricity, gas and water – which explains the 20 per cent of industrial employment, quoted from World Bank sources, in Table 1.2).

With half of the industrial employment in textiles, clothing and leather, and one-quarter in food, beverage and tobacco, these two sectors have constituted 75 per cent, both in employment and in output, of the typically pre-take-off structure.[63] This, together with deficient infrastructure, low productivity and poor effective demand of the large rural market, explains the only marginally higher share of manufacturing in output than in employment.

The Syrian industrial strategy aims at a change in this structure. In the 1970s, 30-40 per cent of total investment has been channelled in to industry, fuel and power generation, apart from nearly 25 per cent allocated to the Euphrates high dam. Two-thirds to three-quarters of industrial investment has been made in the public sector, which produces vegetable oil, beverages, canned food, matches, textiles, but also chemicals, refrigerators, batteries, cement, glass, power, and has launched new ventures in petroleum and phosphates. Private industry concentrates on food, chocolate, silk and cotton textiles, tricot, stockings, soap and some pharmaceuticals.[64]

A recent change in Syrian industrial strategy resulted in a number of inducements offered to domestic and foreign private capital, including free zones, repatriation of profits, and encouraged repatriation of Syrian capital from abroad. Agreements with other Arab countries promised not to engage in nationalisation. Syrian attempts at industrial expansion and diversification, however, continue to accord primary importance to the public sector, which mainly enjoys the investment budget designed to achieve the aspired structural change, while private entrepreneurship cannot be relied upon to undertake new and risky ventures. The Supreme Planning Council is responsible for the investment plans, and government ministries (a separate one for electricity and petroleum) and holding companies (for food, textiles, chemicals and engineering) are in charge of the major sectors. The plan channels about 50 per cent of investment to industry, energy and transportation (industry alone receives 33 per cent), and over 30 per cent to agriculture, including the Euphrates works.[65] Twenty per cent of power capacity, destroyed in the October War, had to be recovered.

A steep rise in industrial imports has been accompanied by only slow growth in industrial exports. So far, Syria has not had very much to offer to foreign markets, apart from raw cotton (up to 50 per cent of exports), crude petroleum (15 per cent), and textiles (10 per cent). Her imports still include 18 per cent foodstuffs and 10 per cent textiles, while imports of machinery, equipment and metal products – 35 per cent of total imports – are constantly growing, both in quantity and prices.[66] According to processing stages, exports consist of 80 per cent raw materials, 7 per cent semi-finished goods, and 13 per cent finished products; and imports of 20 per cent raw materials, 31 per cent semi-finished goods, and 49 per cent finished products.[67] This is a good illustration of both the present state of trade (reflecting the structure of the economy) and the potentials of domestic processing either for the local or for foreign markets.

Following the growing disparity between exports and imports (including intermittently substantial quantities of cereals), the trade deficit has continually deteriorated, and would be only offset on current account by services, such as oil-transit payments, and various transfer payments, e.g. by Syrians abroad or Arab grants.

Despite close Syrian relations with the Soviet bloc, only its exports to that area (at about 30-32 per cent) equal those to the European Community, while in imports the Socialist bloc participates with 18 per cent only and the European Community with 40 per cent (this excludes, of course, military supplies). Though Syrian trade with other Arab countries exceeds Egyptian trade levels, it still marks time at 13-15 per cent in both imports and exports, of which only 6-8 per cent is with the Arab Common Market countries.[68]

This trade direction prevails in spite of free admission of agricultural imports from Arab countries. A slight fall in the share of Arab trade can even be observed, accompanied by a share increase in trade with the EEC and other European countries.[69] It may be assumed that following increasing liberalisation, this trend can gain in strength, despite the existence of a still prohibited import list and a suspended list, both of which will have to be re-checked and possibly revised, if not cancelled, as a result of EEC's agreements with the Mashreq countries.

A change in the general trade structure and in Arab-Syrian trade can be envisaged only if certain fundamental changes in Arab industrial strategy are carried out, regarding complementarity, competitiveness and streamlining of more integrated industrial development. It is much more than restructuring foreign trade; it has bearing on the whole product and employment structure, and the aggregate value-added constituting the national income and affecting its levels. The issue is partly taken up by the new five-year plan, 1976-80,[70] which envisages development of infrastructure for the benefit of production expansion and diversification, and closer co-operation with other economies, e.g. with Great Britain, in 'synchronising' industrial development (which actually means British assistance in mutually agreed new Syrian plants), with the Saudi-Arabian Research and Development Corporation in an electronic assembly plant (with 55 per cent Syrian participation), and with Romania in a new Banias oil refinery (with 51 per cent Syrian participation).

Jordan

Jordan's economy has experienced many ups and downs in her relatively short history, owing to three major factors: (1) the relative poverty of the country in physical and human resources; (2) protracted dependence on foreign assistance for both capital and current expenditure; and (3) recurrent wars with Israel, even though Jordan was virtually uninvolved in the recent 1973 war. Damages inflicted on Jordan and the loss of the West Bank belong to this third factor, although admirably and even somewhat paradoxically, Jordan has substantially recovered from its misfortunes. In the early 1970s, industry's contribution to GDP was estimated by international sources at 12 per cent,[71] while Jordanian sources set it at 15.6 per cent for 1975.

In February 1975, an economic mission of the IDA visited Jordan and submitted its report on 24 May 1976.[72] The $2,371 value-added per employee was unevenly distributed among agriculture ($816, or 34 per cent of the total average), services ($2,700, or 113 per cent), and industry ($5,808, or 245 per cent). The per capita GNP in 1975 was somewhat lower in real terms than in 1966, and real growth during the plan period 1973-5 fetched only 3 per cent per annum, due to wars and agricultural drought, as well as a temporary stop in financial support by Kuwait and Libya. The gradual recovery continues, however, based on substantial imports, on the one hand, and large inflationary public expenditure and investment (up to 28 per cent of GDP in 1975), on the other. The steepest growth was registered in cement (about 600,000 tons in 1975), then in pharmaceutical products (liquid – 300,000 litres, other – 113 tons, in 1975), phosphates, paper, electricity and detergents, in that order. The small iron sector also developed rapidly.

By modern standards, Jordanian industry is still a nucleus only. In the East Bank, only 36,000 employees work in about 7,500 mining and industrial enterprises, which immediately reveals the small-scale structure of the sector. Particularly so, as 36 larger enterprises (50-plus workers each) employ 57 per cent of all workers, and the 8 largest plants employ 38 per cent of the total. Small-scale workshops constitute 90 per cent of all establishments, but employ only 30 per cent of industrial workers. The small and medium-sized firms engage in food processing, textiles, clothing, footwear and some metals, while only the larger undertake production of durable consumer, investment and capital goods.

By 1975, industry has become, according to IDA's findings, the largest single contributor to gross domestic product, while agriculture's share has declined.[73] An increase in Saudi-Arabian assistance, the revival of tourism, an upsurge in the phosphates industry, and Jordanian workers' remittances from abroad have all supported the accelerated growth.

The new five-year plan, 1976-80, envisages an annual growth of industry of as much as 26.2 per cent, which should lead to industry's share in GDP of 28.3 per cent by 1980. The growth target looks too ambitious,[74] both in view of past performance and in consideration of factor endowments available, but the strategy looks sound and appropriate under prevailing labour and market conditions. The emphasis is placed on phosphates potentials, which may supply not only the domestic but also the foreign market on competitive terms, along with such sectors as the food industry, potash, cement, oil refining, fertiliser, and the pharmaceutical industry, the latter perhaps on an all-Arab scale.[75] Most of the new ventures are planned as large-scale capital-intensive projects, due to labour emigration (including skilled manpower).[76] To attract investors, Jordan, which does not have the socialist inhibitions of Egypt, Syria or Algeria, offers numerous incentives, such as tariff protection of 10 to 50 per cent on foreign-financed domestic produce (while allowing imports from the Arab Common Market without tariff barriers). To achieve the industrial targets, Jordan's investment plan for 1976-80 allocated approximately 30 per cent to manufacturing and mining, in addition to complementary infrastructure.

Jordan has also induced the well-managed Industrial Development Bank, established in 1965, as well as other financial agencies, to assist not only the larger enterprises, but also very small firms[77] and this has become one of the first institutionalised efforts to reach the small entrepreneurs, a matter, unfortunately, so often neglected in countries at this stage of development.[78]

Industrial development in Jordan is relatively more tied to the issue of integration, since her exports have been heavily dependent on the Arab market, rising to 75 per cent of her total exports, i.e. exceeding by far, in proportion, those of any other Arab country.[79] Therefore the issue of adjustment and complementarity in the framework of an Arab economic and industrial community is of major importance for Jordan, unless she finds new and different avenues of industrial specialisation.

Iraq

Iraq has in the past been subject to particular instability, adversely affecting overall economic and especially industrial development.[80]

Of the present population of 11.5 million, about 25 per cent live in larger cities, and of 14 million expected by 1980, the rate and not only the absolute number of urban population will probably increase, following the continuous process of urbanisation.[81] However, only some 5 per cent of all earners are occupied in manufacturing proper, mainly in producing light consumer goods, half of them in small-scale establishments. Manufacturing contributes 9-10 per cent to GDP and oil another 27 per cent, although the latter's share in employment reaches only 0.5 per cent. The average rate of industrial growth between the early 1960s and early 1970s amounted to 7 per cent (with agriculture remaining stagnant). The main growth sectors have been foodstuffs, including dairy products, olive and vegetable oils, meat and sugar, tobacco and textiles – chiefly for local consumption. The fastest growing sectors have been chemicals, petrochemicals and fertiliser, tyres and pharmaceuticals.[82]

The potential for further industrial development and diversification derives from existing raw materials, such as agricultural commodities, phosphates, sulphur, salt, limestone, marble, and of course petroleum and gas, the latter still largely burned away. Due to a lack of metal ores, which are still under exploration, heavy and electronic industry is at present possible only with imported raw materials.

The industrial sector in Iraq has remained small in comparison with other activities, whether agriculture or oil-related. The main reason lies in the lack of human resources, which constitutes the chief restraint due to the shortage of skilled manpower and management, but the limited domestic market, inadequate capital allocation, restrictions on private entrepreneurship (under the centralist socialist regime), and export difficulties play their part.[83] Apart from oil, exports consist of 70 per cent agricultural products and 30 per cent mineral and industrial goods, the latter mainly to Arab countries. These exports have so far experienced little growth.[84]

As a member of the OPEC club, though not a leading one, Iraq accumulates significant oil incomes and is set on using part of them for accelerated industrial development. Unfortunately, despite lip-service to the importance of human resources, insufficient attention and resources are channelled to training.[85] If top priority is not given to the human factor, this serious shortcoming is bound to affect the development drive adversely, as it has done in the past.

The plans stress the importance of self-sufficiency in food production, and of expansion and diversification in the manufacturing sector to reduce dependence on oil. A number of large-scale projects have been launched or are in progressive stages of preparation. The chemical industry is growing fastest, in fertiliser products, pharmaceuticals, rubber, plastics, all partly destined for exports.

Construction materials and machinery – tractors, cars, electric equipment – are under way, and enjoy extensive capital allocations. An engineering complex at Suweira is designed for production of cars, trucks, other vehicles and diesel motors (in co-operation with Volkswagen). Rural electrification has been accorded high priority.[86]

All of these projects originate in a number of development plans, started as early as the 1958 revolution. Since then three plans have been launched, but new attitudes have been generated by the 1968 revolution, which – in the 1970-4 plan – presented new, socialist objectives, with an increasing stress on industry and on restructuring the economy. The latter plan was revised and outlays were increased as a result of substantial growth in resources since 1973. By 1975, the industrial share in total investments increased significantly, from 21 per cent allocated in the previous plans, to 42 per cent in the revised plan.[87]

More recent planning attempted to adhere to a careful procedure, which should be successful. The authorities undertook surveys, examined industrial and inter-sectoral requirements, available resources, technology and export prospects, and envisaged co-operation with the Arab Common Market. In the last five years, following feasibility studies, 100 major projects have been selected with attention to commercial and social profitability.[88]

The official order of priorities lists the following:

1. consumer requirements;
2. processing of local raw materials for domestic and foreign markets;
3. production of machinery and equipment for future development.

Under the recent 1976-80 plan, ID 3.6 billion are earmarked for industry, and, if efficiently invested and utilised, this could produce about ID 1 billion of additional annual industrial output upon the maturation of the investments.

Also Iraq, though with greater reservations than Egypt or even Syria, has entered a period of new co-operation with foreign countries and enterprises. Know-how, training, new technologies, equipment and feasibility studies are all needed. The best technology is in the hands of the big corporations, transnationals, and this raises a dilemma between expected benefits and fear of foreign control. Iraq has been looking for readjustments in agreements with the corporations, to be based on mutual benefits, full availability of technological information, training of local staff (particularly stressed in recent agreements), availability of experts, repairs and spare parts, assistance for local R & D, and preference for contracting foreign firms without their financial participation, and only against cash and royalty payments.[89] (The latter is a reversal of the old system of oil royalties paid by the oil companies to the country.)

Iraq is aware that industrial development increased interdependence – in markets, supply of inputs, technology – and it aims at a proper balance, safeguards against any new forms of imperialism, and secure development targets. Arab-European co-operation is considered crucial to an accelerated growth of industry and to opening up prospects for industrial exports, if large-scale projects are to be economically viable.[90]

Algeria

Algeria has put emphasis on industrial development since the early days of its independence in 1962. Under its development plans, nearly 45 per cent of investments were earmarked for industry, which was largely taken over by the government, and now 75-80 per cent of industrial output and 90 per cent of employment belong to the public sector.

Due to its oil and gas endowments, hydro-carbons and gas-liquefaction have become the mainstay of Algeria's modern industry. However, despite quite rapid industrial growth, manufacture has not so far exceeded 12-13 per cent of GDP. A certain declining trend even set in during 1975. The reasons are manifold: shortage of skilled manpower (along with general unemployment), a management and workforce unfamiliar with up-to-date methods and technology, higher productivity and competitiveness; too little attention, and resources, for traditional manufacturing; and stagnant agriculture, with an increasing food deficit, exercising an adverse impact on agricultural supply and on effective demand for manufactured goods. While food industries seem to be fully utilised, other light industries suffer from under-utilisation (up to 20 per cent), which affects the new and inexperienced heavy industries even more.

The industrial development strategy grants high priority to petro-chemicals, iron and steel projects and to heavy mechanical and electrical industry, with continued care for Algeria's pioneering and world-important gas liquefaction industry, which, apart from plants, has launched a gas pipeline under the Mediterranean to Italy.[91] Internal regional development is also included in the industrial strategy.

Although agro-based industries (cereals, olives, grapes, hides and skins) are among the officially listed priorities, the relative neglect of agriculture, in favour of the large-scale, capital-intensive heavier industry for which Algeria clearly opted, reduces prospects in this area.[92]

Algeria's industry faces a number of unresolved issues, on which its future development depends, such as management, co-ordination of investment, storage (in view of accumulating stocks), and marketing.[93] The latter issue gave impetus to an export drive, not only for oil, gas and petrochemicals, but also for other sectors, such as cement, or products of light industry, recently again under review and greater care.

The latest adjustment of the 1974-7 plan envisaged an outlay of $32 billion, of which 44 per cent have been designed for industrial development projects. The largest Middle Eastern petrochemical complex is being constructed at Skikda in northern Algeria for producing polyethylene, ethylene, polyvinyl chloride, vinyl chloride, xylene and aromatics.

The extensive industrial development plans, deriving from available oil-capital resources, require serious marketing adjustments in the Arab area and/or with African and overseas partners. While her Arab economic connections do not appear to be strong or promising, Algeria, along with other countries in the region, initiated associate arrangements with the European Community, along the general outlines for the Maghreb area.

Morocco

Morocco is close to a case of mono-product due to its rich phosphates reserves, and as in other monocultures – of an agricultural or mineral primary-producer type – its main development targets are: first, domestic processing of the mono-product in order to derive maximum profit from all values-added to be accumulated in this process; and second, to diversify the production and trade structure, to reduce dependence on one product.[94]

In fact, the national product has not risen rapidly in the fifteen years since 1960; its growth is estimated at only 4 per cent in constant prices[95] per annum, namely some 1 per cent per capita, reaching an income level of about $300 per capita.

About 25 per cent of the population live in urban areas,[96] where manufacture is estimated to contribute 15 per cent to GNP, with another 6.5 per cent from mining, 5.3 per cent from construction and 3.6 per cent from energy.[97]

IDA sources estimate value-added per worker in Morocco in the mid-1970s at US $926. Value-added per capita in agriculture is estimated at US $514 (56 per cent of the total average), in services at US $1,675 (185 per cent), and in industry at US $1,526 (165 per cent). This confirms, more or less, other estimates according to which 25 per cent of total value-added is contributed by industry, with only 15 per cent of employment – but both figures should be related to a loose definition of industry, covering manufacturing, mining, electricity, gas and water.

Thanks to cumulative though not impressive growth, manufacturing has doubled production in the last 15 years, with textiles leading the list (over 300 points on the 1960 index), chemical industry, construction materials, and electricity (about 250), vegetable and animal fats, other foodstuffs, paper, metals and leather, in that order. This survey excludes firms with less than ten employees and may therefore be biased against foodstuffs, leather and metalworking.[98] Canned food is also missing from the list, although elsewhere it is shown that the canning industries have enjoyed rapid development during recent years.[99]

The country is in dire need of developing the still infant industry, if issues of labour absorption and per capita income are to be adequately solved.[100] The emphasis here is on light and consumer goods industry, although beginnings have also been made, apart from foodstuffs and paper, in cement, chemicals and even motor car assembly.

Morocco's industry currently consists of 63 per cent consumer goods, 24 per cent intermediate goods, and 13 per cent capital goods. As to the size of industries, data exist on some of them: in foodstuffs 43 per cent of firms employ over 40 workers, in textiles and leather only 17 per cent, and in metals 16 per cent.

Phosphates are mainly exported as raw material and contribute 25 per cent to merchandise exports, with citrus fruit, vegetables and other goods in the balance. Morocco is the second largest world producer in phosphates (with an estimated 60 per cent of world reserves), and the largest exporter (one-third of world total). Its output has more than doubled in the last ten years, and in the early 1970s it reached 15 million tons of phosphate rock, of which 13.5 million tons were exported.

Another important item is phosphoric acid, which is the main intermediary product for processing high-grade phosphate fertiliser, or of sodium tripolyphosphate (STPP), used by the detergent industry.

Developments in other mining concerns are uneven, as in manganese and lead ore, while a decreasing trend has been observed in iron ore, zinc ore and crude oil (though oil refining increased to 1.2 million tons per annum).[101]

The government's stake in industry is not clearly defined. There is a tendency towards Moroccanisation but not nationalisation. However, the phosphates sector is largely concentrated in the fully state-owned Office Cherifien des Phosphates (OCP), as the biggest single producer and exporter of phosphate rock in the world. OCP is also responsible for the processing fertiliser plant and the projected phosphoric acid plant (which can be converted into monoammonium phosphate). The latter is expected to profit from economies of scale based on recent trends of growing demand for final and intermediate products. To meet transport demands, a new company was set up with specialised ships and routes to Europe, India and South America.

Exports fluctuate heavily, though phosphates have recently enjoyed growing demand and in 1974 alone their prices increased by 2.5 to 3 times, as compared with 1973.[102]

Despite substantial food exports – nearly 50 per cent of total – the country still has to import some foods to the extent of 23 per cent of the total imports bill, along with other finished and semi-finished consumer goods, and a relatively small margin has been left so far for investment and capital goods. Thus the structure of foreign trade is even inferior to most other countries in the area, at more than 85 per cent primary exports (except the purely oil-exporting countries), and too few development- and investment-oriented imports.[103]

Since 1973, new measures have been taken to encourage industrial investments, *inter alia,* through association of foreign investors with Moroccan nationals. The third development plan (1973-7) aims at an 11 per cent annual growth in industry (13 per cent growth in mining), at at least 85 per cent of capacity utilisation (currently low), regional diversification through spreading of investment in the areas of Casablanca, Rabat and the Northwest coastal plain, job creation by supporting small-scale enterprises, and support for large-scale enterprises designed as capital-intensive, and encouraging both export-drive and import-substitution in foods, textiles, chemicals and motor vehicles.

The investment climate still remains uncertain. Substantial resources are required for importation of intermediate goods, raw materials and equipment needed to spur the industrialisation process. Co-operation with extra-regional economies is essential, in view of the fact that Morocco's trade with Arab countries ranges from 3 to 4 per cent only, and perhaps also in consideration of its political and geographical distance from what is called the Middle East. The country can take advantage of its rich endowments in some minerals and some agricultural sectors, and it depends on their early and proper utilisation, whether a structural change will prove feasible.

Tunisia

Tunisia's 14 per cent of labour in industry (including manufacturing, mining and energy) has contributed by the mid-1970s about 15.5 per cent of GDP, with manufacture alone responsible for 9.1 per cent. Since population has grown faster than job opportunities, significant emigration has taken place, at the average annual rate of 15,000-18,000 people. These emigrants later transfer part of their incomes as remittances from abroad, a revenue quite important to the Tunisian balance of payments.[104]

As the Tunisian economy is different from most other economies in the area, there has been a long-term decline in the ratio of mining to overall industrial output. As a matter of fact, light industries, such as textiles, garments, shoes, paper, furniture and even synthetics, have also been lagging and even declining. Foodstuffs, engineering and electrical industries, gas, fertilisers, pesticides, cosmetics and pharmaceuticals, on the other hand, have been on the increase. Phosphates dominate the mining sector with 70 per cent of its output value, but they encounter difficulties and losses due to low-grade obsolete mining equipment, growing competition on foreign markets and intermittently falling prices. Mechanisation and modernisation may increase productivity but reduce employment.

Food processing has retained its dominant position, with 40 per cent of total manufacturing, hence the continued dependence on agriculture (particularly in olive oil).

The total manufacturing index (1960 = 100) for 1974, has shown 133.2, with mechanical products 165, food and tobacco 146.2, chemicals 128.5, textiles 120, and leather and shoes 98.[105] In 1975 and 1976, only a slight increase took place in the general industrial index, as manufacture rose by another 5 per cent, electricity and gas by 11 per cent, and mining fell in 1976 over 1975 by nearly 13 per cent. This fall occurred in crude oil, phosphate rock and iron ore, while phosphoric acid, bricks and triple superphosphate grew.[106] The low-grade iron ore (800,000-900,000 tons annually) is mainly exported in crude form (75 per cent of total).[107] Crude oil (5 million tons) and refined oil (1 million tons) account for 6-7 per cent of GDP, and have been produced with Italian and then French participation.

The small market made the growth of heavy industry difficult, while export markets were limited. However, efforts have been made to invest in conventional heavy industry – 43 per cent of total investment in manufacture – namely in iron and steel and in engineering. One major steel mill processes part of the iron ore.

The fourth plan (1973-6) expected a more impressive growth of 10 per cent per annum, following a planned 32 per cent of total investment channelled to industry (with an expected 24 per cent of the total from foreign sources).[108] But, as pointed out above, several factors have reduced the rate of implemented growth.

Despite the non-socialist structure of the economy, the role of public investment in manufacturing gathered momentum, reaching over 60 per cent in total manufacture, with nearly 90 per cent in construction materials, nearly 80 per cent in chemicals, over 60 per cent in food processing, and 55 per cent in metal and engineering industries. Wood and furniture are at the bottom of the list with 9.4 per cent only. Substantial public investment is made in petroleum, which together with food contributes 66 per cent to exports.[109] But private investments, mainly by foreign companies, also go to the oil sector. Forecasts for the future envisage an equal share of public and private investments in industry.

The Tunisian strategy emphasises import-substitution, but narrow domestic markets and high production costs call for protectionist measures and quasi-monopolies, thus complicating economic decisions and considerations. Excessive administrative control and managerial shortcomings render co-ordination and efficiency difficult, mainly in public enterprises.

Since 1970, measures were taken for liberalisation, fewer controls and restrictions, a better supply of raw materials and spare parts. A special agency was set up to promote this trend, namely the Agence de Promotion des Investissements, in March 1973.

Foreign trade is unbalanced both on goods and on current account, despite surpluses in services, which are, however, unable to equilibrate the goods deficits.[110] Even with oil included, the terms of trade were adverse until the upsurge towards the end of 1973.

In exports, primary and processed agricultural products contributed about 45 per cent to export returns. Petroleum and its products contributed 36 per cent, and the remaining 20 per cent or less was distributed among other mining, chemicals, textiles and miscellaneous.[111] Since 1974, an estimated increase to nearly 30 per cent (in total exports) took place in the industrial share.

In imports, finished consumer goods (apart from semi-finished) still require 30 per cent of the total, but the share of fuels, oil prospecting equipment, other capital goods and inputs to export industries is increasing.

Gradual diversification in exports is taking place in order to find a partial substitute for olive oil. Impressive steel complexes, cement plants and engineering industries (for motors, cycles, pumps, etc.) are also planned to replace some of the present imports and to provide for extended future supply. This, however, as in other countries of the area, raises all the issues relevant to large-scale modern ventures, in this case with particular attention to the intra-Maghreb homogeneity and therefore complicated trade relations, but also potential for integration.

So far the European Community constitutes Tunisia's largest market, with both exports to and imports from the EEC amounting to nearly 63 per cent of the total (and France's share still outstanding).[112] Tunisia's association with the Common Market is believed to assist in streamlining her exports and indigenous development.

Other countries of the area have not been included in this short survey of selected countries, either due to their distance from the Mediterranean, or owing to their almost exclusive oil economy, or, finally, as in Lebanon, because of the very particular and rather protracted political situation, which renders evaluation even more difficult than in the confrontation countries. However, their stake in the Arab and inter-Arab industry is brought out intermittently in the more comprehensive discussions of the Arab industrial scenario and strategy. It should, perhaps, be added that the conspicuous large-scale plans, largely in heavy industry, characteristic of the capital-abundant desert oil economies, are exemplary instances of industrial ventures, which can hardly succeed without thorough thinking and planning of manpower, technology, production patterns and markets, all making co-operation and perhaps even integration indispensable, if the ambitious programmes are to materialise in an efficient way and not to result in too well-known frustration.

Just at the end of this survey, and with reference to Lebanon, it is worthwhile to quote a passage from an interview with Mr George Asseily, the President of the Lebanese Industrialists' Association, which may be of interest to the more general issues and conditions of industrialisation in most LDCs:[113]

> Political stability and economic recovery in Lebanon are linked in a tight and vicious circle. Without confidence that the present peace is permanent, investors will not be willing to put their money back into rebuilding their business. Without the employment opportunities necessary to turn fighters into workers, the country cannot become politically stable.

The Strategy of Industrialisation in the Arab Countries

Confusion of terms and concepts frequently renders analysis and projections difficult. In discussing strategies and scenarios, it is important to draw clear dividing lines between extrapolated genuine trends, choices between realistic options, and strategies employed or recommended for the achievement of desired targets under optimal conditions. What should mainly be avoided is a certain tendency in developing countries to mix up real-life-oriented options and wishful scenarios, which may or may not be rooted in realistic assessments of prevailing conditions and available, or at least prospective, resources.

The industrialisation drive and strategy are now a new phenomenon in the southern and eastern Mediterranean, but they gathered momentum with the spread of the concept of a new international economic order and a revision in the North-South relationship, accompanied by the relocation of industry and change in the periphery-centre dependence. They also gained new support from Wassily Leontieff's recent study,[114] in which he reinforced the view that no economy can develop rapidly without accelerated industrialisation, reduction of industrial dependence and increase in industrial exports.

In the Arab context, one particular element has proved to be of paramount importance to industrialisation strategies, namely the push-pull effect on rural-urban migration, which created a tremendous challenge to cope with, namely that of shantytowns (or, bidonvilles), strangling the cores of the major cities with millions of their largely under-employed inhabitants, in Cairo, Alexandria or Baghdad. This economic and social menace alone could justify a dynamic industrialisation drive, and immediately set its pattern of *employment-oriented* strategy. Although this is by no means tantamount to extreme labour-intensive industry, the technology and production lines to be adopted must accord priority to the employment consideration.

In the two preceding sections we tried to set the stage for a stocktaking of prevailing industrial conditions in the Arab countries and pointed out the difficulties and drawbacks of an industrial newcomer.

The Fourth Conference for Industrial Development in Arab Countries,[115] at which delegates from 19 countries met in Baghdad on 12-19 December 1976, is considered as a major event in the Arab world and a signpost of new strategies of Arab industrial development and inter-Arab co-operation. Even though the conference was strongly politically oriented (anti-imperialist, anti-colonialist, anti-Zionist) and its main decisions called for more conferences in the future rather than for well-designed development actions, it also dealt with important aspects of industry proper as well as with research, co-operation, North-South relations and other relevant issues.[116]

The importance of this and a number of similar conferences, which have actually become permanently institutionalised, lies in the growing consciousness in Arab countries that modern industry is not just another branch or sector of the economy which can be tackled casually, as it had been intermittently in past policies or development plans. It should rather be considered a complicated, many-sided socio-economic phenomenon, which must be faced with utmost caution and circumspection, to minimise failures and maximise chances of success. Although the issue of inter-industry and inter-Arab integration will be discussed later on, it should be stressed at the outset that following a large measure of frustration with nationally designed industrial ventures, particularly those conditioned by economies of scale, the integration concept appears high on the agenda of Arab industrialisation scenarios, as well as in numerous official proclamations and documents, though practically it is still in its initial stage.

Industrialisation, as economic development in general, cannot be dealt with in purely economic terms. Social, demographic and political factors weigh heavily on all development decisions and strategies in all LDCs, including the Middle East. Here, the Arab-Israeli conflict, and the sudden avalanche of oil riches and its repercussions, largely outweigh reasonable considerations of economic efficiency.[117] Large-scale projects and military acquisitions and industry of doubtful value are the offspring of these factors.

Very recently, the euphoria of oil riches and power is gradually giving way to the premonition of depleted oil reserves in a generation or so. Without trying to analyse all the true, false or deliberately biased reasons for this premonition, it transpires that the Arab world has become conscious of the limitations of its oil resources, which, by the way, have so far been of only marginal help to the have-nots.

Consequently, this consciousness enforces other arguments in favour of diversification of the economy and of external trade, mainly through industrialisation, in the framework of which wide vistas are open to oil and gas processing, in view of the current abundance of Arab crude oil at an annual production of over 900 million tons (out of a world total of over 2,800 million tons), 76 billion cubic metres of oil gas, and 115 billion cubic metres of natural gas.[118]

Although many Arab observers are critical of the prevailing patterns of oil capital investment (largely abroad) and of exorbitant military spending of $8 billion-10 billion annually,[119] thus helping out mainly foreign arms producers, most of them do not suggest cuts in this spending to channel more resources into the civilian sector, but instead, they support building up of domestic military industry on a large scale, including expansion of the maritime power.[120]

In fact, industrialisation was given high priority in Arab national development plans and strategies, with the following main *targets:* structural change and diversification of employment and production; increasing employment opportunities; accumulating value-added (thus raising per capita income) ; improving the balance of payments through both import-substitution and larger, diversified exports; and last but not least, improving the quality of factors of production via modernisation, skill and efficiency – akin to an industrial society.[121]

The Arab countries are no more opting for a kind of industrialisation whose failure in early nineteenth century Egypt was explained away by Muhammad Ali by his saying that it had not been his target to actually industrialise the country, but rather to educate people towards industrial and modern thinking and attitudes (which had been hardly more successful).[122] The present focal target of industrialisation is a structural change of the economy and its sustained real growth.

How should this Arab industrialisation proceed?

A host of answers, options, scenarios and strategies, often conflicting and contradictory, is raised in an effort to find the adequate solution, in view of many misfortunes, experienced by numerous attempts at industrial transformation in the past and in recent times. It is also doubtful whether one all-embracing strategy can be formulated for 21 Arab countries, differing in basic factor endowments (as reflected in their productive structure and natural resources), in size and quality of population, as well as in ideology and in political, social and economic regimes, and their respective targets.[123] It is not enough to make an assumption, based on extrapolated trends, but amplified by development targets, that by the year 2000, industrial employment in Arab countries will reach a total of 22-30 million, of which 3.3-4.4 million will be engineers, technicians and administrators; 14.9-19.9 million, skilled labour; and 4.5-6.1 million, unskilled manpower.[124]

Apart from productive job opportunities, an extensive network of complementary infrastructural facilities must be built up, in areas such as education, technical and vocational training, transportation and communications, construction, energy supply and distribution – most of which are at present totally inadequate.

The Industrial Development Centre of Arab countries attempted to meet this challenge by laying down a series of measures to be adopted as a framework of industrial strategies, through raising the quality of manpower, utilisation of economic and political capacities, strengthening Arab economic independence, consolidating material and social infrastructure, and furthering Arab economic integration.[125]

Against this background, a closer examination follows of Arab industrial options, scenarios and strategy. Arab industrial options can be presented in two contexts of possible scenarios: (1) the Israeli-Arab context; (2) the global LDCs' context.

The Israeli-Arab Context

The Israeli-Arab context is only a partial one, since it is mainly politically oriented and chiefly representative of the so-called 'confrontation countries' (Egypt, Syria, Jordan and partly Iraq and Lebanon). However, in view of the existence of the Arab League's Arab boycott, the OAPEC impact and activities, the declared belligerency of Libya, and the massive military and financial support of Saudi Arabia and Kuwait, mainly for Egypt, the Israeli-Arab context assumes greater proportions both statically and dynamically. The Arab countries consider Israel not only as a military but also as an industrial power, which should be counter-balanced by rapid Arab industrialisation. This assumption even leads to a reasoning that a prospective integration of Israel in the Middle Eastern community may create a new centre-periphery relation, namely, a division of labour in which Israel will retain industrial preponderance, while the Arab economies mark time as primary producers. On the other hand, it can be argued that Israel's integration with the Arab economies could infuse modern entrepreneurship and know-how into the Arab industrial sector (and the economy at large), and also render possible the effective application of the principles of comparative advantage and economies of scale for mutual benefit; Bent Hansen projects three possible scenarios in this context:[126]

a. *status quo ante bellum* with full economic co-operation;
b. *status quo ante bellum* without economic co-operation;
c. *status quo post bellum,* which implies no co-operation.

Hansen clearly favours the first scenario as most conducive to peace, co-existence, co-operation and economic progress. Its precondition, of course, is a peace agreement between Israel and the 'confrontation countries', which will do away with economic warfare and divert resources from military to economic uses.

The Global LDCs' Context

The other scenario, in the global LDCs' context, draws on Leontieff's projection,[127] according to which the GNP gap between the industrial world and the LDCs by the year 2000 will be 12:1, if the LDCs grow by 6 per cent annually and the industrial countries by 4.5 per cent. This gap can be reduced if the LDCs grow by 6.9 per cent and the industrial world by 3.6 per cent, which might be realistic targets on the assumption that prices of raw materials rise substantially and simultaneously that a rapid process of industrialisation occurs in the developing countries.

New investment opportunities, now missing in many LDCs, can emerge; despite competition, certain products may prove cheaper due to lower labour and material costs; and growing effective demand in the LDCs themselves will improve market conditions.

This *general* scenario meets the Arab development targets referred to earlier in this chapter. Within this framework, a number of possible strategic *Arab* scenarios can be selected from a myriad of imaginable combinations:

Scenario A: Large-scale *plus* outward-oriented (or export-drive-oriented) *plus* capital-intensive industry;

Scenario B: Small-scale *plus* inward-oriented (or import-substitution-oriented) *plus* labour-intensive industry;

Scenario C: Large-scale *plus* capital-intensive *plus* Arab and/or globally integrated industry;

Scenario D: Industrial development based on comparative advantage *plus* economies of scale = combination of large and intermediate industry, capital and labour intensity according to factor endowments and technical production functions, and outward- and inward-oriented production.

The choice among the scenarios will largely depend on policy decisions regarding priorities to be accorded to growth, employment or equity, on the assumption that the balance equation does not allow the maximisation of all targets at once due to prevailing scarcities and the danger of imbalances. The same is true of priorities to be accorded, at least in the short run, to basic industries, light industries, and, as a particular case, to agro-industry.

Since the scenarios and combinations listed above are, at least to a certain degree, arbitrary though not incoherent, it is preferred here to discuss their major components, represented in one or more of them, and following their analysis in the Arab context, to try to reach the most favourable – and feasible – scenario, which may or may not correspond exactly to one of the models above.

Let us first see what are the aims of Arab industrialisation as reflected in development plans, proclaimed policies, inter-Arab meetings and conventions, and views submitted by Arab analysts and communication media. Then, following a critical review of prevailing targets and strategies, a scenario will be suggested which might offer an optimal strategy combining targets with feasibility.

Even under conditions of low per capita consumption of industrial goods in Arab countries, a significant gap has been exposed between domestic production and consumption, bridged over by imports. Naturally, import-substitution has become a major target of industrialisation. Arab countries, however, as other developing economies, have been importing not only consumer goods, including durable ones, but also capital and investment goods. Even some of the imported (mainly durable) consumer goods are quite sophisticated and their efficient production depends on the size of the market. Much more so are the capital goods, in particular if their quality is to match modern, high technological standards.

On the assumption of an import-substitution strategy, the Arab countries are still faced with the dilemma between import-substitution of consumer or producer goods. Some believe that even though consumer goods might be more easily substituted, given prevailing skill, know-how and market-demand conditions, consumption itself should be checked and suppressed, in order to release human and capital resources for developing domestic import-substituting heavy industry and capital goods, for three main reasons: (1) to set up basic industries as a precondition of future accelerated growth of the national product; (2) to overhaul the structure of the economy; and (3) to relieve the country concerned from the grip of foreign and multinational suppliers and to further its economic – political – independence.

Some countries have clearly opted for modern, large-scale industries, with emphasis on heavy industry, hydrocarbons and cement. It is believed, though not necessarily borne out by experience, that modern enterprises require less skilled labour, promise higher productivity and competitiveness, and familiarise the population and its manpower with up-to-date methods and technology.[128]

This strategy looked so attractive that many Arab countries launched gigantic investment projects either upon their access to independence or following domestic *coup d'états* and the emergence of new leaders. To a certain degree, the notorious conspicuous spending has been replaced by new conspicuous investment. Steel plants, car assembly plants and high dams are cases in point.

Although this strategy has not been given up so far – and some foreign powers and transnationals seem to encourage it for their own reasons[129] – a measure of disenchantment and re-consideration of the dilemma can be observed. Plans and plants are being subjected to critical and more objective reviews, to market analysis, to alternative costs examination, to balance of payments considerations, to checking the true success and costs of enterprises, including the impact of external economies and diseconomies, to analysing the impact of inflationary pressures, and to confronting the feasibility and desirability of super-modern with intermediate technologies. All this is amplified by the hardly changing product and income per capita, the growing population pressure and the recurring issue of import-substitution of consumer goods, on the one hand, and of the potentials of the export drive, mainly of goods enjoying comparative advantage, on the other.

In view of the poor competitiveness of Arab industrial products on Western markets, recent Arab analysts support concentration on African and Asian markets, in addition to import-substitutes. According to them, export industries require adequate division of labour, redistribution of markets, unification of market conditions and prices, co-ordination and association of partners. Consequently, both strategies are recommended, but successively – import substitution first (in the shorter run), and then export industries (in the longer run).[130] This attitude compares rather favourably with some LDCs' beliefs that difficulties with their existing and potential industrial exports can be solved by removing tariff and non-tariff barriers in the West.

Whichever strategy is adopted – import-substitution, export promotion, or an equilibrium between both – it will depend on domestic decisions, but also on the behaviour or reaction of the market, particularly on the northern strategy – whether it is adverse, neutral or favourable.[131]

The interesting point is that some sources contend somewhat misleadingly that so far the main Arab strategy has been the policy of import-substitution.[132] This creates an impression that substitution concerns imported consumer goods, or eventually, efficiently and economically replaced producer goods, while in fact the largest amounts of scarce resources have been channelled into dubious large-scale capital projects, requiring competitiveness and extensive markets. If these are to be met, at least some form of integration, Arab or more global, is inevitable. This important issue will be dealt with in the next section, but it must be referred to here as it sheds more light on the choice among the various scenarios.

An indication of newly emerging strategies can be found in the reformulation of development targets, with an emphasis on balancing the import-substitution and export-drive approaches, on securing the supply of basic consumer goods, and on Arab and international co-operation as a means of extending the market and increasing efficiency. Though still called 'an inward-oriented strategy', designed to achieve independence from foreign influence, it nevertheless represents actually a significant departure from semi-autarchic tendencies. In this context food and agriculture are accorded a paramount importance, and 'Arab self-sufficiency' is above all required for agriculture-oriented activities, in view of the rather gloomy prospects if a radical transformation does not take place. The grain imports are expected to increase to 22 million tons by 1985, and to 34 million by the year 2000. Also imports of 4.6 million tons of nitrogen fertiliser, 2 million tons of processed phosphates, and 710,000 tractors are envisaged.[133] If these import surpluses are fully or at least partly domestically substituted, through both agricultural and industrial development, the most acute issues of the Arab economies could be solved, and development strategy might enter new, promising and more feasible avenues.

Arab planners suggest that certain preliminary steps should be taken to render industrial strategy successful, namely:[134]

Inventory of the present state of industry in all Arab countries, in all sectors, including small industries and all basic requirements

Investigation of kinds and quantities of consumer goods desired

Setting objectives of production, investment and productivity

Examination of internal and external trade patterns, scope and potentials

Identification of new investment potentials and exploration of backward and forward linkages

Expansion of markets, inside and abroad

Unification, exchange and development of Arab technology

Determining adequate prices for the lower strata of population

Development of infrastructure – transport, communication, ports, storage facilities, construction and energy.

One can hardly deny the crucial importance of each of the steps, advocated by Arab analysts, but upon closer examination it transpires that some of them are preconditions, others the result of industrial development; a key sector such as infrastructure must be carefully planned and integrated with the producing sectors, in order not to violate the basic requirements of Hirschman's model of SOC and DPA relations. A further condition of an adequate industrial strategy is not only a proper balance between productive sectors and infrastructure, but also the building up of a well-integrated industry, namely one in which different areas of activity are complementary and support each other.[135]

What is clearly missing from the measures indicated is the emphasis on human resources as a decisive factor in a modern industrialisation process and the related issue of employment opportunities. In this regard, the issue of bureaucracy, which flourished on the fertile ground of both inherited and newly public-oriented attitude and setup, has become a major menace to any strategy of development. Here is the blunt description of Egyptian bureaucracy by an acute observer, as 'a parasitic class, fulfilling no other function than that of conserving their own positions and preventing the system from being changed . . . This parasitic class has to be weeded out as one of the preconditions for increased efficiency and growth in Egypt.'[136] Industrial growth, which is inherently conditioned by flexibility and efficiency, is certainly handicapped by this state of affairs. An Arab source enforces the attack on the 'paralytic, corrupted and wasteful bureaucracy', largely responsible for Egypt's industry 'operating at about 30% of capacity'.[137]

Another rather surprising shortcoming of the various attitudes to development and industrialisation schemes is a practical neglect of any serious planning for the absorption of growing labour surpluses, particularly in the shantytowns. Planners and governments are carried away by multi-purpose or individual projects, paying no more than lip-service to the major issue of employment both for the investment and production stages. If estimates of 'industrial employment' of 22 million - 30 million in Arab countries by the year 2000 (referred to above) prove correct, it is essential to build up a strategy which will lead to an efficient absorption of this manpower in an efficient industry.

Coming back to tentative scenarios, two principal approaches can be adopted:

1. Individual scenarios for each Arab country, in view of the differential structures, rates of total and industrial growth, population growth, trade and investment trends, and factor endowments.
2. One or more global scenarios for the Arab countries, envisaging or disregarding integration.

In both approaches, realistic scenarios should be based on extrapolated trends and careful assumptions which, while tested, may or may not be proved, depending on the quality and strength of their basis and of changing conditions.[138]

In the present context we opt for outlining a feasible but dynamic industrial scenario for the whole Arab area, without elaborating on individual national scenarios, but with due attention to the differentials existing side by side with common characteristics and targets. Industrial activity, just because it is relatively new in the area, may become a focus for integrated, or at least co-ordinated, Arab development, and combine human and natural resources in modern efficient ventures. Their success will depend on three conditions: (1) a full utilisation of present and realistically potential factor endowments; (2) adherence to the principle of (dynamic) comparative advantage; and (3) an optimal degree of integration aimed at economies of scale and adequate division of labour.

These are the principal assumptions underlying our integrated scenario for Arab industrialisation, which will take account of the four alternative scenarios indicated earlier, but will be free to combine their elements according to the three conditions listed above.[139]

This scenario is based on the following strategy:

A. Arab countries should continue to expand processing of domestic agricultural and mineral raw material and primary commodities, involving dynamic agro-industry and all stages of processing. This implies primarily the full utilisation of all potentials and capacity in agriculture, which is still the main source income for the majority of the population, and, under improved conditions, of capital accumulation. However, since our premisses are that industry is the major potential leading sector of growth and structural change, no opportunity should be neglected to design industrialisation according to priorities, envisaging domestic demand and market, comparative advantage and alternative costs – in particular with regard to new lines of production and to export-oriented industries – and shelving all kinds of conspicuous investment. At the same time, certain modern and new directions of activity need to be sympathetically investigated, e.g. petrochemicals or solar energy, even though technically complicated and sophisticated, but with great initial advantages.[140]

On the other hand, it is very doubtful whether sophisticated arms production and construction of nuclear reactors should be undertaken, although these are sensitive areas in which political decisions may over-rule economic considerations, such as high costs, scant know-how, danger of pollution and other risks involved.[141] Under these conditions, national and regional independence may be even more jeopardised than under the old imperialist system.

B. Import-substitution policies should be related to existing and realistically potential factor endowments, on the one hand, and to the larger all-Arab area, on the other – in order to take advantage of all available resources, of a wider market, and consequently, of greater efficiency on a regional level.

C. The choice of technology is to be made not on the basis of abstract *a priori* theory, but according to the real factor endowments, namely, raw materials, capital, labour, skill and management available (in quantity and quality), and economic and technical production functions. Even handicraft – such as carpet-weaving or repair shops – may peacefully co-exist with the intermediate technology such as is required in some agro-industry or even in manufacturing, and with the more sophisticated technology which may be needed in desalination processes, water supply, refineries and petrochemical complexes, gas liquefaction, nuclear and solar energy, fertiliser, or steel mills. Here, in particular, factor and market considerations lead to the inescapable integration issue.[142]

D. Location, or even re-location and streamlining of industries, according to optimal division of labour, both internally, to minimise the centre-periphery polarisation, and on a regional basis, to secure the most efficient employment of production factors as well as a more equitable distribution of benefits.[143]

E. The issue of export orientation must be solved in the context of regional, Arab, Middle Eastern or Mediterranean integration (in a tighter or looser form), and of wider international co-operation on the earlier raised assumption that without the goodwill of the northern industrial economies, export drive and even import-substitution cannot survive in the longer run, despite – or because of – double-edged protectionist measures. International co-operation, despite setbacks, is more viable than a 'collective' or individual self-reliance strategy, which is hardly compatible with a dynamic industrial drive.[144]

F. More adequate national planning must precede Arab or regional planning and co-ordination. Among the many political, financial and administrative stumbling blocks in inter-Arab conferences on integration was the lack of clear national economic and industrial targets, which could have been confronted and eventually streamlined in the common interest. Nevertheless, it is an inescapable conclusion from the preceding components of this scenario that greater and more effective co-ordination and, preferably, integration – inter-Arab as well as regional and international – are a condition of a fully-fledged, successful industrialisation drive.

It transpires that scenario D, presented earlier in the global LDCs' context, is the closest to our present comprehensive scenario, which takes account of comparative advantage, economies of scale and priorities. It is not determined by abstract doctrines nor by wishful thinking and arbitrary targets imposed by governments, but qualified by social and economic needs, on the one hand, and by domestic and international realities, on the other.

Any scenario or plan involves economic policies conducive to the optimal implementation of the envisaged strategies. An examination of Arab development plans and policies clearly indicates an overall preference for an industrial drive, for the establishment of basic industries and for public entrepreneurship in these areas. Therefore, reasons for setbacks and for achievements falling short of targets must not be sought in inadequate official approach to industrial problems but rather in more objective causes, such as factor endowments, market and effective demand, infrastructural conditions, and the general character of a non-industrial society.

With regard to policies themselves, they did not prove to be doctrinaire. Despite the declared socialist, public-oriented, economic concept, the respective Arab governments, such as in Egypt, Algeria and Syria, have shown significant flexibility in the course of the 1970s[145] by adopting new measures for far-reaching encouragement of private and foreign investment, such as full repatriation of profits and capital at free exchange rates and fiscal exemptions for a number of years; even the domestic bureaucracy has begun to show the first tentative signs of more responsive attitudes.[146]

Foreign-financed projects, mainly in Egypt, include a wide spectrum of consumer goods (cotton and textiles), steel complexes, the chemical and petrochemical industry, oil, and power generation, as well as some horizontal agricultural projects, such as land reclamation. Most of these are still at the exploratory stage.[147] The interesting, and encouraging, aspect of the recent Egyptian planning (for 1976-80) is that first, substantial funds are allocated for complementary infrastructure, and second, most planned investment is designed for the completion of existing projects, and increasing utilisation of capacity and efficiency. The implementation of these policies may constitute a major breakthrough in Egypt's industry.[148]

There is growing awareness and declared strategies pronounce in favour of consumer goods, agro-industry and processing domestic raw materials, in response to a critical reassessment and an appreciation of the requirements of factor endowments, comparative advantage and competitiveness, as well as of socio-economic pressures. Despite this, most of the larger Arab economies feel, and exercise, particular responsibility for setting up heavy industries as a basic condition of a *national* independent economy.

This attitude, apart from the objective difficulties discussed earlier, partly explains reservations concerning feasibility and even desirability of inter-Arab economic and industrial integration.[149]

Arab Integration

Following political and economic transformation on the heels of the Second World War and particularly in the two recent decades, various economic blocs and associations came into being all over the world, with diversified aims and varying degrees of cohesion. Their central declared purpose was to minimise adverse cyclical fluctuations and to maximise international welfare. The EEC and Comecon have become the outstanding instances of integration among more developed countries, while the developing countries, some of them very new national and economic entities, have attempted to follow suit through regional organisations, specific commodity groups (the most effective and audible being OPEC), or 'the 77', with the UN agencies, and particularly UNCTAD, in the background.

Integration has become a catchword which caught the attention of governments, planners, political scientists and economists. It gathered momentum with the onset of another catchphrase, the 'new international economic order'. The flood of professional and amateur literature on the two subjects makes it impossible, and unnecessary, to discuss the issue in our present context. However, since the industrial scenarios for the Arab countries are closely related to the issue of integration, whatever form it may or should take, a few specific comments may be helpful and clear the way for area-bound analysis.

Although, for the sake of simplicity, we shall mainly employ the term 'integration', it should be understood that its exact interpretation would mean full and far-reaching partnership (short of total unification) between several units, or between a large body and a unit adjoining it, be it political or economic. Consequently, a number of concepts have been employed to express various degrees of such a partnership, starting from 'adjustment', then 'harmonisation', 'co-operation', 'co-ordination', 'association' and finally 'integration', with the latter as the most accomplished form of partnership.[150]

In referring to 'integration' in the context of Arab industrialisation, we shall not go into the intricate theoretical and empirical details of each form of partnership, as this could carry us away from our main interest in *any* form of partnership required or desired to spur the industrialisation process. However, intermittently, and where necessary, the general term 'integration' will be more closely qualified, and its 'lower' forms will be spelled out. What should bc emphasised here is a certain basic difference between the mainly anti-cyclical and welfare character of, for instance, European integration (EEC), and the growth-oriented, prospective rather than actual, integration among the LDCs (including the Arab countries), whose development and industrialisation depend in the final analysis on the effective application of comparative advantage and economies of scale, in order to cut production costs and make modern industries economically viable.

Arab industrial strategy aims not just at an accidental and marginal growth but at a structural change, which would shift the main contribution to the national product and balance of payments from low-level, primary to high-level, modern secondary sectors. This necessarily raises issues of economies of scale linked to demand and markets, and of comparative advantage allied with industrial location and respective factor endowments – in raw material, capital, skills – with regard to both inward-oriented (import substitutes) and export-oriented industry. Despite some setbacks in nationally based modern industries, even large-scale enterprises requiring modern technology, adequate capital and absorptive markets can be run efficiently under conditions of genuine integration among the economies concerned, and co-operation (or even association) between them and wider regional and global entities.

Arab sources favouring import-substitution admit that in order to enjoy economies of scale and fully utilise the existing or necessarily built-up capacity (of large-scale projects), the total Arab region must be considered as a statically and potentially wider market.[151] This requirement gains in importance if export industries are to be encouraged, in face of occasionally cut-throat competition on the international market. Arab integration is considered by some Arab observers as a matter of political will rather than of economic feasibility.[152]

The creation of an all-Arab data bank must precede any serious attempt at the *implementation* of Arab integration. Industrial and consumer surveys belong to this stage, which may be followed by planning joint goals and, possibly, changing patterns of investment and consumer demands through increased productivity and income and its redistribution.[153]

A number of requirements conducive to accelerated and successful industrialisation can be met on an integrated basis. Among them are: production for a domestic (integrated) market; greater integration between industry and agriculture, as well as between primary commodities, such as crude oil or phosphates, and the processing and marketing of finished, high value-added products; more effective independence of export sectors from foreign impact and, at the same time, a firmer basis for co-operation with foreigners in technology, marketing and joint ventures; a well-adjusted regional infrastructure; greater justice in the distribution of benefits between the stronger and weaker Arab countries; and a comprehensive Arab industrial philosophy, with a less 'nationalist' philosophy and strategy.[154]

On this last subject, differences of opinion exist on whether national industrial strategy is a precondition for a global Arab strategy or whether it is rather a hindrance. With strong nationalist feelings and policies in the individual Arab countries prevailing, it is difficult to imagine an integrative Arab industrial strategy without due consideration of national options and strategies.[155] In practical terms, however, this is largely a non-issue, since in most Arab countries there is actually no national industrial strategy to speak of. This appraisal, submitted by Arab observers, seems to be extreme, especially in formal and institutional terms, as reflected in numerous development plans and industrial projections. It can be substantiated by empirical evidence, however, which shows the lack of a sustained, consistent and implemented strategy, and industrialisation attempts launched rather sporadically and unorganically. True, this pessimistic view does not help much in instituting Arab integrated strategy. The reason does not lie in lack of needs and desirable targets which may be more easily achieved on an integrative basis. Main handicaps are in disparity in statistical evidence, in manpower, in socio-economic structure and in lack of functional implementation facilities even for existing common institutions. This leads sceptics to the conclusion that only co-ordination of national plans (in whatever form they exist) and indicative rather than mandatory industrial planning are feasible.[156]

This same scepticism also draws on a specific, but focal issue – at least in static terms – of the present structure of Arab trade, which is deeply associated with the most essential problem of the overall Arab primary economic structure, the competitive rather than complementary character of the national economies, and the development and industrialisation efforts requiring vast imports of capital and investment goods from outside the area (apart from military and conspicuous imports).

According to estimates for the period 1965-73, only 5.1 per cent of total Arab exports went to Arab countries.[157] The EEC countries have become the Arabs' biggest partner. In 1970-73, Arab exports to EEC ranged from 43 to 70 per cent of their total exports; Arab imports ranged from 44 to 48 per cent of their total. In 1974, EEC's supplies to the area nearly doubled.[158] Although in recent years inter-Arab trade has been on the increase[159] – particularly in exports from non-oil countries, e.g. Egypt, Jordan and Syria, and imports mainly from oil-rich states, e.g. Kuwait and Saudi Arabia – the picture has not changed much in principle. The oil boom on the one hand, and tariff deductions in the EEC on the other, again pushed Arab trade in the direction of Western Europe.

All this, however, does not mean that outward trade flows – due to lack of regional complementarity and other reasons[160] which might impede integration on static grounds – necessarily prevent integration within a dynamic concept of industrialisation. On the contrary, to avoid future competition under growth conditions and to secure better domestic as well as foreign markets, a large degree of integration seems essential. As one source puts it, rather bluntly, 'the real choice is between foreign domination or integration on an equal footing'.[161]

The validity of the integration concept would certainly profit from including in its framework other countries in the region, such as Israel, Turkey, Cyprus and Iran. Each of these countries has its own specific contribution to offer to an integrated industrialisation drive – experience and know-how, non-negligible resources, rich oil endowments and development resources. Taken together these countries could contribute a market of about 75 million people, with effective demand above average in the Arab part of the area. Their foreign trade is extensive, with significant deficits on current account (including even Iran, due to its huge military and investment spending), and import-substitution on a *regional* basis may offer new opportunities and cost savings.

Non-Arab countries cannot expect profit-sharing in Arab oil revenues, but even the non-oil Arab countries have not enjoyed adequate assistance from this source to meet their consistent trade deficits and accumulating debt burden (with the exception of some military undertakings).[162] The reasonable and economically justified solution would be harnessing all available resources in the area – human and material – to a joint Arab, or preferably regional, integrated industrial drive. On the assumptions of larger and higher effective demand, greater efficiency of large-scale, properly located industry, diversification of production, consumption and trade, cost-saving transportation and insurance, the area should become a more equal partner in international trade and development, not on account of political pressures and quasi-monopoly in oil, but in its own right as a modern industrial entity, economically attractive to any partner.

Although it is difficult to imagine genuine integration in one sector only, such as industry, we shall concentrate on the industrial aspect of inter-Arab co-operation.

Attempts at Arab industrial co-operation have been made by the Arab League since the early 1950s.[163] Over 25 years, programmes have been drafted, conferences convened (i.e. a Pan-Arabic Congress on industrial growth in Kuwait, in March 1966), seminars and symposia held on the importance and feasibility of a common Arab industrial strategy, all within the general framework of an Arab Common Market launched in the period 1957-60, and in operation since 1964. In 1964,

Arab Economic Unity was established, and its Council (CAEU) designed plans to develop Arab economic strategy, along lines similar to those of the European Community. Its membership increased from the initial 5 to 13, and joint Arab strategy, with a time horizon of 20 years for its implementation, was approved in March 1976 by the Arab League's Council, which set up a group of experts for further study and recommendations.

In 1969, the Industrial Development Centre for Arab States (IDCAS), in Baghdad, was formed to assist in the working out and in the implementation of joint Arab industrial ventures. In the course of the 1970s, on the heels of the oil boom, the euphoria of a new international order, and resumed negotiations with the European Community, the issue of a common Arab industrial strategy was reinforced. The Fourth Arab Industrial Conference in 1976 in Baghdad was preceded in June 1976 by an Arab Industrial Co-ordination Seminar in Alexandria, held under the joint sponsorship of IDCAS and CAEU, with the participation of more than 80 ministers, industrialists, experts and representatives of OECD and the UN agencies.[164]

The Alexandria Seminar and the Baghdad Conference were aware of 'the obstacles and difficulties that have to be overcome to bring about rapid Arab industrial integration which is essential to the future success of economic development in the Arab world'.[165] The meetings drew on the experience of various economic blocs in the industrial field, and their eventual lessons for a new Arab scenario, and studied the procedure for co-operation and co-ordination of joint efforts, markets, capital supply and other relevant factors.

Unfortunately, the main upshot of the Seminar and the Conference was a decision to set up a three-minister committee (representing Iraq, Algeria and Saudi Arabia) for a follow-up, and to convene another ministerial meeting in Tunis in 1977 and another session of the Conference in November 1978. Articles published by Nabil Sabbagh in *Al-Ahram Al-Iqtisadi*, with the titles 'This Planning – Between Wishes and Reality', 'In Spite of All That, the Road is Long', or 'Why this Gathering' – are the *cri-du-coeur* of a well-wishing but frustrated observer.[166]

Arab economists[167] take a sober view of the prospects of Arab industrial integration. Among the favourable and supporting factors, they list common Arab interests, abundant capital and labour, large markets, similarity of tastes and consumption patterns, proximity of states, and the geographical location of the region; among the main adverse conditions they cite different stages of development of the national economies and different economic and political regimes. Others concentrate on national egoism and hypocrisy, Arab mutual mistrust and lack of confidence in the potential of the Arab community as the crucial factors working against Arab integration.[168] Some of the obstacles mentioned are certainly not insurmountable, but experience has proved that since integration is to a large degree a matter of political will, the different adverse factors cannot be disregarded. Also some of the favourable factors indicated above may have a double-edged impact, or may be of a more complicated character, such as 'common Arab interest', or 'similarity of tasks and consumption patterns', which can have a market effect, but can also restrict diversification.

The oil-rich countries are regarded with a great deal of suspicion (usually from the non-oil-producing circles). They are thought to prefer imported technology and capital intensity (explained by scarce labour in their own countries) to native technology, research and labour intensity. Also doubts are raised with regard to joint ventures of oil countries with foreigners, ventures which are competitive rather than complementary and working in fact against Arab integration.[169]

An examination of integration efforts in the last two decades reveals the disturbing fact that although, in addition to policy statements and conferences, a large number of common Arab arrangements, institutions and companies have been set up, aiming at vital long-term targets such as industrial division of labour, equity, integration and efficiency,[170] so far only poor results could be registered, in particular in the industrial field. The list of relevant bodies is impressive: The Arab Common Market, Arab Mining Company, Arab Company for the Development of Animal Resources, Arab Pharmaceutical Industry Company, Arab Company for Industrial Investments, or the already mentioned Industrial Development Centre for Arab States. In addition, joint Arab ventures were launched, such as the Arab Maritime Petroleum Transport Co. (in Kuwait), the Arab Shipbuilding and Repair Yard Co. (in Bahrain), the Arab Petroleum Investment Co. (in Saudi Arabia) and the Arab Petroleum Services Co. (in Libya),[171] as well as a new line of sectoral branch unions, such as fertilisers, steel, engineering, textiles, and recently projected in fish industry, cement, paper and ports construction.[172]

Very little has been performed so far in the actual implementation of Arab integration, however, whether via the Arab Common Market, interested mainly in rather static trade aspects,[173] or via the more comprehensive but hardly implemented programme of the Arab Economic Unity Council aiming at a complete freedom of movement of people, capital and trade between the member countries.[174]

A relatively new element in recent attitudes is the growing emphasis on integrated investment and production rather than on an integrated market and trade.[175] Accordingly, producer federations should be given priority, similar to OAPEC, and, following market research, mainly export products should be identified and planned, with the proviso that in the export concept, chiefly though not solely, Arab integrated markets are included.[176]

Investment in total Arab enterprises confirmed is estimated at US $8 billion, while potentials are set at three times that amount. Some of the common enterprises (particularly fertilisers, textiles and engineering) have set comprehensive targets which should include production, marketing and training.

Several instances related to our scenario and to its integrated implementation can illustrate the avenues of Arab integrated industry, most of them building, as yet, on the recent trend of integrated sectoral branches, and less on an overall integrated Arab industry.

In consumer goods, four main examples can be quoted:

a. *Textiles.* Most countries of the area are endowed in cotton, wool and in artificial fibres. Processed products in the form of textiles have already become an important component of national industrial output and exports. In view of competition and restraints in foreign markets, production must be streamlined, its utilisation of capacity optimised, and its efficiency increased. Bottlenecks and shortages exist in some countries in reserve weaving and spinning machines, or in the form of outdated equipment, or in under-utilised capacity.[177] The defensive measures taken by the USA and the Common Market in this particular sector highlight the importance of the recent Arab attempts to integrate this sector.

b. *Sugar.* Present imports by Arab countries amount to about US $1 billion annually. More local refining should be planned and adequately located according to preferable conditions, e.g. in Sudan.[178]

c. *Pharmaceuticals.* Thirteen Arab countries have joined a special Arab company for this sector, to complement the existing plants and production, and mainly to initiate serious market research, identify new high-standard products, and utilise modern technology. While domestic location of this industry should be decided upon according to efficiency considerations, co-operation with parallel enterprises abroad may be of particular advantage in this field.[179]

d. *Petrochemicals.* This sector bridges over the consumer and producer sectors as it usually serves both. On the one hand, it supplies plastic goods of various kinds, and on the other it produces industrial fibres, pipes, nitrogenous fertiliser, etc. Despite its quite rapid development in the area, it is still a young industry, in need of capital and skill. Due to its potentials and complex forward and backward linkages as a leading sector, it requires a great deal of co-operation with regional as well as external economies. So far, potentials for import-substitution exist, but this sector is designed intrinsically to become not only an exchange-saver but also an exchange-earner, if efficiency, competitivity, and markets are ensured.[180]

The investment and capital goods sector, which is considered by all developing countries to be a fundamental condition of 'self-reliance' and the industrialisation drive, has already attracted the largest shares of domestic and foreign capital resources in some Arab countries. Some of them have very good chances of success, owing to both supply and demand conditions; others must be carefully re-examined, on the basis of experience and actual performance, and in the light of prevailing and potential factor endowments and market conditions.

The following comments will touch upon select branches only.

a. *Cement.* Present Arab demand for cement amounts to 24 million tons. It is estimated that the expected Arab production in 1980 will be 40 million tons, and thus, even given increased domestic demand, some surplus may be left for exports. An Arab Union of Cement Factories is to aid in furthering know-how, setting up new factories and expanding production and markets in order to achieve the targets.[181]

b. *Liquefied Petroleum Gas (LPG).* A number of Arab countries enjoy a significant comparative advantage in this sector, and plants are spreading over most oil-producing economies. Exports are already substantial, in particular to Japan and the United States, but co-ordination of further development is essential in view of designed capacity of 40 billion tons per annum by 1981.[182]

c. *Tractors.* Following demand investigations, more than 300,000 tractors will be needed by the Arab countries till 1985. Expansion opportunities exist in Egypt, Syria, Iraq, Algeria and Morocco, but not without ensuring greater adjustment, uniformity and integrated planning and investment.[183]

d. *Iron and Steel.* The widespread support for this sector in LDCs, and in most Arab countries, stems from its strategic aspects, backward and forward linkage effects, contribution to skill and technology, and diversification of output and trade, away from traditional structure. On the whole, a U-curve reflects this industry's efficiency, either at very small-scale or very large-scale production. Thus, economies of scale and the allied market issue are decisive, along with the location aspect, according to comparative advantage. The per unit cost of a 1-million-ton capacity steel plant is estimated at 60 per cent of the respective cost in a 50,000 tons plant. Existing projections of demand and supply are often contradictory and confusing, and a serious effort must be made to identify true data and more reliable projections, at least in the short run. Total Arab steel consumption of 25 million tons projected for 1985 seems highly exaggerated, on the basis of trends extrapolated from the also rather exaggerated estimate of present consumption of about 7 million tons. If the optimistic projections prove true, significant import-substitution should be allowed for, but even that should be on an integrated basis. However, if all the economies of the area proceed successfully with their impressive investment programmes in this sector, unexpected and unco-ordinated surpluses may appear, turning excessive demand into excessive supply, while the high production costs will presumably make competitiveness on the external market doubtful.[184]

This sector requires very careful planning, with considerations of scale, raw materials, market conditions, technology, skill and management, in view of the many setbacks experienced in this particular industry in the Middle East. There are reasonable potentials in Algeria, Morocco, Egypt, Iraq, Sudan, Syria and Kuwait, but the components of these potentials must be closely examined, the plans co-ordinated, and the whole sector – perhaps more than most others – regionally integrated.[185]

Arab planners are aware of the issues involved in developing modern industry under conditions prevailing on the international market on the one hand, and in the regionally co-ordinated and self-centred national economies in the area on the other. In February 1976,[186] the Arabian Gulf Organisation for Industrial Consulting (AGOIC) was set up, with the support of Saudi Arabia, Kuwait, UAE, Qatar, Bahrain, Oman and Iraq (with residence in Doha, Qatar), to streamline national plans and to avoid duplication of industrial projects through regional planning and co-ordination, feasibility studies and technological co-operation.

As we have shown, not all industries require large-scale enterprises and their efficiency mainly depends on other factors, such as skill, management and other factor endowments leading to comparative advantage. However, certain other industries, which are found to be central to Arab industrial strategies, such as steel, chemicals and petrochemicals, refineries, engineering industry and even modern textile plants, are dependent on a pool of technological and financial resources and on the economies of scale achieved through more integrated production and marketing.

Arab Co-operation with other Areas and Entities

The integration issue, with particular reference to industrial development, requires at least a short discussion of the Arab relationship with other major partners, chiefly with the European Community (EEC), and, more concisely, with the USA, Israel, OPEC and Africa.

Since its inception, the European Community attempted to compensate the developing countries for the Zollverein-like new economic bloc, and it set up a network of trade and financial arrangements for the LDCs. The special position of the Mediterranean, with its colonial heritage, oil resources and geo-political location, accorded it particular importance for the EEC. By 1972, the European Community had signed agreements with almost all Mediterranean countries, except Algeria, Syria, Libya and Albania, but the pattern of preferences and discriminations was not uniform nor consistent, although it largely followed the outlines of the agreements with Spain and Israel.

EEC-Mediterranean relations have gained particular significance since 1973, although even earlier oil supplies to the EEC countries on the one hand, and the Common Market's exports to the Mediterranean on the other, had been substantial. The Mediterranean constitutes about 12-13 per cent (equal to the USA) of EEC trade, which absorbs 50-60 per cent of total Mediterranean exports. Despite huge oil supplies by OAPEC to EEC, the trade balance is in favour of EEC, and for instance in 1975, the Maghreb and Mashreq countries, together with Mauritania, Somalia and Sudan, registered a trade deficit of US $3 billion with the European Community.[187]

Apart from the oil issue, the main bone of contention between the two partners are tariffs imposed by EEC's Common Agricultural Policy (CAP) on competitive agricultural imports from the Mediterranean. Recent agreements with the Maghreb (Algeria, Morocco and Tunisia) and Mashreq countries (Egypt, Syria, Lebanon and Jordan), in April 1976 and in January 1977, respectively, and with Israel, have introduced a degree of uniformity and reduced tariffs on most of these imports by 40 to 80 per cent, and promised 100 per cent tariff cuts on non-agricultural Arab exports as from 1977.[188]

The European character of the Community prevents North African and Middle Eastern countries from joining the Community as full members; only Greece, Turkey and Malta are eligible for such a membership. For the others, the association option is reserved. Association with EEC is possible through Art. 238 of the EEC Treaty, or Articles 131-136 on 'Associations of overseas countries and sovereign territories', but the term 'association' itself is not defined in the Treaty and therefore it is open to interpretation and negotiations. The term 'co-operation', not mentioned in the Treaty at all, is widely used in the negotiations, and agreements are made by the EEC with individual states and not with more or less integrated blocs. It is therefore difficult to envisage an official agreement with an integrated Arab multi-state entity, and this should be taken into account in integration planning or in an integrated industrial export drive. Nevertheless, a strong element of *regional* considerations can be detected in EEC's attitude to the countries of the area.

The European-Arab dialogue, which has gathered momentum since 1976, originated in the Arab summit meeting in Algiers before the oil crisis in 1973 and in a statement which read: 'Europe is linked to the Arab countries across the Mediterranean through cultural affinities and vital interests such as develop only in the compass of trusting co-operation and mutual benefit.'[189] Algeria itself was until 1962 a member state of EEC, because of its links with France, but since its independence new arrangements had to be worked out, more or less in the general framework of EEC's relations with the Maghreb countries, and similar to the association agreements with Tunisia and Morocco since 1969.

Three main issues have become focal in the EEC-Arab relations:

1. Arab pressure on EEC's political stand on the Middle East, Israel and the concessions granted to the latter by EEC.
2. Arab demands for tariff-free, unrestricted access of agricultural produce to the EEC markets.
3. The issue of reciprocity in tariff reduction on industrial goods, a matter on which, for instance, Israel can be more (though not fully) responsive than the less efficient and less competitive Arab industries.[190]

The Arab countries requested a non-reciprocal removal by EEC of tariff and non-tariff restrictions on Arab goods, and better terms of trade at large, to be achieved through price-indexing raw materials and stabilising Arab export earnings. Massive financial participation by the EEC in Arab economic ventures – up to 50 per cent – was among the Arab demands.[191]

Following protracted negotiations, the two sides agreed on a *status operandi,* although intermittently the Arab-European dialogue 'was not so much a dialogue but two monologues being delivered at roughly the same time'.[192]

Gradually, a global Mediterranean policy (GMP) has evolved (initiated by the European Parliament in 1970-71), which envisaged a free trade area along the Mediterranean littoral. The EEC published a pro-Arab declaration regarding the Middle East dispute, it granted preferential i.e., lower tariff rates on citrus to the Maghreb countries; it also granted more generous concessions on industrial rather than agricultural imports (in which Mediterranean competitiveness, with France and Italy particularly is significant); and allocated concessionary loans and grants to the Arab associates.[193] But the major underlying issue remained the economic competitiveness of Arab industry. In many cases even a zero tariff on Arab industrial goods would not help on the international market, while on the domestic Arab market, industrial products from abroad, though easier to contain, have remained a lasting menace to domestic production. Both internationally and domestically, industrial efficiency, as discussed earlier in the context of Arab strategy and integration, will have the decisive effect on the prospects of a structural change, especially in view of the fact that in the industrial field Mediterranean producers have little control of the market,[194] while the Community apparently developed a 'neo-mercantilist orientation [which] is not confined to the agricultural sector'.[195]

In the longer run, a large degree of reciprocity in tariff reductions or abolition must prevail. The EEC, in common with other economic blocs, cannot become a fully-fledged partner to Arab integration, in the latter term's strictest and fullest sense, but various aspects inherent in association, co-operation and adjustment can and should be envisaged in the streamlining of the Arab industrialisation process – namely, transfer of domestically adaptable technology; supply of capital goods essential for industrialisation; improved market conditions for Arab industrial exports; and investment stimuli and resources. These are, as a matter of fact, the Arab expectations from the European Community.

In programming an industrial scenario related to the EEC and other extra-Arab economies, the existing and potential Arab industries must be subjected to an analysis differentiating between various sectors and their relative strength on the international market. For instance, the Moroccan phosphate industry, which with one-third of total world supply and in great demand can largely dictate its terms (in 1974 its prices were quadrupled), is quite an exceptional case. Egyptian textiles and garments are representative of a long series of Arab industrial consumer goods, where an imposition of an even small duty involves reduction in prices and/or quantities sold. Since it can be hardly expected that the Community, with all its internal problems, will accommodate or even less likely integrate its industrial ventures with those of the Arab countries, except in some very particular cases or transnational undertakings, the onus of adjustment must stay mainly with the Arab economies and the inter-Arab, or Middle Eastern regional integration.

The Arab-US relations have been long since marred by the Israeli-Arab conflict, with recurring Arab attempts to convince the US that her (and the whole West's) economic interests lie with the Arabs and not with Israel.[196] *The Economist* quotes, without critical comment, sources which state that the two-way Arab-American trade, with $20 billion, is more than ten times as big as American-Israeli trade, and that Arab reprisals, which might follow American anti-boycott legislation, may constitute a threat to 500,000 American jobs, to billions of dollars of national income, to important sources of energy and to the overall American influence on the Middle East.[197] In a similar way, Dr Ibrahim A. Obaid[198] defines Israel as 'the only obstacle that stands in the way of ushering in an era of mutual and lasting co-operation' with the West, and states that 'had it not been for the said [Arab-Israeli] conflict the oil weapon would not have been unleashed'. This largely contradicts his own other contentions and complaints regarding Western exploitation, losses, soaring prices of industrial products, commodities prices indexation, etc. Most of Obaid's reasoning has been either partly refuted or flatly rejected by another participant in the same publication.[199]

A stick-and-carrot policy has been employed by the Arabs with regard to America, with the weapon of oil supply and prices as the stick, and petrodollars and Arab orders and markets as the carrot, and with the Soviet alternative permanently looming in the background. In fact, the US has been less dependent on the Arabs economically than

Europe. Its deficit with the Arabs of $2.5 billion in 1976 (in contrast with EEC's surplus)[200] has not been necessarily an economic incentive (particularly in view of its aid commitments), and in the longer run it is the American partner which seems to the Arab partner to be more essential politically and economically.

The United States, more than any other single country, is a powerful agent of industrial development, of supply and demand for any industrialising country, of almost unlimited potentials for alternative energy and other commodities sources, and, at the same time, her economic responsibility is of a global nature. Under these circumstances, the Arab countries' own interest in economic and industrial development will profit from close Arab-American economic partnership not by threatening with the oil weapon and counter-boycott measures nor at the expense and exclusion of some other countries, but rather with their full co-operation.

Political and national interests are absolutely legitimate and frequently enjoy higher rating than economic ones, but the latter are unjustly confused with material or even materialistic aspirations. Genuine economic interests in the final analysis, best serve the true social and national interests. If the Arab countries enter the path of an irreversible and sustained industrial growth, this will more effectively promote their aims of true political independence and of greater international and domestic social equity than any boycott, double-edged oil weapon or refusal to close ranks with an economic counterpart like Israel, which might be a bridge rather than a barrier, and a genuine partner in regional, integrated development.

This should prove true not only because 'some trade is always better than no trade',[201] but mainly due to the prospective and more promising spread of the industrial mentality and to the potentials of hammering out industrialisation patterns related to the area's realities, and to a stronger integrated supply and demand unit. In an integrated Arab-Israeli scenario, some of the partners may gain more, some less, but, for a combination of reasons, such as trade diversion and trade creation, reallocation of resources (mainly from military to civilian uses), and more efficient industrialisation planning, all should gain from a full utilisation of the options of a peace economy and more diversified regional trade.

It may be interesting to follow an Egyptian view on the economic impact of peace, much more constructive than that of Dr Obaid, mentioned earlier. Abdel Maguid, the Minister of Planning, submits that the first direct result will be the decline in total defence expenditure.

Then, Arab (oil) aid could be diverted from defence to economic purposes. Third, upon returning Sinai to Egypt, new oil potentials may be discovered. Fourth, peace conditions will endorse and sustain the momentum of development, and an improved economic atmosphere will increase confidence, accelerate the flow of foreign funds as well as of the remittances from Arabs working abroad.[202] This is *one* of rather few statements of this kind, but it presumably reflects the undercurrents of Arab thinking, which may not only stimulate Arab development strategy, but possibly also certain forms of mutually beneficial integration with Israel. The growing peace mentality is also reflected in actual measures taken, for instance, in the Suez area, designed to become, on the one hand, a free-zone area, and on the other, a focal industrial pole with refineries and a petrochemical complex, fertiliser, cement and other construction material.

The particular fields of industrial co-operation, apart from irrigation projects and desert settlement, could be in highly developed agro-business, desalination plants, fertiliser, pharmaceutical products, nuclear and solar energy, i.e. areas of either clear regional comparative advantage or projects requiring sophisticated technology in which know-how can be shared and based on regional R & D. This does not preclude profitable Israel-Arab co-operation in sectors whose efficiency is dependent first of all on Arab integration itself, such as oil refining, petrochemicals, gas liquefaction, steel plants and other large-scale ventures.

The Arab-Israeli conflict and the delicate relations with the outside world mollify Arab (and African) non-oil countries' grievances, nurtured against the OPEC and OAPEC on two accounts: (1) the inflationary, unbalancing and counter-development impact of soaring oil prices; and (2) the refusal of the 'haves' to share their riches and profits with the 'have-nots' on the latter's terms, either through outright grants, or at least by adequate concessionary loans and investments.

While some sources, such as the official Damascus daily *Al-Baath*, accuse the oil-rich Arab states of accumulating 'illegitimate wealth at the expense of the martyrs of the October (1973) war',[203] and receive the support of other have-nots in this outcry, OPEC sources, for instance in Kuwait, claim that the confrontation countries alone have received total aid of US $40 billion since 1967, and now 'the donors would like to have a better idea of what happened to that huge money'.[204]

African countries, either with close direct relations with Arab states, or in the framework of the Arab multilogue with African countries and other LDCs, intermittently speak out on the oil and OPEC subject, although they do it openly couched in the cautious terms of a desired economic co-operation. President Kaunda of Zambia is quoted in this respect: 'Many African countries still buy Arab oil through New York and many Arab countries still buy Ghana's cocoa and other African resources through British markets. With our established Afro-Arab solidarity, we must now build a new interdependent economic system, otherwise we shall remain at the mercy of industrialized countries.'

The African frustration, following high hopes raised after the 1973 Arab-Israeli war and the African declaration of solidarity with the Arabs, has been only partly mollified by launching various assistance and investment programmes, such as OPEC's Special Fund, the IDB (Islamic Development Bank), the KFAED (Kuwaiti Fund for Arab Economic Development), the SDF (Saudi Development Fund), or ABEDIA (Arab Bank for Economic Development in Africa, which took over SAFA – the Special Arab Fund for Africa). Despite largely concessionary terms, the funds were insufficient, actual disbursement falling behind nominal allocation, and hardly balancing the actual losses resulting from the rise of the oil bill. One of the major resentments was against the allegations concerning OPEC's investments and deposits in the West, which paid 5 per cent interest, and which were then re-lent to the LDCs, often at 15-20 per cent interest.[205] Another source of African discontent are the EEC agreements with the Mediterranean countries, which provide for closer trading and economic relationships than those under the Yaoundè and Arusha agreements, regarding the African countries.

Although clashes between close neighbours are often more frequent and more harsh than disputes between more distant counterparts, it is evident that the first and foremost partners for integration and industrial adjustment are the Arabs themselves, for cultural, national, geographic and economic reasons. If this partnership is still of limited practical value and success, it cannot be expected that salvation will come from more distant corners, where different, but similarly complex conditions and problems prevail. Nevertheless, successful Arab industrialisation is strongly related to the international economic community, its global and regional organisations, and its ability and willingness to meet the Arab development aspirations half-way. Even if fully-fledged integration of this kind is out of the question, mutual understanding and co-operation is certainly in the best interests of all parties concerned, and a realistic assessment of obstacles and prospects can help in thrashing out reasonable solutions.

Concluding Remarks

'Collective self-reliance', which is deemed to constitute the backbone of the new international economic order and of the prospective emergence of the third world as a major unified industrial power, involves many inherent contradictions and paradoxes. These are related to issues such as indexation, stabex, buffer stocks, free admission to international goods and capital markets, preferably on concessionary terms, and transfer and adjustment of technology, to accelerate the industrialisation process – all with the proviso of non-interference in the LDCs' own national, economic and social systems and aspirations. This set of issues belongs to a different area of study, but their complex and heterogeneous character highlights and partly explains the difficulties and bottlenecks facing Arab industrialisation and integration. Therefore, although Arab industrial strategy must take account first of all of its own premisses, endowments, conditions and targets, it cannot disregard the wider spectrum of ideas, strategies and actions in its immediate neighbourhood and in the larger, global dimension.

The effects of economies of scale cannot be very impressive on a static basis due to the limited size of the present Arab industry. A still unpublished investigation[206] of some 30 industrial sectors has shown that only 12-15 qualify for advantages resulting from economies of scale, while the remainder can reach optimal efficiency in smaller units. The total annual savings through eventual aggregation and integration are estimated at no more than 50 million-70 million dollars. Most of them are in chemicals, iron and steel, cement and car assembling. However, the order of magnitude will change radically under dynamic assumptions of a rapidly developing industry, modelled on modern technology and designed for both domestic import-substitutes and export-oriented products. This will require concentration of certain industries and even their relocation, according to the comparative advantage of the partners in the integrated area.

Comparative advantage itself should be considered from a dynamic rather than from a static angle. Otherwise, decisions taken may be both nationally unjust and economically inefficient in the longer run. The dynamic optimal advantages depend on exploration, applied technology, new inventions and production functions, and patterns of demand for consumer and capital goods.

The main variables concerned are: raw materials, labour, energy,[207] financial resources – their quantities, qualities and relative prices. Experience and know-how may be added as a variable deserving particular consideration. One variable alone cannot serve as an exclusive criterion. For instance, wages in select industries (textiles, wood, chemicals and metal products) in Israel in 1970, have been on average, around five times higher than in Egypt, while the estimated ratio of productivity per worker has been between 3 and 4 to 1. From this it might appear that the location of industries involved might be preferable in Egypt, but the inexactness of estimates, including the recalculation in terms of unsettled rates of foreign exchange, the wide differences between individual industries, the disparities in factor endowments (though partly reflected in labour costs), do not so far permit any conclusive projections.

With regard to the variables most relevant to location decisions, Egypt leads in raw materials and labour, Iraq in energy, Israel in capital intensity (but not in capital resources) and in technology and know-how, with other Arab countries joining those mentioned in certain variables. Although in terms of experience Egypt and Israel take the lead, still in 9 out of 23 individual industries *all* countries share similar experience.

In non-integrated economies, the size of the individual country's market (population and effective demand) is a decisive factor of location according to economies of scale, while desired location based on comparative advantage depends on the largest concentration of the relevant variables in optimal proportions. A combination of the two principles would give preference in most industries to either Egypt or Israel, on a static basis, but if integration, on the one hand, and dynamisation (time dimension) of the two principles, on the other hand, are envisaged, more countries may efficiently (and justly) participate in the industrial division of labour.

More extensive and detailed surveys and analysis of industries, including linkages and external economies and diseconomies, are required before well-founded criteria for division of labour between the Arab countries, or in the whole region, might be worked out. This division of labour, which largely reflects the overall issue of Arab industrialisation, is amplified by the secular trend in terms of trade, which, despite periods of commodity booms – correlated with upswings in the industrial economies but also sharing responsibility for their recessions – does not run in favour of primary producers, and constitutes a continuous menace to national income and balance of payments.[208] This adds another important dimension to Arab industrialisation, both from the indigenous structural angle and the global international aspect.

In conclusion, Muhammad Ali in Egypt and one hundred years later Kemal Ataturk in Turkey may not have been so wrong in stating that the main and foremost target should be to educate people to industrial thinking and mentality. The correlation between the latter and the successful process of industrialisation is evident. The only question, hard to answer, is that of sequence and causality, namely whether mentality is a prerequisite of industrialisation or the other way round. This will presumably remain one of the continuously disputed issucs.

Notes

1. This does not prevent the primary sectors from becoming leading sectors in development, or sources of capital accumulation, or high-earning sectors in their own right in periods of booming demand for and high prices of commodities.

2. See the discussion of Kuznets's and Myrdal's assertions of initial adverse effects of industrialisation on income equality, in H. Chenery and M. Syrquin, *Patterns of Development 1950–1970* (London, Oxford University Press, 1975), p. 60.

3. Cf. G. Myrdal, *The Challenge of World Poverty* (London, Pelican, 1970), p. 93, and H.W. Singer, *The Strategy of International Development* (London, Macmillan, 1975), p. 37.

4. J.B. Donges, 'A Comparative Survey of Industrialization Policies in Fifteen Semi-industrial Countries', *Weltwirtschaftliches Archiv*, band 112, 4 (1976), p. 642.

5. Ankie M.M. Hoogvelt, *The Sociology of Developing Societies* (London, Macmillan, 1976), pp. 80–1.

6. M.J. Williams, 'The Emerging New Realism in North-South Cooperation Development', *OECD Observer*, Nov./Dec. 1976.

7. Cf. H. Brookfield, *Interdependent Development* (1975), p. 72.

8. J. Tinbergen (Co-ordinator), *RIO, Reshaping the International Order, A Report to the Club of Rome* (New York, E.P. Dutton, 1976), p. 142.

9. Cf. W.G. Hoffman, *The Growth of Industrial Economies* (Oxford University Press, 1958), *passim.*

10. Cf. UN, *Monthly Bulletins of Statistics, passim.* See also our introductory remarks, above.

11. UN, *The Growth of World Industry 1938–1961* (NY, 1963), and UN, *Monthly Bulletins of Statistics, passim.*

12. P. Bairoch, *The Economic Development of The Third World since 1900* (London, Methuen & Co., 1975), p. 52.

13. C.V. Vaitsos, *Intercountry Income Distribution and Transnational Enterprises* (Oxford, Clarendon Press, 1974), p. 3.

14. J. Tinbergen, *Economics in the Future,* p. 43. This definition is qualified by the possibility that in time the mix of factors may change, either by different technology, or by new factors endowment, and therefore it assumes

dynamic dimensions.

15. Cf. Chenery and Syrquin, *Patterns of Development*, p. 33.

16. Raymond Vernon, 'International Investment and International Trade in Product Cycle', *Quarterly Journal of Economics*, 80 (1966), pp. 190–207.

17. This point will be referred to on an empirical level below.

18. Harry G. Johnson, *Technology and Economic Interdependence* (London, Macmillan, 1975), p. 36.

19. Cf. J.B. Donges, 'A Comparative Survey', p. 654.

20. Similarly, export drive may rely on heavy subsidy rather than on efficiency. In the final analysis, the issue is driven back to the Heckscher-Ohlin model of international trade, where its direction and nature are determined by the differences in the relative factor endowments. Cf. Harry G. Johnson, *Technology and Economic Interdependence*, p. 34.

21. Cf. IDCAS, UNIDO, *An Approach to Industrial Development Strategy and Arab Industrial Cooperation*, Working Paper (original, Arabic), *Document No: IDC 4/WP*, Baghdad, 1976 (Later quoted: *IDC 4/WP*, Baghdad).

22. See items on manufacturing in Table 1.2, as well as our discussion below.

23. Cf. Table on Select Economic Indicators of Arab Countries and Israel; *IDCAS*, 'L'industrie de transformation dans certains pays arabes', Tripoli Conference, 7–14 April 1974; and *Acier Arabe (Al-Sulb Al-Arabi)*, Revue mensuelle publiée par l'Union du Fer et de l'Acier, Alger, 43/1977.

24. R.B. Sutcliffe, *Industry and Underdevelopment* (London, Addison-Wesley, 1971), pp. 17–18.

25. Cf. Gian Paolo Casadio, *The Economic Challenge of the Arabs* (London, Saxon House Lexington Books, 1976), pp. 116–17.

26. UN sources.

27. Egyptian planners are proud of the already significant electricity supply of 8 billion KwH, and expect 18 billion KwH by 1980, and 29 billion KwH by the mid-1980s. But apart from the feasibility of the targets themselves, the rate and efficiency of utilisation depend on simultaneous growth of demand, or, eventually, sales to bordering countries.

28. Cf. *Memo*, Middle East Money, Beirut, 25.10.1976. Also B. Hansen is highly critical of excessive investments in the steel and automobile industry, which handicaps modernisation of the textile industry and expansion of cement production. Cf. B. Hansen, in A.S. Becker, B. Hansen, M.H. Kerr, *The Economics and Politics of the Middle East* (New York-London-Amsterdam, Elsevier, 1975), p. 23.

29. *IDC 4/WP*, Baghdad, *passim*. Estimated Arab iron ore reserves are 8,000 million tons, but even in 1985 expected (though hardly feasible) Arab steel production will be only 16 million tons, thus leaving a margin of nearly 10 million tons for required imports. See, *Acier Arab*, 43/1977.

30. *Al-Ahram Al-Iqtisadi*, 15.6.1976.

31. *IDCAS*, 1974.

32. Cf. 'Common Market and Economic Integration in the Gulf', *Al-Ahram Al-Iqtisadi*, Cairo, 15.5.1975.

33. *Memo*, 6.9.1976.

34. Cf. Table 1.2, and *IDC 4/WP*, p. 3. See also R. Mabro and S. Radwan, *The Industrialization of Egypt, 1939–1973* (Oxford, 1976), p. 219.

35. See the article by Nabil Sabbagh, in *Al-Ahram Al-Iqtisadi*, Cairo, 1.7.1976. It should be added that the degree of concentration in overall Arab exports is particularly striking. It is a double concentration, reflected in the preponderance of primary exports *and* of one major commodity. In the late 1960s and early 1970s, *oil (plus*, in some cases, gas or asphalt) constituted 73.4 per cent of total exports in Algeria, Iraq 90 per cent, Kuwait 93 per cent, Libya 99.7 per cent,

Oman 99 per cent, Saudi Arabia 99.8 per cent; *raw cotton* contributed in Syria 40.9 per cent, Egypt 47.2 per cent, South Yemen 46.5 per cent, Sudan 60.9 per cent; *coffee* in North Yemen 38 per cent; *live animals* in Somalia 52.5 per cent. In other countries single commodities contributed less, but in some cases 25–30 per cent. Cf. Kuwait Fund for Arab Economic Development, *Key Indicators of Arab Countries,* April 1975, Table 6.3.

36. In Egypt, a committee headed by the Deputy Minister of Finance, Ibrahim Kotb estimated Egyptian war losses since June 1967 at US $40 billion, including $3.7 billion unearned Suez Canal revenues, $4.4 billion lost oil revenues, and military losses, training costs and destruction of housing and installations. Cf. *Memo,* Beirut, 26.4.1976.

37. As already indicated, detailed figures must be considered with great reservation, due to variety of differing sources and insufficient definitional clarity of industry or manufacturing. It is rather the order of magnitude which counts and which may be considered reliable if extrapolated from a longer trend. Cf. Table 1.2, and Kuwait Fund for Arab Economic Development, *Key Indicators of Arab Countries,* April 1975, Table 5.1, as well as *Business International,* March 1976, p. 33, and data of Egyptian Agency for Public Mobilisation and Statistics; also, *Financial Times,* 28.6.1976.

38. In the last 20 years, average annual agricultural growth ranged from 2.6 per cent in Syria, to 3.2 per cent in Egypt, and 3.4. per cent in Iraq, thus leaving only a marginal per capita growth of 0.5-1.0 per cent only. Cf. Bairoch, *Economic Development of the Third World,* pp. 20–21.

39. The prevailing urban low-income (an average £E 175 p.a.) family in Egypt spends 67 per cent on food and beverages, while the high-income (£E 1,800 p.a.) spends only 43.8 per cent.

40. *Memo,* Beirut, 26.2.1976.

41. *Business International,* March 1976, p. 43.

42. The absence of foreign competition, cut off from the domestic market by government measures, often led to less productivity.

43. *Memo,* Beirut, 25.10.1976.

44. B. Hansen has this to say on the subject: 'Stability in totalitarian systems is conducive to the emergence of a parasitic class without genuine development interests surrounding the rulers.' Cf. A.S. Becker, B. Hansen, M.H. Kerr, *Economics and Politics of the Middle East,* p. 26.

45. These were partly at least the results of the Egyptian government's undertaking to employ all university graduates.

46. *MEED,* 25.2.1977. In Jordan, out of 31 vocational schools, 14 are industrial. 300,000 Jordanians are now working abroad. Jordan is called a 'victim of its own developed education and training system'.

47. A very good discussion of these issues can be found in Nabil Sabbagh, in *Al-Ahram Al-Iqtisadi,* 1.7.1976.

48. Cf. SIPRI, *World Armaments and Disarmament,* current Yearbooks, *passim.*

49. It should be noticed, however, that overall Egypt's share in world exports constantly fell, from 0.8-1 per cent by 1947/8, to 0.2 per cent throughout 1970–74. UN, *Yearbooks of International Trade Statistics, passim.* See also, Egyptian *Statistical Handbooks,* and publications of the Federation of Egyptian Industries. More recent estimates set Egyptian industrial employment at about 16 per cent.

50. Cf. Z.Y. Hershlag, *The Economic Structure of the Middle East* (Leiden, E.J. Brill, 1975), pp. 118–20.

51. With regard to electricity, see our comments on industrial indicators, above. Cf. also, *Arab Oil & Gas,* 1.2.1977, pp. 18–19; *Al-Ahram Al-Iqtisadi,*

15.1.1977.

52. See *The Economic Structure of the Middle East*, p. 120.

53. In the later 1960s and early 1970s, even a fall in labour productivity was observed, though this may be due to statistical over-estimates of labour inputs.

54. IMF, *International Financial New Surveys, passim; Al-Ahram*, 1.4.1972.

55. For larger nationalised industries, but rather neglecting the small enterprises.

56. This issue has been referred to in this study in a more general context, but it might be instructive to read a quotation from *MEED*, 28.1.1977, p. 5: In Egypt, the open door policy only 'exposed the administration as being ineffective and chaotic and has been little more, so far, than an invitation to rich Egyptians and foreigners to open up night clubs and take out agencies. The result was that Arab aid fell last year to around half the $2,000 million level it had reached in 1975; the Arab oil producers had no wish to pour their money down what they termed "an open drain".'

57. Cf. R. Mabro and S. Radwan, *The Industrialization of Egypt, 1939–1973, Policy and Performance* (Oxford, Clarendon Press, 1976), pp. 30–31.

58. Cf. *Business International, Egypt*, March 1976, pp. 51 ff. In the mid-1970s, Egypt exported about £E 200 million industrial goods. Plans for 1980 envisage £E 500m exports but still over £E 1 billion imports of industrial goods.

59. *Memo*, Beirut, 22.11.1976, pp. 10–11.

60. Ibid.

61. *Statistical Abstract of Syria*, 1975; UN, *Statistical Yearbooks*, annual; *Al-Ishtiraki*, Damascus, 13.5.1974.

62. A survey on a weaving factory in Aleppo found that labour productivity there stood at one-twentieth only of that in a parallel industry in the US. Cf. *Al-Iqtisadi*, Damascus, 1.11.1972.

63. Syria, *Statistical Abstract*, 1975.

64. Syria, *Statistical Abstract*, 1975.

65. Syria, Ministry of Planning, *Appropriations for the Third Five-Year Plan for Economic and Social Development*, 1971–5.

66. Syria, Central Bureau of Statistics and General Directorate of Customs – current publications.

67. *Statistical Abstract*, 1975.

68. Syria, Central Bureau of Statistics and General Direction of Customs sources.

69. Ibid.

70. *Memo*, Beirut, 6.9.1976.

71. UN, *Yearbooks of National Accounts Statistics, passim.*

72. The data referred to are quoted from that report.

73. IDA *Report*, and *Memo*, Beirut, 6.9.1976. This statement, however, may be exaggerated in comparison with other sources. See above.

74. Although it includes mining, the development of which may be more rapid than that of manufacturing. In 1974, iron ore deposits were discovered on a promising scale.

75. *Memo*, Beirut, 12.7.1976, and IDA, *Report*.

76. We referred elsewhere in this study to the labour issue of Jordan.

77. Which are so far responsible for 90 per cent of all establishments, as indicated above.

78. IDA, *Report*.

79. Cf. Jordan's *Statistical Yearbooks*, and Central Bank's *Monthly Statistical Bulletins*.

80. Cf. S.S. Sedki, 'Industrial Development of Iraq in the Context of Over-all Economic Plans' (PhD Thesis, School of Business, University of Northern

Colorado, Microfilm), 1974.

81. Cf. *MEED,* 4.3.1977.

82. *The Arab Economist,* January 1974; Republic of Iraq, Ministry of Planning, *Industrial Development of Iraq,* Potential Areas of Co-operation with Developed Countries, Sept. 1975, pp. 3–4; *Memo,* Beirut, 6.12.1976.

83. Cf. S.S. Sedki, 'Industrial Development of Iraq'.

84. *Memo,* 6.12.1976.

85. Cf. Iraq, *National Development Plan, 1970–75, passim.*

86. Ibid.; *Memo,* 6.12.1976.

87. *Industrial Development of Iraq,* p. 10.

88. Ibid., p. 11.

89. Ibid., pp. 1–2, 15–16.

90. Ibid., pp. 22 ff.

91. *Memo,* 26.12.1976. As already indicated, at an annual gas production of 8 billion cubic metres, Algeria's present total capacity of liquefaction reaches 5 billion c.m. Liquefied natural gas is produced entirely for export.

92. Cf. Murque, in *Actuel Developpement,* GEDITEC, 3–4/76.

93. For instance, production of fertiliser in 1973/4 was estimated as meeting domestic demand. Even if this increases, the expected further growth in this sector necessitates extensive market outlets.

94. Cf. IBRD, *Current Economic Position and Prospects of Morocco,* Feb. 1974.

95. If recent estimates for 1974–7 prove true, the annual rate of growth may reach 7 per cent, and the per capita over 4 per cent (IBRD sources).

96. Some sources quote the figure of 35 per cent, which includes smaller urban centres possibly disregarded in the previous figure.

97. *Memo,* 12.4.1976.

98. Cf. Morocco, Secrêtariat d'Etat au Plan publications, *passim.*

99. Ibid., *passim.*

100. It should be noted that the phosphate sector is based on labour-intensive extraction, with 14,000 employees, mostly unskilled and semi-skilled.

101. IDA sources.

102. Sources of Secrêtariat d'Etat au Plan.

103. Cf. *Memo,* 12.4.1976.

104. Cf. Ministère du Plan, *IVe Plan.*

105. *Memo,* 26.7.1976.

106. Data of the Central Bank of Tunisia.

107. *IVe Plan de Developpement Economique et Social, 1973–76.*

108. Ministère du Plan projections.

109. *Memo,* 26.7.1976.

110. Institut National de la Statistique, *Statistiques du Commerce Extérieur de la Tunisie.*

111. Ministry of Planning Data.

112. IMF, *Direction of Trade, Annual Reports.*

113. *MEED,* 28.1.1977, p. 8.

114. W. Leontieff, in UN, *The Future of the World Economy* (NY, 1976). Cf. also *D & C,* Bonn – Berlin, 2/77.

115. *IDC 4/WP,* Baghdad, 1976.

116. Cf. *Acier Arabe,* 43/1977.

117. Cf. B. Hansen, *Economics and Politics of the Middle East,* p. 37.

118. Cf. Petroleum Economist Data, *Arab Oil & Gas,* 1.2.1977.

119. It might be interesting to compare the average *annual growth of military spending* of 19 per cent in the Middle East, with *national product growth* of about 5 per cent (apart from sudden jumps in oil countries), and industrial growth of

6.2 per cent. The M.E. confrontation countries' case, except Israel (and temporarily only), does not confirm the Benoit (1973) thesis of a positive correlation of levels of military spending and non-military growth rates. Moreover, the causal direction of this correlation is not established.

120. *Al-Mejella Al-Askariyah*, Damascus, August-September 1975, pp. 13–29. Only few, as we shall see below, speak out clearly against waste of resources on arms and in favour of a peace strategy.

121. Cf. Dr George Tomeh, in Edmond Völker (ed.), *Euro-Arab Cooperation,* (Leiden, Sijthof, 1976), p. 198; Cf. also *IDC 4/WP,* p. 10.

122. See my *Introduction to the Modern Economic History of the Middle East* (Leiden, Brill, 1964), Chs. on Egypt.

123. Cf. *IDC 4/WP,* p. 1.

124. Ibid., p. 19.

125. Cf. Azam Rifaat, 'New Strategy for Arab Industry', *Al-Ahram Al-Iqtisadi,* 15.7.1975, pp. 12–13.

126. Cf. B. Hansen, *Economics and Politics of the Middle East, passim.*

127. W. Leontieff, *Future of the World Economy.*

128. Cf. Murque, in *Actuel Developpement*, revue bimestrielle, GEDITEC, Paris, 3–4/76.

129. These reasons can be illustrated, *inter alia,* by the fact that the value of foreign contractors' works in the Arab countries for the period 1975–80 has been estimated at US $28.2 billion by the *Financial Times,* according to *Acier Arabe,* 43/1977.

130. *Acier Arabe,* 44/1977.

131. Cf. *A Global Model,* Princeton, *passim.*

132. Cf. *IDC 4/WP,* 3 ff.

133. *IDC 4/W,* 12 ff.

134. Cf. *Acier Arabe,* 43, 44/1977; Azam Rifaat, 'New Strategy for Arab Industry', *Al-Ahram Al-Iqtisadi,* 15.7.1975, pp. 12–13.

135. Cf. Bernard Murque, in *Actuel Developpement,* no. 12, March-April 1972, p. 27.

136. B. Hansen, in Becker *et al., Economics and Politics of the Middle East,* p. 25.

137. *Memo,* 6.12.1976.

138. For a more general discussion of the issue, see W. Leontieff, *Future of the World Economy, passim.*

139. Cf. Tomeh, in Edmond Völker (ed.), *Arab Co-operation* (Leiden, A.W. Sijthof, 1976), p. 198 and *passim.*

140. *Middle East Economic Digest,* 20.5.1977.

141. An Arab source comments: 'A push-button system needs *more* than just pushing the button.' *Memo,* 25.10.1976.

142. Cf. *Egyptian Gazette,* Dec. 1976, especially on water and power supply and utilisation. See also, *Arab Oil and Gas,* 1.2.1977.

143. See in this respect, *El-Mal Wa'altegarah,* Oct. 1976.

144. Cf. Nabil Sabbagh, in *Al-Ahram Al-Iqtisadi.*

145. See, for instance, President Sadat's 'October Paper' of 1974, on the issues of liberalisation, decentralisation, encouragement of private foreign investment and inter-Arab co-operation.

146. *Arab Oil & Gas* published by the Arab Petroleum Research Center, Paris-Beirut, vol. V, no. 129, 1.2.1977, pp. 18–19. The process of decentralisation and reorganisation of the public sector was set into motion in Egypt, but it remains to be seen whether the vested interests can be overcome. See *Business International,* March 1976.

147. Arab Republic of Egypt, Ministry of Planning, *Memorandum on*

Programs and Projects Suggested for Foreign Financing, February 1977.

148. *Al-Ahram Al-Iqtisadi*, 25.4.1976; *Business International*, Egypt, March 1976, p. 43.

149. Cf. *Acier Arabe*, 1977/45.

150. The differences between most of the terms mentioned are discussed in Peter Gonschior's 'Impediments to the Co-ordination of National Cyclical Policies in the EEC', *Intereconomics*, no. 1/2, 1977.

151. Azam Rifaat, 'New Strategy for Arab Industry'.

152. *Acier Arabe*, 43, 44/1977.

153. Cf. Nabil Sabbagh, *Al-Ahram Al-Iqtisadi.*

154. *El-Mal Wa'altegarah*, Oct. 1976.

155. See our comments in the preceding section, in the passage on the comprehensive scenario, point F, p. 62.

156. *El-Mal Wa-altegarah*, October 1976.

157. *Al-Ahram Al-Iqtisadi*, 15.6.1976.

158. Cf. Ibrahim A. Obaid, in Völker, *Arab Co-operation*, p. 172; and, *Business International*, March 1976, pp. 51 ff.

159. Cf. IMF, *Direction of Trade*, Washington, December 1976.

160. In fact, inter-Arab trade has been also adversely affected by trade barriers between Arab countries, either due to shortages in supply (on the export side), or due to the competitive rather than complementary character of production (on the import side). Cf. *Al-Ahram Al-Iqtisadi*, 15.6.1976.

161. *IDC 4/WP*, pp. 8–9.

162. See IMF, *IFS, passim.*

163. Earlier forms of regional co-operation, such as the Middle East Supply Centre, or the Customs Union between Syria and Lebanon, belong to the past, but they may still serve as interesting models of certain forms of integration. See, my *Introduction to the Modern Economic History of the ME*, 1964, and, *The Economic Structure of the ME*, (1975), *passim.*

164. Cf. R.W. MacDonald, *The League of Arab States* (Princeton, 1964), *passim; Al-Gumhuriya*, 21.6.1976.

165. *IDC 4/WP*, p. 33.

166. Nabil Sabbagh, in *Al-Ahram Al-Iqtisadi, passim*, 1976. Cf. also *MEED*, 7 January 1977, p. 9.

167. See *Al-Tāliyah*, May 1976; and, *Tishrin*, Syria, 21.1.1977.

168. Cf. Amin Dahbar, *Etude Analytique et Statistique sur le Marché Commun Arabe, et l'Oeuvre Economique de la Ligue Arabe* (Damas, n.d.), p. 103.

169. *Al-Tāliyah*, May 1976.

170. *IDC 4/WP*, p. 25.

171. Tomeh, in Völker, *Arab Co-operation*, pp. 198–9.

172. Cf. *Al-Ahram Al-Iqtisadi*, 15.6.1976; George Tomeh, in Völker, ibid., *passim.*

173. The restricted line of thinking of the Arab Common Market is reflected, *inter alia*, in its emphasis on reaching a common Arab customs barrier by 1978. Cf. *Alrai*, 6.10.1976.

174. Tomeh, *Arab Co-operation.*

175. *Al-Tāliyah*, May 1976.

176. *IDC 4/WP*, pp. 8–9.

177. *Iraqi News Agency*, 2.5.1977.

178. *Egyptian News Agency*, 3.5.1977.

179. *Al Gumhuriyah*, 30.4.1977.

180. Cf. Dr Hamid Omar, in *Al-Ahram Al-Iqtisadi*, 15.1.1977.

181. *Al Gumhuriyah*, 27.3.1977.

182. *Arab Oil & Gas*, 1.2.1977.

183. *Al Gumhuriyah,* 5.3.1977.
184. *Business International,* March 1976.
185. *Al Gumhuriyah,* 21.1.1977.
186. Cf. *MEED,* 25.2.1977.
187. *MEED,* 25.2.1977.
188. *MEED,* 25.2.1977.
189. Quoted in Rudolf Regul, 'The State and Prospects of the Mediterranean Policy of the EEC', *Intereconomics,* no. 1/2, 1977, p. 19.
190. In the Israel-EEC agreement, Israeli customs duties on EEC's industrial products should be abolished by 1 January 1989, while EEC's duties in Israeli products were to be reduced by 60 per cent immediately, by 80 per cent on 1 January 1976, and abolished completely by 1 July 1977.
191. Regul, 'The State and Prospects of the Mediterranean Policy', p. 22.
192. *The Economist,* 19 February 1977, p. 58. This is a reference to the Tunis Arab-European meeting on 13 February 1977, where EEC refused to discuss an overall preferential treatment of the Arab League. Cf. *MEED,* 18.2.1977.
193. *MEED,* 25.2.1977.
194. Cf. Avi Shlaim, 'The Community and the Mediterranean Basin', in K.J. Twichett (ed.), *Europe and the World, The External Relations of the Common Market* (London, Europa Publications, 1976), pp. 90 ff.
195. Ibid., p. 100.
196. I.A. Obaid, in Völker, *Arab Co-operation,* p. 177.
197. *The Economist,* 14 May 1977, p. 47.
198. In E. Völker, *Arab Co-operation,* pp. 176 ff.
199. Dr Louis Metzemaekers, in Völker, ibid., *passim.*
200. *MEED,* 20.5.1977.
201. Cf. A.S. Becker, B. Hansen, M.H. Kerr, *Economics and Politics of the Middle East,* pp. 30–31.
202. *MEED,* 13.5.1977.
203. Quoted in *MEED,* 4.3.1977.
204. Ibid.
205. Ibid., 4.3.1977, and 18.3.1977.
206. Most of the data and findings referred to in this summary originate in a study carried out under the direction of the author, on the economic implications of peace in the Middle East, at the Horowitz Institute, Tel-Aviv University.
207. For instance, energy costs seem at the moment to be higher in Syria, Lebanon, Jordan and Iraq than in Israel, but presumably lower in Egypt, despite the sub-optimal efficiency of the hydro-electrical plants in that country. However, upon the development and implementation of hydro-electric and possibly solar energy in other countries of the region, the relative costs may change.
208. UN, *World Economic Surveys, passim; Yearbooks of International Trade Statistics, passim;* UNCTAD, *Trade and Development Policies in the 1970s,* 1973.

2 ARAB ECONOMIC CO-OPERATION: IMPLICATIONS FOR THE ARAB AND WORLD ECONOMIES

Samir A. Makdisi

The purpose of this study is four-fold: the first is to portray the current status of Arab economic co-operation. What progress has been achieved among the Arab countries in terms of the goals of multilateral economic co-operation which they have set for themselves? The second is to assess some of the major factors which govern the effectiveness of Arab economic co-operation and explain its present limitations. The third is to analyse the potential gains from a closer and more effective Arab economic co-operation. What are some of the major prerequisites for realising any potential gain and in what area are they expected to manifest themselves? The fourth is to examine briefly some of the implications of an assumed close Arab economic co-operation to the world economy.

The study is accordingly divided into four main sections: (1) The form and extent of Arab economic co-operation; (2) Arab economic interdependence: effectiveness and limitations; (3) gains from more effective Arab economic co-operation; and (4) some implications of Arab economic integration to the Arab and world economies. A final section contains concluding observations.

Arab Economic Co-operation: Form and Extent

Meaning of Co-operation and Integration

When a group of countries aims at integrating their economies, the implication is that they aim at abolishing all restrictions on the movement of goods, permit a high degree of mobility of resources and co-ordinate their economic and developmental policies in order to realise any potential gains from integration. Economic integration thus reflects an advanced stage of economic co-operation where individual countries have agreed to give up their sovereignty over certain important economic policy issues in favour of the joint sovereignty of the group. This type of co-operation is often referred to as an economic union.[1] The free trade area, customs union, joint ventures, preferential payments arrangements, etc. are, in turn, alternative forms of economic co-operation, which are designed to achieve closer economic interdependence among groups of countries.[2] Each of these arrangements has its own implications for the nature of economic interdependence which is likely to arise as well as to the potential gains (and losses) which are likely to accrue to the individual countries which have decided on any of them. Historically, moves towards closer economic interdependence have been gradual. In a number of cases, their ultimate objectives were not realised[3] and we therefore often find prevailing arrangements among groups of countries that do not go beyond the extension of certain forms of trade and/or payments privileges, though originally these countries had been bent on achieving much closer economic co-operation and interdependence.

Measures to effect multilateral economic co-operation among the Arab countries go back to the early postwar period[4] (see following section). The achievement of some form of economic unity among the Arab countries has always been a declared objective of the Arab League. It has not been realised, despite various efforts at drawing up agreements designed to move the Arab economies in that direction. Whatever form Arab economic co-operation has taken, whether it was intended as a full customs union, or a common market, or simply the extension of certain trade and payment privileges, or more recently joint ventures, two features of this co-operation stand out. The first concerns the implementation of the agreed measures. Generally this has been limited in nature. This statement is perhaps more applicable to measures that were intended for the Arab countries as a whole rather than to preferential measures which are applicable to sub-groups of these countries. The second feature relates to the type of co-operation which has been envisaged among the Arab countries. At present it would be difficult to classify it other than to state that it comprises certain trade and other preferential arrangements. That is, the type of economic co-operation which prevails today among the Arab countries, or among sub-groups of these countries, cannot be described as a truly free trade area, a customs union, a payment arrangement or any other specific arrangement. The reason is that while, in principle, moves in the direction of specific economic arrangements were imitated, in practice, they faced hindrances which prevented the attainment of this goal.

Accordingly, when one refers to Arab economic co-operation one has to differentiate carefully between measures agreed in principle and adopted *de jure* and the actual steps taken towards their implementation. One has also to differentiate between overall Arab multilateral action and actions taken by sub-groups of the Arab countries.[5] Only then can one hope to establish a clear picture of the present status of Arab economic co-operation, and what it implies to the individual Arab economies, and to the outside world.

Multilateral Trade Privileges

The initial step towards Arab multilateral economic co-operation was taken by the Arab League on 7 September 1953 when it drew up a trade and transit treaty the primary purpose of which was to facilitate trade and transit movements among the Arab countries.[6] The main provision of this treaty relates to the extension of preferential treatment in customs duties. Agricultural and animal produce were to be exempted from those duties. Industrial and intermediate products[7] became subject to a reduction of 25 and 50 per cent respectively in the applicable duty.[8] Thus as it stood this treaty fell far short of establishing a free trade area or a customs union. It did not provide for the elimination of all customs duties, nor did it deal with other trade barriers particularly those of an administrative nature such as licensing or quotas. Further, it did not call for the establishment of a common external tariff *vis-à-vis* the outside world. It was a very limited move in the direction of closer multilateral trade relationships. Even then it was not effectively applied by the signatory countries.[9]

On 3 June 1957 another attempt at multilateral co-operation was initiated. The Treaty of Arab Economic Unity was drawn up establishing the Council of Arab Economic Unity (CAEU). The treaty was not approved however, until mid-1962 and the initial efforts of the Council to effect multilateral co-operation were not begun until 3 August 1964. At that time a decision was taken to establish an Arab Common Market (ACM).[10] While the ultimate objective was a full economic union, this was to be attained in stages beginning with the gradual implementation of a free trade area among the signatory countries. In practice, only four countries, namely Egypt, Iraq, Jordan and Syria, have so far agreed to implement a free trade area[11] which, as of the end of 1970, was in operation at least as far as the abolition of customs duties is concerned.[12] Important obstacles which still remain in the face of the free movement of goods among these four countries pertain to trade regulations of an administrative nature, e.g. licensing, *ad hoc* decisions by public sector organisations, etc. Existing evidence appears to indicate that these regulations have continued to act as hindrances to the free movement of goods.[13] To that extent a truly free trade area among these four countries has not yet been fully established.

Exchange Policies and Capital Movements

Exchange Policies. In contrast with the trade field, Arab multilateral co-operation at the level of payments has been almost non-existent.[14] As in trade policies, the evolving exchange systems and policies of the various Arab countries have differed greatly: from complete freedom of exchange operations to very strict controls over current and capital transfers. Similarly, exchange rate policies have also differed, with most countries up to 1971 maintaining fixed and unified exchange rates and subsequently linking their currency to the dollar or the SDRs.[15] Others have maintained unified floating rates. A few countries have maintained dual or multiple rates.

At present the prevailing exchange systems of the Arab countries may be divided into three categories.[16] The first would include countries maintaining a liberal exchange system with no restrictions being imposed on international economic transactions, i.e. Lebanon, the Yemen Arab Republic and the petroleum exporting countries of Bahrain, Kuwait, Qatar, Oman, Saudi Arabia and the UAE. The exchange rate policies presently followed by members of this group differ. Bahrain, Oman and the UAE have the dollar rate of their national currencies fixed. Accordingly, the value of their respective national currencies *vis-à-vis* one another is also fixed. Saudi Arabia and Qatar have linked their currencies to the SDRs: their value *vis-à-vis* other currencies (not linked to the SDRs) will therefore fluctuate in accordance with the fluctuations of the SDRs. The currency of Lebanon and the Yemen Arab Republic are market-determined.[17]

The second category would include countries which maintain controls over current economic transactions but follow a liberal policy, at least with respect to a large portion of import items. Included are Jordan and the North African countries of Libya, Tunisia, Algeria and Morocco. In the case of Algeria and Libya, the public sector has a monopoly over the importation of several important commodities. Payments for invisibles are normally subject to certain limits depending upon the purpose of the payment. The Jordanian currency is linked to the SDRs, the Moroccan currency to the French franc and the Libyan currency to the US dollar. Both Algeria and Tunisia maintain independent exchange policies, i.e. daily rates are established by the Central Bank.

The third category would include countries the current international economic transactions of which are subject to strict controls although the degree of their severity may differ from one country to another. Included are Egypt, Iraq, Syria and Democratic Yemen. In all of them the public sector plays an important role in foreign trade. Payments for invisibles either require a licence or are subject to specific limits. The national currencies of all four countries are presently linked to the US dollar. Egypt maintains, in addition, a parallel exchange market which applies to less essential imports and specified invisibles (e.g. travel allowances).[18] The rate in this market is determined in the light of evolving foreign exchange conditions.

Capital Movements. Concerning the first category of countries, capital movements are unrestricted. Kuwait, however, requires that at least 51 per cent of new Kuwaiti companies must be held by Kuwaiti nationals. Similarly, Qatar requires a minimum of 51 per cent participation of its nationals in certain industrial enterprises.

The other Arab countries apply strict controls over capital movements, though they have all enacted foreign investment laws designed to encourage the inflow of capital: repatriation of profits and principal is permitted in accordance with specified schedules. In the case of Syria special facilities for investment apply to Arab capital.[19] In 1975 an Arab institution for the guarantee of investments began operations.[20] Its primary objective is to ensure Arab investors against non-commercial risks. As such it is expected to help stimulate inter-Arab investments though its financial facilities are judged to be relatively limited while certain improvements in its legal set-up and policies seem to be called for if it is to serve its objective effectively.[21]

It may be noted, therefore, that with the exception of Syria no special facilities are extended to Arab investments by the Arab countries and no specific inducements apart from the above mentioned investment guarantee have been established to encourage inter-Arab capital flows.

Impact of the Growth in Financial Resources of the Arab Petroleum-exporting Countries on Arab Economic Co-operation

The dramatic growth in the financial resources at the disposal of the Arab petroleum-exporting countries[22] has had an important impact on the efforts to achieve Arab economic co-operation. This impact has manifested itself in at least two ways: the first is the induced shift in the nature of economic co-operation from the trade to the financial spheres.[23] The regional and national financial institutions which have been established[24] have acted as a channel for the multilateral transfer of Arab funds among the Arab countries, in addition to direct bilateral transfers which have taken place for economic and non-economic reasons.[25] This is an important form of co-operation because the flow of capital has been induced generally in accordance with certain criteria designed for this purpose. In the absence of such institutions these flows may not have occurred, at least their level and geographic and investment pattern would have been different, being then governed by autonomous decisions based on a calculus of private costs and benefits. The second is a renewed emphasis on multilateral economic co-operation which was stimulated by the substantial growth in the financial resources of the petroleum exporting countries.[26] The fact that this renewed emphasis could take the form of financial flows rather than the further extension of trade and payments privileges may have acted to ease efforts to achieve effective multilateral co-operation. The concept of economic co-operation is perhaps less difficult to accept and implement when it manifests itself in bilateral and/or multilateral financial flows than when it requires the abolition of trade and payments restrictions or the co-ordination of economic policies. While efforts to attain closer inter-Arab economic co-operation and interdependence in the trade and payments spheres have not ceased, indeed in recent years have intensified, it may be said that a parallel and perhaps potentially more effective channel for this co-operation is the financial channel. Progress in this area may so far have been relatively limited, as demonstrated in the preceding section. But it could act as the new stimulus for closer economic integration among the Arab countries. Free capital movements (whether induced or autonomous) may in this case precede and ultimately lead the way to the free movement of goods and (to a certain degree) labour.[27]

Arab Economic Interdependence: Effectiveness and Limitations

Inter-Arab Trade

Two aspects of inter-Arab trade which would need to be considered are (1) the magnitude of this trade and (2) its composition. Further, both aspects would need to be examined first with respect to the countries of the Arab Common Market (ACM), i.e. those which have already taken some steps towards establishing multilateral trade co-operation, and secondly the other Arab countries, thus covering the Arab world as a whole.

Trade of Member Countries of the ACM. Tables 2.1 and 2.2 indicate the export and import trade of the ACM countries for the two years 1970 and 1973 with respect to other members of the market, to other signatories of the Council of Arab Economic Unity (CAEU) which have not as yet become effective members of the common market and finally with respect to the other Arab countries.[28]

Looking at inter-ACM trade, it appears to form a small portion of the combined total trade of the member countries of the market, comprising less than 6 per cent in 1970 and a much lower ratio in 1973.[29] For recent years (e.g. 1976), this ratio appears to have dropped. The aggregate ratio for inter-ACM trade however conceals important differences among individual members of the common market. On the export side, Jordan and Syria appear to be the most important trading partners of the Arab market. Jordanian exports to the ACM averaged for the two years about one-fourth of the total. Syrian exports averaged about one-fifth of the total, but with a marked difference between the two years. On the other hand, Egyptian and Iraqi exports to the ACM comprised exceedingly small portions of their total exports respectively.

ACM exports to the other members of the CAEU indicate that at present the latter are of very minor importance as export outlets to the ACM countries. Overall ACM exports to other members of the CAEU averaged about 2 per cent of the total for the two years under consideration. With the exception of Jordan, the export ratios for the individual members of the ACM were very small. That of Jordan was a little over 10 per cent.

Considering the non-CAEU Arab countries as a group, they absorbed, on average, about 4 per cent of total ACM exports for the two years. However, while the ratios for Egypt and Iraq were very small, those for Jordan and Syria were much higher, about one-fourth and one-sixth respectively. Taking all the Arab countries as a group they absorbed, on average, about 10 per cent of total ACM exports in the two years. But again for Jordan and Syria the Arab markets constituted an important export outlet while for Egypt and Iraq they were relatively unimportant.

Similar observations seem to apply to the ACM's import trade (Table 2.2). Inter-ACM trade was 3-5 per cent of the total. ACM imports from the other members of the CAEU are even more limited. The ratio of ACM imports from the other Arab countries to total imports was also less than 5 per cent. For all the Arab countries this ratio was close to 10 per cent. As is the case of exports, the Arab

Table 2.1 The Arab Common Market: Pattern of Trade Exports (in Millions of Arab Dinars)

From/To:	ACM		CAEU		Other Arab countries		Total Arab countries		Total exports	
	1970	1973	1970	1973	1970	1973	1970	1973	1970	1973
Egypt										
Value	7.85	5.17	9.02	9.30	4.82	7.65	21.69	22.11	233.20	311.40
% of total exports	3.36	1.66	3.86	2.98	2.06	2.45	9.30	7.10		
Jordan										
Value	2.80	3.42	1.30	1.77	2.69	3.50	6.79	8.69	10.30	16.10
% of total exports	27.18	21.24	12.62	11	26.11	21.73	65.92	53.97		
Iraq										
Value	10.56	5.75	4.99	5.64	12.79	6.08	22.34	17.47	364.57	663.80
% of total exports	2.89	0.86	1.37	0.85	3.51	0.916	6.12	2.03		
Syria										
Value	17.44	6.34	1.73	1.99	12.80	10.22	32.00	18.55	54.30	93.90
% of total exports	32.11	6.75	3.18	2.11	23.57	10.89	58.93	19.75		
Subtotal	38.65	20.68	17.04	18.70	33.10	27.45	82.82	66.82	662.37	1,085.20
Per cent of total exports	5.8	1.9	2.6	1.7	5.0	2.5	12.5	0.2	100	100

Note: Values for total exports taken from *IFS.*
Sources: Council of Arab Economic Unity (CAEU), ***Annual Bulletin for Arab Countries Foreign Trade Statistics 1970 and 1973***
International Financial Statistics.

Table 2.2 The Arab Common Market: Pattern of Trade Imports (in Millions of Arab Dinars)

From/To:		ACM		CAEU		Other Arab countries		Total Arab countries		Total imports	
		1970	1973	1970	1973	1970	1973	1970	1973	1970	1973
Egypt											
Value		4.89	5.50	6.52	6.05	4.50	6.16	15.91	17.70		
% of total	c.i.f.	2.03	2.18	2.70	2.40	1.86	2.44	6.60	7.03	240.80 (c i.f.)	251.70
imports	f.o.b.	2.23	2.40	2.97	2.64	2.05	2.69	7.26	7.73	218.90 (f.o.b.)	228.90
Jordan											
Value		5.24	1.33	0.46	0.04	7.79	1.14	13.48	2.51		
% of total	c.i.f.	9.39	1.45	0.82	0.043	13.96	1.24	24.15	2.73	55.80 (c.i.f.)	91.70
imports	f.o.b.	10.52	1.62	0.92	0.048	15.64	1.39	27.06	3.06	49.80 (f.o b.)	81.90
Iraq											
Value		6.17	4.77	0.69	1.42	5.40	4.28	12.26	19.48		
% of total	c.i.f.	3.65	1.89	0.40	0.56	3.19	1.70	7.25	4.17	168.90 (c.i.f.)	251.20
imports	f.o.b.	4.09	2.12	0.45	0.63	3.58	1.90	8.13	4.67	150.70 (f.o.b.)	224.30
Syria											
Value		13.42	11.91	0.25	1.43	8.13	10.83	21.80	24.18		
% of total	c.i.f.	13.93	7.26	0.25	0.87	8.44	6.60	22.63	14.74	96.30 (c.i.f.)	164.00
imports	f.o.b.	15.06	7.84	0.28	0.94	9.12	7.13	24.46	15.92	89.10 (f.o.b.)	151.80
Subtotal		29.72	25.51	7.92	8.94	25.82	22.41	63.45	54.87	561.80 (c i.f.)	758.60
										508.50 (f.o.b.)	686.90
Per cent of	c.i.f.	5.29	3.09	1.40	1.18	4.59	2.95	11.29	7.23		
total imports	f.o.b.	5.84	3.42	1.55	1.30	5.07	3.26	12.47	7.98		

Note: Values for total imports taken from *IFS.*
Sources: CAEU, *Annual Bulletin for Arab Countries Foreign Trade Statistics 1970 and 1973* International Financial Statistics.

Table 2.3 ACM Countries: Per Cent of Manufactures in Total Trade[a]

Exports	ACM		CAEU[d]		Other Arab Countries		Total Arab countries		Total[b]	
	1970	1973	1970	1973	1970	1973	1970	1973	1970	1973
Jordan	27%	56%	13%	12%	21%	26%	22%	35%	16.5%	21.6%
Value	(0.75)	(1.90)	(0.16)	(0.21)	(0.56)	(0.89)	(1.47)	(3.00)	(2.94)	(6.00)
Egypt	64%	46%	68%	68%	26%	32%	57%	50%	30%	25%
Value	(4.96)	(2.34)	(6.09)	(6.28)	(1.22)	(2.43)	(12.27)	(11.05)	(24.54)	(22.10)
Iraq	10%	21%	39%	55%	6%	25%	12%	33%	5.15%	1%
Value	(0.73)	(1.18)	(1.91)	(3.06)	(0.76)	(1.52)	(3.40)	(5.76)	(6.80)	(11.52)
Syria	14%	43%	66%	67%	6%	30%	14%	39%	18%	16%
Value	(2.43)	(2.70)	(1.14)	(1.33)	(0.68)	(3.04)	(4.25)	(7.07)	(8.50)	(4.14)
Total ACM, value	(8.87)	(8.12)	(9.30)	(10.88)	(3.22)	(2.88)	(21.39)	(26.88)		
ACM, excluding Egypt	(3.91)	(5.78)	(3.21)	(4.60)	(2.00)	(5.45)	(9.12)	(15.83)		
Imports										
Jordan	28%	(–)[c]	24%	(–)[c]	33%	(–)[c]	31%	(–)[c]	69%	29%
Value	(1.47)		(0.11)		(2.57)		(4.15)		78%	32%
									(8.30)	
Egypt	13%	21%	8%	7%	70%	78%	27%	36%	58%	49%
Value	(0.65)	(1.15)	(0.54)	(0.41)	(3.13)	(4.80)	(4.39)	(6.36)	63%	53.5%
									(8.64)	(12.72)
Iraq	81%	91%	84%	22%	80%	80%	81%	.8.09	77%	73%
Value	(5.02)	(4.34)	(0.58)	(0.31)	(4.31)	(3.44)	(9.91)	(8.0)	87%	81.6%
									(19.82)	(16.18)
Syria	17%	16%	24%	21%	29%	32%	22%	24%	70%	62%
Value	(2.30)	(1.89)	(0.06)	(0.29)	(2.35)	(3.45)	(4.71)	(5.63)	75%	67%
									(9.42)	(11.26)

Notes: The totals of trade of ACM statistics did not appear to be always reliable for example, the addition of the subtotals sometimes exceeded the indicated grand total; sometimes the subtotals do not add up to the grand totals.

a. Manufacture includes codes 5, 6, 7 and 8 of the SITC.

b. Total trade figures are taken from the IFS. c.i.f. and f.o.b. totals are used.

c. The additions of codes 5, 6, 7 and 8 exceed total imports.

d. Yemen PDR, Yemen AR, Mauritania, Libya, Kuwait, Somalia, Sudan, UAE.

Sources: CAEU, ***Annual Bulletin for Arab Countries Foreign Trade Statistics, 1970, 1973,*** International Financial Statistics, 1967.

markets are relatively more important (taking the average of the two years) for Syria and Jordan than they are for Egypt and Iraq. However, the Arab markets occupy a lesser importance in terms of the import trade of Jordan and Syria than they do as export outlets for these two countries.

To summarise, as it stood in recent years overall ACM trade with the rest of the Arab countries remains limited. Secondly, for individual countries (i.e. Jordan and Syria) the Arab markets assume much greater importance than they do in the case of the other members, especially on the export side. But thirdly, to have a better understanding of the actual and potential prospects for expansion in inter-ACM trade and in ACM trade with the rest of the Arab world, we should also examine ACM's broad composition particularly as between manufacturers and non-manufacturers.[30] The potential for regional trade expansion is to a large degree linked to the potential for increased trade in manufactures which itself is dependent upon the level and pattern of development of the countries concerned (see pp. 115–20).

Table 2.3 summarises the data concerning inter-ACM trade in manufactures and ACM trade in such goods with the rest of the Arab countries. Several comments are in order. First, in relative terms inter-ACM exports in manufactures appear to be more important than the common market's total inter-export trade. To a lesser extent, the same may be said of the ACM's manufactured exports to the rest of the Arab countries. Secondly, the Arab markets constitute a relatively important export outlet for Egyptian manufactures, absorbing over one-half of the total for the two years under consideration. The portion of Iraqi manufactures going to the Arab markets is also considerably higher than its corresponding portion for overall trade. Thirdly, with the exception of Egypt, the total of ACM manufactured exports going to the Arab countries has risen substantially from 1970 to 1973.[31] Fourthly, for all four countries (except Syria in 1970) the portion of their trade comprising manufactures is greater with respect to the Arab countries than it is with respect to the rest of the world. Fifthly, on the import side, with the exception of Iraq the order of magnitude of these ratios is reversed. That is as may be expected, ACM imports from the outside world are largely manufactures whereas, excepting Iraq, the larger portion of their combined imports from the Arab countries comprises non-manufactures. The high ratios for Iraq with respect to both Arab and non-Arab trade may perhaps be explained by the availability of domestic agricultural produce and the strict control over import licensing, the public sector determining the pattern of imports. It may be conjectured that, in an Arab context, for the relatively developed Arab countries of the ACM, trade in manufactures – as might be expected – affords a wider opportunity for trade expansion among themselves as well as with the rest of the Arab countries than would trade in other commodities. This aspect of the analysis is dealt with below (pp. 116–17).

Trade of Other Arab Countries.[32] Tables 2.4 and 2.5 summarise the pattern of trade of certain selected Arab countries for the years 1970 and 1973. (A somewhat similar pattern applies to more recent years.) For most of them, i.e. excluding Kuwait and Lebanon, the portion of their exports (excluding oil) absorbed by the Arab markets was relatively small. For Kuwait and Lebanon, by contrast, the Arab markets are very important export outlets. Overall, the portion of total exports (excluding oil) of the countries under consideration which was destined for the Arab countries did not exceed 5 per cent in both years. Were oil exports included, this ratio would be much lower. When the pattern of import trade is examined, it is apparent that, overall, inter-Arab import trade occupies a relatively more important position than does inter-Arab export trade. Nevertheless, the ratios of Arab total imports are relatively low with no single Arab country being heavily dependent on the Arab markets as sources of imports. The main reason for this phenomenon is, of course, the important position which manufactures occupy in the imports of the Arab countries and which are mainly supplied by the industrial countries. This is reflected in Table 2.7. For most of the listed countries imports of manufactures comprised about 50-75 per cent of the total of which a small portion originated in the Arab countries. In contrast, Arab exports of manufactures to the Arab countries generally accounted for a much larger portion of total exports of manufactures (Table 2.6). For Kuwait and Lebanon the Arab markets absorbed a major portion of their manufactured exports. These markets also constituted important outlets for Tunisian and Moroccan exports of manufactures.

Reasons for Limited Effectiveness

The factors which account for limited effective Arab economic co-operation are to a large extent of a non-economic nature. The Arab world has its share of political and social differences among the countries which it comprises. Varying political ideologies, the desire to retain control over national destinies, vested political interests, real or imaginary fear of ultimate subordination or annexation on the part of

Table 2.4 Selected Arab Countries — Patterns of Trade: Exports (value in million Arab Dinars)

	ACM		CAEU		Other Arab Countries		Total Arab Countries		Total Exports[a]	
	1970	1973	1970	1973	1970	1973	1970	1973	1970	1973
Kuwait[b]										
Value	4.05	4.06	3.01	16.87	6.83	28.50	13.09	51.53	35.04	80.94
% of total exports	11.55	7.48	8.59	20.84	19.49	35.30	37.34	63.66		
Lebanon[f]										
Value	—	22.30	—	30.00	—	32.08	—	84.53	64.08	170.20
% of total exports	—	13.10	—	17.60	—	18.84	—	49.60		
Libya[b]										
Value	—[c]	12.80	—	—	0.04	1.15	0.05	14.02	3.27	(146.6)[d]
% of total exports	—	8.73	—	—	—	0.78	—	9.50		
Morocco										
Value	0.015	—	0.15	—	0.53	—	0.72	—	155.63	245.60
% of total exports	0.03	—	0.09	—	0.34	—	0.46	—		
Saudi Arabia[b]										
Value	2.36	—	2.25	—	38.58	—	43.20	—	—[e]	—[e]
% of total exports		—		—		—		—		
Sudan										
Value	5.32	4.82	0.23	4.79	2.40	3.85	7.97	13.47	100.00	122.70
% of total exports	5.32	3.92	0.23	3.90	2.40	3.13	7.97	10.97		
Tunisia										
Value	0.16	0.60	5.63	5.72	3.01	2.48	8.81	8.80	61.00	107.40
% of total exports	0.26	0.55	9.20	5.30	4.93	2.30	14.40	8.19		
Total %	0.80	1.32	0.76	1.63	3.47	1.98	5.00	4.89		

Notes: a. Total export figures are taken from the IFS.
b. Excluding oil.
c. Not significant.
d. Since according to given IFS data, total exports are less than the sum of the subtotal as given by CAEU it was decided to use the total given by CAEU instead.
e. Grand total and sum of subtotals could not be reconciled.
f. Estimates for 1970 are not available.

Sources: *International Financial Statistics;* CAEU, *Annual Bulletin for Arab Countries Foreign Trade Statistics 1970 and 1973.*

Table 2.5 Selected Arab Countries — Patterns of Trade: Imports (c.i.f.) (value in millions of Arab Dinars)

	ACM		CAEU		Other Arab countries		Total Arab countries		Total exports[a]	
	1970	1973	1970	1973	1970	1973	1970	1973	1970	1973
Lebanon										
Value	19.90	25.76	0.96	2.00	2.71	5.72	(23.67)[b]	(33.46)[b]	217.85	359.97
% of total imports	9.13	7.16	0.44	0.55	1.24	1.58	10.81	9.30		
Kuwait										
Value	7.28	9.00	0.45	2.60	10.05	13.86	17.79	25.47	208.69	293.00
% of total imports	3.50	3.07	0.21	0.90	4.81	4.73	8.52	8.70		
Sudan										
Value	5.34	3.28	0.23	3.36	0.50	1.69	6.07	8.32	96.20	122.40
% of total imports	5.55	2.70	0.24	2.74	0.52	1.38	6.30	6.80		
Saudi Arabia										
Value	9.07	—	13.55	—	30.69	—	53.30	—	236.86	555.80
% of total imports	3.82	—	5.72	—	13.00	—	22.50	—		
Libya										
Value	2.03	8.30	0.11	1.28	12.00	24.80	14.16	34.40	184.00	482.20
% of total imports	1.10	1.72	0.05	0.27	6.52	5.14	7.69	7.13		
Tunisia										
Value	1.81	3.35	0.05	0.23	0.97	4.49	2.83	8.08	102.16	182.30
% of total imports	4.77	1.84	0.05	0.13	0.95	2.46	2.77	4.43		
Morocco										
Value	0.01	—	0.002	—	0.52	—	0.54	—	218.70	307.08
% of total imports	0.004	—	0.001	—	0.24	—	0.24	—		
Totals %	6.58	6.17	9.89	1.97	14.11	12.07	29.20	20.31	387.90	552.20

Notes: a. Taken from *IFS*.
b. The CAEU data appeared to be greatly under-estimated. *Direction of Trade* data were used instead.

Source: CAEU *Annual Bulletin for Arab Countries Foreign Trade Statistics, 1970 and 1973,* International Financial Statistics.

Table 2.6 Selected Arab Countries: Exports Per Cent of Manufactures in Total Trade (value in million Arab Dinars)

	ACM		CAEU		Other Arab countries		Total Arab countries		Total Trade	
	1970	1973	1970	1973	1970	1973	1970	1973	1970	1973
Kuwait[a]										
Value	(2.97)	(3.29)	(2.26)	(11.40)	(3.84)	(18.99)	(8.68)	(30.67)	(16.02)	(49.9)
% of total	73.00	54.30	75.00	67.50	56.20	66.39	66.00	59.5	45.7	61.6
Lebanon										
Value	–	(14.9)	–	(24.27)	–	(26.13)	–	(64.45)	–	(116.89)
% of total	–[c]	66.80	–	80.90	–	81.45	–	76.25	–	68.67
Libya										
Value	–	–	–	–	–	(0.0028)	–	(0.0028)	(0.0031)	(0.0028)
% of total	–[b]	–	–	–	–	0.24	–	0.02	0.09	0.002
Morocco										
Value	(0.014)	–	(0.022)	–	(0.307)	–	(0.347)	–	–	(79.87)
% of total	31.00	–	15.17	–	57.90	–	48.00	–	–	32.50
Saudi Arabia										
Value	(0.039)	–	(0.30)	–	(0.23)	–	(0.57)	–	(0.805)	–
% of total	1.65	–	13.30	–	0.59	–	1.32	–	0.11	–
Sudan										
Value	(0.004)	(0.038)	–	(0.026)	(0.0057)	(0.0008)	(0.0057)	(0.028)	(0.068)	(0.105)
% of total	0.08	0.78	–	0.55	0.24	0.03	0.07	0.21	0.07	0.08
Tunisia										
Value	(0.0098)	(0.42)	(0.96)	(1.63)	(2.52)	(1.63)	(3.50)	(3.68)	(11.64)	(22.8)
% of total	6.12	70.00	17.05	28.50	83.70	65.00	39.72	41.80	19.08	21.20

Notes: a. Per cent of total exports destined to each group of countries.
b. Not significant.
c. Estimate not given.

Source: *International Financial Statistics;* CAEU *Annual Bulletin for Arab Countries Foreign Trade 1970, 1973.*

Table 2.7 Selected Arab Countries: Imports (c.i.f.) Per Cent of Manufacture in Total Trade (value in million Arab Dinars)

	ACM		CAEU		Other Arab countries		Total Arab countries		Total imports	
	1970	1973	1970	1973	1970	1973	1970	1973	1970	1973
Kuwait	49.5%	55.4%	30.4%	1.6%	52.0%	59.8%	51.0%	54.1%	73.0%	79.0%
% value	(3.60)	(4.99)	(0.137)	(0.043)	(5.22)	(8.29)	(9.15)	(13.77)	(152.83)	(232.11)
Lebanon	—	—	—	—	—	—	—	—	61.0%	69.0%
% value	—	—	—	—	—	—	—	—	(114.34)	(267.78)
Libya	41.4%	55.2%	17.3%	0.3%	46.9%	72.0%	47.9%	66.0%	68.7%	75.7%
% value	(0.84)	(4.58)	(0.019)	(0.004)	(5.63)	(17.9)	(6.79)	(22.75)	(126.56)	(365.40)
Morocco	—	—	70.0%	—	14.5%	—	15.3%	—	6.1%	—
% value	—	—	(0.0014)	—	(0.076)	—	(0.082)	—	(13.59)	—
Saudi Arabia	59.8%	—	21.0%	—	54.4%	—	46.7%	—	41.7%	—
% value	(5.40)	—	(2.84)	—	(16.66)	—	(24.9)	—	(98.93)	—
Sudan	77.8%	89.3%	100%	99.0%	91.4%	88.7%	79.7%	93.0%	67.2%	67.3%
% value	(4.15)	(2.93)	(0.23)	(3.34)	(0.457)	(1.50)	(4.48)	(7.77)	(64.70)	(82.42)
Tunisia	9.1%	2.7%	5.2%	6.9%	24.0%	11.2%	13.0%	74.3%	58.1%	64.2%
% value	(0.107)	(0.092)	(0.0025)	(0.0158)	(0.243)	(0.503)	(0.352)	(6.01)	(59.36)	(117.0)

Source: *International Financial Statistics;* CAEU, *Annual Bulletin for Arab Countries Foreign Trade Statistics, 1970 and 1973.*

the politically weaker countries, etc. have all affected national attitudes and have acted as an important constraint on possible forms of economic co-operation when such possibilities looked promising from a purely economic point of view. This aspect of the problem, however, does not concern us here and we shall therefore turn to some of the economic factors which may account for the limited effectiveness of Arab economic co-operation.

Two sets of factors may be distinguished. The first concerns those which may have acted to discourage moves towards closer economic co-operation or integration. The second would include those factors which tend to limit the impact of closer Arab economic integration even if one assumes proper implementation of agreements to co-operate closely, or to integrate. The first set of factors would comprise, among others, different national economic policies, competitiveness of national economies which in the event of integration implies initially a serious burden or cost arising from the required adjustment in domestic production. The second set would include disparities in the level of development, small size of the national markets, heavy dependence on outside markets for export products, inability to co-ordinate economic policy, etc. The two sets overlap. For example, economic policy has a great influence not only on moves to effect closer integration but on sustaining it as well once some form of economic co-operation has been achieved.

Looking at the contemporary Arab economies it may be argued that the limitations of inter-Arab interdependence may be ascribed to the following three basic factors: (1) marked disparities in the level of development; (2) the structure of contemporary Arab economies, e.g. the present dependence of a number of Arab economies on a few primary products which rely on foreign markets; in this connection one may analyse the issues of competitiveness and complementarity of these economies; and (3) divergences in national economic policies.

Disparities in Levels of Development. The criteria for comparing levels of development are numerous: per capita income, level of technology, level and quality of education, level of infrastructure, degree of industrialisation, etc. Whatever criteria one adopts, disparities in the level of development among the various Arab economies can be demonstrated. Obvious contrasts are Lebanon and the Sudan. In 1973 Lebanon's per capita income stood at about LL 2,630 (US $1,000 using the average exchange rate as a conversion factor).[33] The industrial sector accounted for about 20 per cent of GDP

Table 2.8 Arab Countries Ranking in Terms of Certain Indicators of Level of Industrialisation

	Ratio of manufactures to total (1974)	% of GDP arising in manufacturing sector (1974)	Income per head (excluding oil countries of Group III)
Group I			
Lebanon (73)	1	1	1
Syria	4	2	2
Egypt	2	3	9
Group II			
Jordan	2	5	6
Tunisia	3	6	5
Morocco	5	5	7
Democratic Yemen (72)	6	4	8
Iraq (73)	7	6	4
Algeria	8	7	3
Group III			
Kuwait (73)	9	10	–[a]
Saudi Arabia (75)	10	9	–[a]
Libya	12	11	–[a]
Group IV			
Yemen Arab Republic (75)	11	9	9
Sudan	12	8	8

Note: a. When included Kuwait, Saudi Arabia and Libya would rank 1, 3 and 4 respectively.
Source: UN (ECWA) *Statistical Abstract of the Arab World* (Amman 1977).

and probably employed more than one-fourth of the labour force. The Sudanese per capita income stood in 1974 at about SL 87 ($250). Income originating in the industrial sector comprised 8 per cent of the total, while industrial employment made up about 5 per cent of total employment. Other contrasts include Egypt and the North Yemen Republic.[34] These contrasts are confirmed by Table 2.8 which ranks the Arab countries in terms of certain indicators of the level of industrialisation. Income per capita apart, Lebanon, Syria and Egypt would rank among the relatively more industrialised countries while Sudan and the Yemen Arab Republic would rank among the least industrialised. The petroleum-exporting countries also rank relatively low. Marked disparities in the level of development on the part of the less developed members of the proposed union or area of closer co-operation involve economic concerns of possible developmental polarisation akin to the existing situation between the developed and developing countries. Similarly, when drawing up their developmental plans, the less developed economies would want to invoke the infant industry argument in a manner similar to that utilised by the developing countries in particular *vis-à-vis* the outside industrial world. Indeed, among proposed unions clauses are often introduced to permit the less developed members of the union to protect their production or certain areas thereof against potential competition from the other members of the union.[35] It is therefore not surprising that among some of the economic groupings which have been formed important constraints on effective co-operation have appeared on account of issues pertaining to a real or imagined inappropriate distribution of costs and benefits among the countries concerned. In part this may be attributed to the nature of the union which may have permitted certain countries to benefit more than others.

Structure of the Arab Economies. The relevance of economic structure to the issue of integration has traditionally stemmed from the importance ascribed to the complementarity and competitiveness of the national economies concerned. It is argued that the more competitive the economies of the countries proposing to form a union (but potentially the more complementary these economies are), the greater are the benefits to be derived from the union. The prospects for trade creation, in other words, became more promising and could very well outweigh costs arising from possible trade diversion.[36] Similarly, the higher the tariff walls between members of the proposed union prior to its formation, the greater are the possibilities of trade creation, and the lower the external tariff walls, the less are the possibilities for trade diversion. The Vinerian analysis rested on certain strong assumptions including fixity in the consumption pattern and a two-country case. Following on Viner's and Meade's analysis (the latter dealt with the consumption effects only by assuming structure of production remaining constant),[37] Lipsey distinguished between inter-country substitution (Viner's trade creation and trade diversion) and inter-commodity substitution (resulting from price shifts). He showed that for the two-commodity case, the net result in terms of welfare depends upon the pre-union tariff walls and the post-union terms of trade. With a three-commodity case, the welfare effects of a customs union – in comparison with uniform tariffs – become inconclusive.[38] Lipsey does conclude, however, that given a country's volume of international trade, the higher is the proportion of trade with the country's union partner, the greater are the chances that a customs union would raise welfare. Similarly the lower the total volume of foreign trade, the more a customs union is likely to raise welfare.[39] Whatever the results of formal static analysis may be, they do not form the basis upon which countries intent on forming a union are likely to dwell. In other words, the issue is not one of comparing the welfare situations of the countries concerned before and after the union is formed. Economic integration is viewed in terms of its potential impact on the process of longer-term economic growth.[40] The immediate effects on welfare, measured in terms of levels of consumption, are marginal to the central arguments for or against economic integration. This does not imply that the concepts of trade creation and trade diversion become irrelevant. But their relevance is now related to their effect on the size of the combined markets of the members of the union. Trade creation could then be interpreted as enlarging the market by permitting a higher level of output from given resources while trade diversion would have the opposite result. The potential advantages of closer economic co-operation are discussed below (pp. 113–20).

Turning to the structure of the contemporary Arab economies, four readily apparent groupings may be listed. The first would include the petroleum-exporting countries the economies of which hinge on petroleum resources (e.g. the Gulf countries and to a somewhat lesser extent Saudi Arabia). The second would include countries the economies of which are endowed with oil as well as with non-oil resources (e.g. Algeria, Iraq). The third would include those countries whose economies are dependent to a large extent on agricultural or other mineral resources (e.g. Morocco, Syria, Tunisia, Yemen Arab Republic). The fourth would include countries the economies of which are diversified but tend to rely substantially on trade and services (Lebanon and to a lesser degree Jordan[41] and Democratic Yemen).

The above groupings are of course, somewhat arbitrary. Thus if comparisons of levels of industrialisation were to be made, a different country classification would emerge. As already pointed out countries such as Lebanon, Syria and Egypt have established a diversified industrial base to a much larger extent than have the other Arab countries. In contrast, countries such as the Yemen Arab Republic or the petroleum-exporting countries have yet to establish an industrial base. In the mid-1970s the portion of GDP arising in the manufacturing sector of Lebanon,[42] Syria and Egypt ranged from 17 per cent to 20 per cent compared with a range of 4-8 per cent in the other group of Arab countries cited above. Similarly industrial employment made up about 13-19 per cent of the total in the three countries compared to a range of 6-9 per cent in the other group of Arab countries. Further, one can proceed with a more detailed classification which would include per capita consumption of electricity, the level of technology in use, the availability of industrial managers and skilled workers, etc. Such comparisons will also reveal that a new grouping of Arab countries will have to be made.

It is obvious, therefore, that when one is comparing national economic structures, the criteria one uses in such comparisons would dictate the nature of the results. Such criteria, furthermore, may either be broad or detailed and this in turn would influence the results of any comparisons.

It may be useful for our purpose to group the contemporary Arab countries into the following four categories. The first would comprise those countries which are in the early stages of their general development, still relying on agriculture as a major source of income and employment, with very limited industrial development, e.g. Sudan, the Yemen Arab Republic. The second group would include countries which have witnessed a certain degree of industrial development but still substantially rely on a few primary products, e.g. Iraq, Syria, Egypt, Morocco and Algeria. The third group would include countries which have established an industrial base with national economies relatively more diversified than those of the rest of the Arab countries, e.g. Lebanon and Tunisia. The fourth would group those countries which are primarily dependent upon petroleum resources and whose industrial development is still very limited.

With this classification in mind it may be useful to bring out some of the elements of competitiveness and complementarity among groups of Arab economies which are relevant to our present discussion and to indicate to what extent those elements might have tended to restrain the process of Arab economic integration. At the level of complementarity we have the Arab economies which have already gone forward with the industrialisation process and those which have yet to do so effectively. We have the strictly petroleum-exporting countries and the rest of the Arab economies. We also have those Arab economies which are relatively diversified and do not depend heavily on agriculture and the basically agriculture economies. At the level of competitiveness, two examples may be mentioned. There is first the group of Arab countries which have already established some industrial base. The structures of their manufacturing sector are to a very large extent similar. There is secondly the primarily petroleum-exporting countries whose economies are similar.

It may be conjectured that on the side of competitiveness, the mutual fears of similarly situated Arab countries tended to dampen enthusiasm for effective moves towards integration. The costs of adjustments on the part of a given individual country which any such integration might have entailed have been viewed (and perhaps continue to be viewed) as being politically and socially intolerable. Further, national pride might not permit certain established industries to face keen competition and possible decline as the price for closer integration even if the ensuing adjustment process could be effected relatively smoothly. It might be argued that joint preparatory studies by the countries concerned relating to co-ordinated plans of regional industrial development might have helped induce those countries to move closer together. However, such a step presupposes the ready acceptance of the concept of integration with its implied submergence of national economic planning into a supra-regional planning. Concerning the petroleum-exporting countries, the element of competitiveness in their national economies is not one that should prevent closer co-operation since the markets for petroleum exports are largely abroad. But again there is the potential competitiveness which arises from the establishment of similar petrochemical and other industries. This could act as a retarding factor unless efforts are made early enough to co-ordinate their industrial programmes.

The existing elements of complementarity among the Arab countries would appear to have varying effects. The disparities in the level of industrialisation act to weaken integration efforts. The complementarity of the primarily petroleum-exporting countries and the other Arab countries is likely to encourage integration, at least on the part of the latter group of countries. Similarly, the complementarity of the trade and services oriented economies and some of the other economies should serve as a positive element in the efforts to integrate. However, the extent to which it may or may not do so would depend upon the nature of economic policies – especially international economic policies – which are followed. The economic policy aspects of any integration process occupy a central position in determining the success or failure of this process particularly as concerns the allocation of costs and benefits associated with it. To the policy issue we now turn.

Divergences in National Economic Policies. Divergences in national economic policies – both domestic and external – act to restrain moves to integrate at two levels. There is first the fear that a move in the direction of policies followed by potential partners could prove to be disadvantageous to national economic interests. An obvious example would be the case of two countries, the first of which follows liberal exchange policies, whereas the second applies strict exchange controls. Or one country applies tariff protection moderately while the other uses it strictly and extensively. On the domestic front one country may be extending tax and other incentives to stimulate local industries while a potential partner does not and may not wish to extend any subsidies at all. Rates of domestic inflation may differ markedly from one country to another as a result of domestic policies and this in itself would tend to restrain the move to integrate among them.

There is secondly the question of policy harmonisation after the initial steps to integrate have already been taken. In practice, this has proved to be a difficult problem to tackle. To the extent that the minimum necessary level of policy harmonisation is not achieved, the process of integration is likely to falter and ultimately to be totally forestalled. It follows that any calculation of costs and benefits associated with the principle of integration with respect to individual countries may turn out, in practice, to be invalid. Instead such costs and benefits could, in due course, become substantially lopsided with most of the benefits accruing to certain members, others sustaining the bulk of the costs.

Concerning the Arab countries, it has already been suggested that the external economic policies differ from one Arab country to another. Of the four ACM countries three members apply strict exchange controls over their current international economic transactions. But again, the severity of these controls may differ from one member to another and with respect to individual economic transactions. The fourth country, Jordan, follows a more liberal policy though it does maintain controls over current economic transactions. Similar considerations would apply to capital movements.

At the domestic level there also exist marked differences in the policies being followed or at least in respect of numerous aspects of such policies. These differences cannot be summarised here. They may be illustrated, however, with one or two examples. In certain Arab countries the use of monetary policy is limited despite the existence of certain monetary instruments, e.g. Syria. Reliance on influencing economic activity rests on the direct participation of the public sector in economic activity and the manipulation of the national budget (fiscal policy). In other countries, monetary instruments play a more important role. Regulations of the interest rate structure in the UAE for example has an important bearing on the level of deposits and lending and therefore on general economic activity. In certain Arab countries the progression in income tax rates is steep, e.g. Egypt. In others it is moderate (e.g. Lebanon). And in still others there are virtually no income taxes at all (e.g. the Gulf countries).

Policy harmonisation may not be regarded as a major prerequisite for the initial steps towards more effective Arab economic co-operation. For example a free trade area may be established without prior harmonisation. A closer form of co-operation, however, may not be sustainable without a degree of policy co-ordination. Indeed even a free trade area may not in the long run be viable or effective, if the tariff or licensing policies of the members vary substantially.

Gains from More Effective Arab Co-operation

Prerequisites for Realising Potential Gains

The preceding analysis has pointed out some of the prerequisites which should be fulfilled if the move to bring about effective economic co-operation or integration is to result in mutual benefits, i.e. to serve the purpose of growth for the countries concerned. It may be useful to group together some of the major prerequisites which are involved.

Given the dependence of the Arab economies on world economy, particularly at the level of trade and technology, one major prerequisite would be that any proposed steps should not be designed to isolate the economies of the integrating economies from world trade and payments. Any proposed integration should endeavour to avoid unnecessary disruptions to economic relations with the outside world. Proper protection of national production should not imply in other words isolation from the world economy, or the undue weakening of economic ties with the outside world.

Viewed in this context, it follows that restrictions on international payments should, as a matter of general policy, be avoided or minimised unless it can be shown that they are essential for the process of development. Admittedly, under certain circumstances (e.g. political turmoil) such restrictions may have to be imposed. But normally, restrictions on trade – whether price or quantitative in nature – should be applied with a view to fostering the process of industrialisation and not for other purposes.[43] Similarly, restrictions on current transfers would ordinarily seem to be uncalled for to the extent that trade policy is being co-ordinated with developmental policy unless again it can be demonstrated that such restrictions are necessary for the development process. Restrictions on current transfers, for payment reasons, may be resorted to in special circumstances, but as a general economic policy it is perhaps more appropriate to avoid their extensive use while relying on other means to cope with balance of payments problems. In practice, the circumvention of existing restrictions on current transfers is commonplace, especially in developing countries where the control machinery is usually weak and inefficient. Finally, to the extent that the domestic political situation permits, restrictions on capital movements should be minimal though, as is often the case in practice, capital inflows may be directed to specified economic fields and not left to the vagaries of market forces.

The importance of policy harmonisation has already been stressed. If the Arab economies are to move closer together in the direction of integration, parallel steps in the direction of policy harmonisation cannot be ignored. Beginning with a free trade area or a customs union some co-ordination of foreign trade policies would become essential. Moving to a common market or an economic union would similarly require co-ordination of other aspects of external and domestic economic policy. Foremost among these would be the exchange, interest rate and industrial policies.

To integrate in the direction of a common market or an economic union implies a policy which would permit a freer movement of resources among the countries concerned. Existing restrictions on inter-Arab capital movements would need to be removed. While a freer movement of labour would also need to be effected, this issue (unlike that of capital movements) is intricately tied to non-economic issues which have to be fully accounted for. The calculus of gains and losses must be broadened to include social costs and benefits resulting from such movements. What would seem to be required, in other words, is a co-ordination of labour policy which would take into account the labour availabilities and needs of each country (for skilled, semi-skilled and unskilled labour) as well as the social and political ease with which non-national labour can be absorbed into the domestic economy. Further, the nature of longer-run industrial policy being envisaged must be accounted for. 'Surplus' labour in certain countries may not be readily absorbed by countries which are in need of additional labour; indeed only a small portion of this labour may be so absorbed. Instead of leaving it for the market to determine the ultimate balance concerning labour movements, with all their unpredictable economic, social and political consequences, such movements must be made subject to the constraints of an overall labour policy based on the relevant elements mentioned above.[44] In brief, the freedom of capital movement in an integrated area is much more readily acceptable than that of labour movement. The former is basically governed by economic criteria (though even here national prejudices may act as a constraining factor) whereas the latter is governed and judged by economic as well as non-economic criteria.

To ensure the success of the process of economic integration, a minimum level of political harmonisation or understanding must be established. It would be difficult to conceive of an economically integrated Arab area if political developments are going to be permitted to disrupt inter-Arab economic relationships. Political understanding among the parties concerned must be reached so that the process of economic integration would not be disrupted by possible differences in political positions. If this proper climate is not ensured then an effective expansion in inter-Arab trade and particularly investment within the framework of an agreed formula for integration can be readily disrupted. A commitment to integrate implies a commitment to gear economic development in individual countries along certain paths which might be different in the absence of such a commitment. Any serious moves in this direction would or should therefore imply the joint acceptance of certain political conditions which would assure the continuation of the process of integration.

Longer-run Gains: Dynamic Aspects of Closer Integration with Special Reference to the Arab Countries

The dynamic aspects of integration relate to the greater possibilities which it would permit for a more efficient use of resources and greater economies of scale as well as the added stimulus provided for industrial production. More concretely, it may be said that the dynamism of integration takes the form of enlarging the combined domestic markets beyond the limits possible for each were they not integrated. In economic jargon, integration pushes the regional possibility frontier outward more than would have been feasible in its absence. The possibility which integration creates for economies of scale and a more efficient use of resources are supposed to be the factors behind the more rapid enlargement in the size of the market or the production possibility frontiers. But then what assures that integration would necessarily lead to such a result without leading to a substantial degree of polarisation in the development of the integrated area?

The answer to the above question is in two parts: the first concerns the identification of those areas of economic activity which are likely to be most promising in terms of potential growth in an integrated area; the second relates to the co-ordinated policy measures which are necessary to ensure an acceptable distribution of costs and benefits among the integrating countries.

It is generally recognised that industrialisation is the key to the process of development. It has also been observed that as industrialisation proceeds, the pattern of manufacturing output tends to change in response to evolving demand conditions. Historically, as industrialisation proceeded the relative importance of industries such as clothing and textiles tended to decline while that of industries such as chemicals and capital goods tended to increase.[45] The latter industries would contribute one major promising area for future development, and the enlargement of the size of the domestic market should be viewed in this context.[46] It has been pointed out that it is trade in durable manufactures which is expected to be of the trade-creating type. As far as developing countries are concerned such manufactures are largely imported from the industrial countries and therefore the immediate effects of integration are not likely to be, on balance, trade creating. The expansion of manufacturing output of developing countries can be achieved through export promotion and/or import substitution though the latter option is much less promising than the former. In either case, the size of the domestic market of individual countries acts as a constraint. The combined markets of individual countries may afford better opportunities to establish viable manufacturing industries especially in those areas which constitute promising growth points and which can support the necessary expansion of industrial exports and/or compete with foreign manufacturers on the local market.[47]

Another area which is expected to prove promising in the event of closer economic co-operation taking the form of integration comprises existing industries and industrial structures. While planning for the future, regional industrial development has to account for the expected changes described above. Integration would or should also lead to a reassessment of existing economic and industrial specialisation among the integrating countries as well as to the examination of new opportunities to exploit existing capacities. The scope for developing traditional industries remains wide particularly in the less developed members of the integrating area. The more limited the given industrial base, the greater is the scope. And the potential for using existing industrial capacity (which is often under-utilised) becomes more promising. The possibilities for a more rational allocation of industrial activities would further be enhanced, though it is recognised that this is a difficult issue to tackle, relating to the criteria to be used in allocating regional industrial activities.

Presumably, the integrated area would offer better opportunities for the achievement of a broad industrial development, the establishment of optimum size plants,[48] the reaping of economies of scale and a more efficient use of resources. It would act as a further inducement to domestic and foreign investments. Taking proper advantage of these opportunities is subject to the maintenance of proper economic policies in the individual countries and in the integrated area as a whole. The sustainability of these opportunities would depend to a large extent on an acceptable distribution of costs and benefits among the integrating economies. This would include the implementation of corrective trade, monetary, fiscal and employment measures, among others, in addition to measures in the field of common services.[49]

Looking at the contemporary Arab economies one immediate observation which comes to mind is the financial wealth which they possess collectively. An economically integrated Arab area need not be concerned, in the foreseeable future at least, with sources of project financing or balance of payments problems. Oil resources are expected to constitute a substantial source of wealth for a number of years to come. Admittedly, with the widening absorptive capacity of the petroleum-exporting countries, balance of payments current account surpluses may not last for many years to come, in which case regional balance of payments problems could become a matter of concern. This longer-run issue, however, does not concern us here.[50] While oil resources will ensure that Arab exports can still act as an important vehicle for growth, this does not lessen the importance of developing other export industries not only for long-run balance of payments reasons but more so for laying the basis for future industrial development. It has been mentioned above that the enlargement of the size of the market will provide opportunities for sustained industrialisation. In line with the experience of the industrial countries the pattern of industrialisation of developing countries is expected to shift in favour of non-traditional industries such as machinery and transport equipment.

Table 2.9 indicates the composition of exports of manufactures for selected Arab countries (including members of the ACM) and their geographic distribution. It is noted, first, that for most countries code 6, representing manufactures by material (e.g. the traditional exports of textiles, cement, paper, etc.) comprise, as might be expected, the larger portion of total manufactured exports. Kuwait is a clear exception.[51] Secondly, the manufactured exports of the non-ACM countries, Lebanon, Kuwait and Tunisia, are more diversified than those of the ACM countries. This is partly seen in the importance occupied by the non-traditional exports contained in code 7 in the case of Kuwait and Lebanon and in code 5 in the case of Tunisia. Thirdly, with the exception of Kuwait and Lebanon, machinery and transport equipment form a small portion of total exports in manufactures. It should be borne in mind, though, that the high ratio registered for Kuwait and Lebanon reflects, in part, the production of industries where the degree of transformation or value-added is limited. Fourthly, for one group of countries, i.e. Egypt and Tunisia, the Arab markets absorb a small portion of their total exports in manufactures. However, it is significant that in the area of machinery and transport equipment the larger portion of Egyptian and an important portion of Tunisian exports go to the Arab countries. For a second group of countries, i.e. Jordan and Iraq, the dominance of the Arab markets in their export trade in manufactures is clear-cut. For the rest of the sample, i.e. Lebanon, Kuwait and Syria, the division of exports between Arab and non-Arab countries is more balanced, though Kuwaiti exports seem to be relatively more dependent upon the Arab markets than are Lebanese and Syrian exports. In the case of Syria, the ratio in favour of the Arab countries is higher for machinery and transport equipment than it is for the other groups of manufactures.

Table 2.9 Selected Arab Countries: Composition of Exports of Manufacturing in Accordance with the SITC (in per cent)

Country	SITC Codes							
	5		6		7		8	
	1970	1973	1970	1973	1970	1973	1970	1973
Egyptian Exports								
Arab countries	17	8	16	15	79	57	20	9
Other countries	83	92	84	85	21	43	80	91
Given code as a % of total manufactures	9	9	73	68	3	2	15	21
Jordanian Exports								
Arab countries	96	93	96	100	100	100	100	98
Other countries	4	7	4					2
Given code as a % of total manufactures	16	18	46	62	19	13	19	8
Iraqi Exports								
Arab countries	99	92	100	96	100	100	76	82
Other countries	1	8	—	4	—	—	24	18
Given code as a % of total manufactures	11	15	79	71	2	1	8	13

Table 2.9 – *cont.*

Country	SITC Codes 5		6		7		8	
	1970	1973	1970	1973	1970	1973	1970	1973
Syrian Exports								
Arab countries	54	32	44	39	88	50	47	86
Other countries	46	68	56	61	12	50	53	14
Given code as a % of total manufactures	3	3	65	64	4	8	28	25
Lebanese Exports[a]								
Arab countries	8	54	36[b]	55	19	49	...	78
Other countries	92	46	64	45	81	51	...	22
Given code as a % of total manufactures	12	11	57	41	31	29		19
Kuwaiti Exports								
Arab countries	29	25	73	87	66	64	68	82
Other countries	71	75	27	13	33	36	32	18
Given code as a % of total manufactures	29	36	15	23	46	30	10	11
Tunisian Exports								
Arab countries	2	1	61	27	15	47	54	45
Other countries	98	99	39	73	85	53	46	55
Given code as a % of total manufactures	51	50	41	42	2	2	6	6

Note: Code 5: Chemicals.
Code 6: Paper, textiles, cement, iron and steel, etc. (manufactures classified by material).
Code 7: Machinery and transport equipment.
Code 8: Clothing, footwear, etc. (other manufactures).

a. For the 1970 data the source is: ECWA, *Foreign Trade and Payments Statistics in Countries of Western Asia,* 77–1031 (August 1977). The ECWA data are not strictly comparable with the CAEU data.

b. Includes code 8.

Source: CAEU, *Annual Bulletin for Arab Countries Foreign Trade Statistics.*

On the basis of the foregoing discussion, three tentative conclusions may be drawn. The first is that moves towards Arab economic integration will afford the Arab countries better opportunities for developing non-traditional industries, the scope of which is still limited. The future needs of the Arab countries and the availability of financial resources to back up the development process provide, in principle, substantial incentives for the development of Arab industry within the framework of an economically integrated area. While some Arab countries have already pushed ahead of others in certain non-traditional industries, there remains a very wide scope for balanced regional development in these fields. This is indicated by the generally limited growth of non-traditional industries and the relatively limited scope in overall trade and inter-Arab trade which exports of non-traditional manufactures occupy. Any envisaged regional co-ordination in this regard would have to account for the elements of complementarity and competitiveness noted above (p. 108). In designing the framework of industrial co-ordination, care must be taken to strengthen the elements of complementarity whether of a potential nature or by design, and to minimise those elements which act to discourage co-ordination. The potential for financial co-operation could be exploited to play a very significant role in inducing industrial co-ordination. That is, available resources can be used to minimise the impact of any required adjustment in national industrial planning and to support the regionally co-ordinated plan. If as a result of an integrated Arab market Arab industry becomes more efficient and competitive, a widening foreign market for Arab industrial products may develop. This would fit into a strategy which aims at gradually reducing Arab dependence on oil exports as a source of foreign exchange. It is unfortunate that in practice there is no apparent co-ordination among the industrial programmes of the various Arab countries or sub-groups thereof.

Secondly, to maximise the benefit from the potential for industrial development offered by an economically integrated Arab market the policy issues discussed above must be fully considered. One additional specific prerequisite may be noted here, namely the rapid development of the transport and communications network among the Arab countries: one major flaw in this area is the non-establishment, so far, of modern pan-Arab highways or the development of an efficient inter-Arab communications network. Again the existence of financial resources could support substantial progress in this regard. Thirdly, the above considerations re-emphasise the importance of financial co-operation among the Arab countries to ensure the availability of financial resources for regional needs and the free flow of funds among the Arab countries. The conscious development of an Arab financial market would greatly facilitate the attainment of these objectives since it would provide the proper links for the flow of financial resources. Joint ventures or other forms of joint economic participation among either the private or public sectors of the Arab countries can also be a promising vehicle for the flow of resources and for the implementation of what is decided upon as a balanced industrial programme in the region as a whole.

Some Implications of Various Forms of Arab Economic Integration to the Arab and World Economies

While the scope of Arab economic co-operation remains limited, it would be useful to examine briefly and tentatively some of the implications of an effective process of Arab economic integration to the Arab and world economies. Such an examination is governed by at least three considerations: the first is the time dimension involved, i.e. whether we have in mind the immediate, medium-term or long-term impact of Arab economic integration. It may be argued, however, that the effects of the integration process will only be felt in the longer run, or that at least any division of time is at best arbitrary since we are dealing with a continuous process. For our purposes we shall therefore not draw a distinction between these periods except when it is found useful to do so. The second consideration concerns the form which the integration process is assuming or has assumed. Specifically we shall be concerned whether it is taking the form of a free trade area, a customs union, a common market and/or joint ventures. The third is the importance or weight which the Arab economies jointly occupy today in the world economy and the degree to which they currently interact with it.

As to relative weight in the world economy, one available indicator is the portion of world trade which the Arab economies jointly account for. It is very small. This comparison, however, conceals two important economic variables which the Arab economies command: their oil resources and their accumulating financial resources. Oil exports are at present and will remain for a number of years to come a strategic item in the economic wellbeing of the industrial world. And again while the total financial wealth of the Arab countries is also relatively small in terms of world totals, their ability to shift their financial holdings between countries and between currencies could have important world financial repercussions. Nevertheless, we can only assume that some form of stable relations in the international economic system will prevail which, in turn, will permit normal operations of international economic transactions.

Tables 2.10 and 2.11 summarise the pattern of trade of eleven Arab countries for the years 1970 and 1973 somewhat differently from the presentation in Tables 2.4 and 2.5. On the export side, it is apparent that the majority of these countries do not rely heavily on the Arab markets as export outlets, the two main exceptions being Lebanon and Kuwait followed by Syria. In contrast, the degree of dependence on West European markets is generally much greater, Jordan being the

Table 2.10 Selected Arab Countries: Distribution of Trade Exports (in per cent)[a]

	Western Europe		USSR & Eastern Europe		USA		Arab countries		Japan		Rest of world	
	1970	1973	1970	1973	1970	1973	1970	1973	1970	1973	1970	1973
Jordan	9	3	2	1	...	...	60	55	...	4	29	37
Syria	32	34	18	23	...	1	24	22	7	...	19	20
Iraq	70	75	1	1	2	1	8	3	...	...	19	20
Egypt	14	21	57	48	1	3	8	8	3	4	17	16
Sudan	37	41	21	5	4	2	9	11	8	11	21	30[b]
Kuwait	64	60	—	—	1	2	2	2	15	17	10	10
Libya	93	77	—	7	3	9	...	...	...	1	4	6
Tunisia	65	63	10	7	1	15	15[c]	8	2	—	7	7
Saudi Arabia	45	60	—	—	1	7	6	1	21	17	27	15
Lebanon	12	26	5	4	4	5	58	40	—	—	21	25
Morocco	76	74	8	7	2	2	4	5	3	1	7	11

a. Rounded ratios.
b. The mainland of China alone represents 15 per cent.
c. CAEU data: (—) = data not available; (...) = data not significant.
Source: IMF/IBRD, *Direction of Trade, Annual 1969–73.*

Table 2.11 Selected Arab Countries: Distribution of Trade Imports (in per cent)

	Western Europe		USSR & Eastern Europe		USA		Arab countries		Japan		Rest of world	
	1970	1973	1970	1973	1970	1973	1970	1973	1970	1973	1970	1973
Jordan	37	32	10	10	11	10	20	20	6	5	16	23
Syria	33	44	21	15	3	4	17	14	7	4	19	19
Iraq	44	39	22	20	4	7	7	5	3	7	20	22
Egypt	37	47	29	17	6	18	6	6	2	1	20	11
Sudan	41	40	16	12	3	8	7	6	6	6	27	28
Kuwait	39	37	5	3	13	13	8	9	15	18	20	20
Libya	55	65	8	6	14	5	8	6	6	6	9	12
Tunisia	64	71	7	4	17	9	—	5	...	1	12	10
Saudi Arabia	34	35	2	—	18	26	19	7	10	23	16	10
Lebanon	48	53	10	6	12	12	13	8	5	5	12	16
Morocco	65	65	9	6	11	11	2	3	2	2	11	13

a. Rounded ratios. (—) = data not available; (...) = data not significant.
Source: IMF/IBRD, *Direction of Trade, Annual 1969–73.*

clear exception. For certain of the petroleum-exporting countries, Japan is an important market; for others, e.g. Egypt, Syria and the Sudan, the USSR and to a lesser extent China constitute or have constituted important outlets. The US market so far appears relatively unimportant. On the import side, the dependence of individual Arab economies on the Arab markets is generally more limited than in the case of exports. On the whole, the West European markets are the most important sources of imports. Again for certain countries the USSR or Japan occupy or have occupied a relatively important position.

At the trade level, the impact of closer Arab economic co-operation on the pattern of trade will be governed by the pattern of Arab development and the degree and extent of commodity substitution one can expect between the Arab and outside markets. Any conclusions in this regard must be based on an extensive examination of the present and projected future composition of commodity trade. This implies, among other things, an assessment of the extent to which the Arab regional market will satisfy future demand for various categories of goods, a task which lies outside the scope of the present study. Nevertheless, three tentative observations relating to this issue may be put forward.

First, during the early stages of integration, the foreign markets which will most likely be affected are those which offer products that can be replaced, in part if not in full, by Arab products. This may affect Arab trading relationships with the other developing countries more than those with the industrial countries. Secondly, as industrialisation proceeds and Arab industry becomes more broadly based, efficient and diversified, the influence of this development will be felt more importantly in the markets of the industrial countries, especially the European markets with which the Arab world maintains close ties, than in other foreign markets. However, given the long-term developmental requirements of the Arab countries, the impact of their own industrial development on the European markets is expected to manifest itself mainly in a changed pattern of trade particularly as concerns manufactures. It will not necessarily lead to a reduced proportion of Arab-European trade to total Arab trade. Indeed, this proportion may increase. Thirdly, let us suppose that Arab economic integration will lead to a substantial rise in the ratio of inter-Arab trade to total Arab foreign trade. While the impact of this development on the Arab economies may be substantial, its effects on the European economies in particular and the world economy in general are expected to be small. On the side of Arab exports, the world economy will in the foreseeable future continue to be the major outlet for the most important Arab export, namely petroleum. This picture will of course drastically change when world dependence on oil is reduced substantially. On the import side, Arab imports from European and world markets constitute a small proportion of the total exports of these markets. Hence, even if one were to assume that Arab economic integration will lead to an increasing proportion of inter-Arab trade with respect to total Arab trade, it would follow that its overall impact is likely to be relatively small, though particular exporters and industries may be considerably affected. Finally, whatever impact closer Arab economic co-operation will have on trade patterns, these effects are likely to become more important as the form of co-operation moves from a free trade area to more advanced stages of integration.

As pointed out below, an effective integration among the Arab countries may have a greater impact, in the foreseeable future, on the world economy in terms of substantial shifts of Arab funds towards Arab markets. But as already mentioned, to the extent that stable international monetary relations prevail, such a shift is expected to be carried out gradually.

With the above considerations in mind let us examine briefly the possible impact of alternative forms of Arab economic integration.

Free Trade Area

A free trade area is commonly taken to imply the removal of all trade barriers among a group of countries. It does not specify any common external tariff wall or agreements on other aspects of foreign trade policies. The present status of the ACM is close to being a free trade area: as mentioned earlier, administrative hindrances to trade have not yet been totally removed.

The impact of an Arab free trade area on the Arab and outside markets would depend on the supply and demand elasticities of the various traded goods and on the prevailing tariff walls in the member countries: these vary considerably, being generally low in the petroleum-exporting countries. Given the composition of trade between the Arab countries and the rest of the world as well as their present level of industrialisation, the short-term impact of an Arab free trade area is likely to manifest itself in three possible conflicting ways. First, for those Arab countries which are already dependent on the Arab markets as export outlets, this dependence, other things being equal, is likely to increase since their competitive edge is expected to be enhanced. For the petroleum-exporting countries the impact is likely to be small. The bulk of their exports is dependent on outside markets while most of what they import from the outside cannot be replaced by Arab products at least for a number of years to come. But since they generally maintain low tariffs they could develop as entrepôt centres for the Arab East. That is, foreign competition in the other Arab markets is likely to increase. Thirdly, as the Arab countries industrialise, their share of trade in manufactures may tend to rise though in the absence of a common external tariff this outcome is very uncertain. For one thing, the future developmental needs of the Arab countries are such that they will continue to depend heavily on outside economies for capital goods; for another, as long as certain Arab countries have low tariffs on outside products, the rest of the Arab economies will continue to face keen foreign competition on these markets. This picture might change over time were the petroleum-exporting countries to raise their tariff walls thereby affording the Arab countries a better competitive edge *vis-à-vis* foreign products. Nevertheless, the full exploitation of this edge can only be realised after their industrial base has been sufficiently developed. The impact of this development might affect more substantially the pattern of inter-Arab trade rather than its proportion to total Arab trade for reasons already noted above. It might also be argued that a free trade area could be detrimental to the general economic development of the Arab countries. This might be the case if it endangers the industrialisation process of a number of Arab countries on account of the unco-ordinated tariff policies of the various members of the free trade area.

Customs Union

The obvious advantage of a customs union over a free trade area is its implied common external tariff. This advantage would be realised if the tariff policy is well designed (see above, p. 108).

Let us assume that the Arab countries decide to establish a tariff wall which reflects a weighted average of the various national tariff walls. The immediate impact of a customs union would manifest itself in two opposing ways: for those countries which then had a lower tariff wall than before, their imports, other things being equal, would be stimulated, assuming import elasticities. The opposite tendency would take place in the countries which faced higher tariff walls than previously. For each member country, and by extension for the union as a whole, the net outcome would depend upon (1) the degree of import substitution which is expected to occur in each case, (2) the competitiveness of the products of each union member with foreign products under the new tariff walls, and (3) the relative weight of each member in the union's trade. If it assumed that the common tariff wall gives a higher average shelter to industrial production than before then an expansion in the inter-Arab trade in manufactures both absolutely and relatively to total Arab trade in manufactures would not be surprising. But even then, the medium- and the longer-term impact on the major industrial markets will be small. In the medium term, a substantial base of Arab industry would not yet have been established. In the longer term, industrialisation in the union may have succeeded in reaping the benefits of a rapidly growing regional market as a unified Arab market would be. This might change the pattern of trade in favour of inter-union trade. But as the experience of the industrial countries suggests, successful industrialisation leads to a more differentiated industrial output accompanied by a growing and not shrinking world trade. Thus, the longer-term impact of a successful Arab customs union would be expected to influence the pattern of trade in manufactures with the rest of the world and especially Europe. Whatever the ultimate effect on the proportion of inter-Arab trade to total Arab trade it will not, on the whole, substantially affect the markets of the industrial economies.

While a customs union may be preferable to a free trade area, it does not ensure on its own a successful integration of the member countries. It does not, for example, permit or ensure a freer flow of resources. Further, as emphasised above, a co-ordination of national economic policies is an essential prerequisite for the realisation of the potential gains of integration. Such co-ordination is an important factor in inducing in particular capital flows among the Arab countries. An Arab customs union may, then, have a limited effect on the overall industrial development of the Arab countries since it does not necessarily ensure the free and substantial movement of capital, and to a lesser extent that of labour among these countries.

The Common Market

A common market implies (1) a freer movement of resources among its members though for certain resources (e.g. labour) this freedom may be subject to certain constraints as discussed above and (2) proper co-ordination of various economic policies partly with a view to ensuring some balance in the distribution of benefits and costs associated with integration.

If successfully implemented an Arab common market could very well create substantially better opportunities for Arab industrial development, by encouraging the movement of resources especially of Arab capital among the Arab countries. Given the availability of financial resources and the co-ordination of economic policies, the potential benefits associated with a unified Arab market may act as important stimuli for attracting Arab capital towards Arab industries. Over time this would accelerate the shift in the pattern of Arab trade in manufactures along the lines noted previously. But again it is not in the trade field that the foreseeable impact of Arab integration on foreign markets will make itself primarily felt. Rather, it is in the pattern of Arab financial flows where the major shifts could occur in favour of the integrated Arab market. This might imply a shift in the pattern of future Arab investments away from international financial and other markets and possibly a return flow to Arab markets of Arab resources already invested abroad. Foreign capital may also be encouraged to enter the Arab market on a substantial scale, assuming that Arab economic policy would favour this inflow. The extent to which foreign capital may be induced to do so might depend on the existing possibilities of setting up joint ventures which make the entry of this capital more attractive from the Arab point of view and provide better guarantees with respect to its treatment.

Joint Ventures

If Arab economic co-operation is to take the form of joint ventures (both inter-Arab and with outside participation), then again its major impact will be felt on the geographic pattern of Arab investments. Three criteria will probably govern the magnitude of the shift in favour of Arab markets. The first is the availability of potentially feasible and rewarding projects at the public and the private sector levels. The second is the degree of relative financial stability which is being maintained, and the third is the degree to which freedom of capital movements and the return of capital is ensured. Indeed existing restrictions on capital movements in those Arab countries which are potential hosts have been emphasised as being a major hindrance to the flow of Arab capital towards these countries and to the development of an Arab financial market.[52] Were such restrictions eliminated – at least with respect to inter-Arab capital movements – a major shift of Arab funds to the Arab markets would not be surprising: there are numerous potentially rewarding projects which can be (and to a certain extent are being) undertaken in the Arab countries.[53] And their financial experience is not generally one of instability, though in certain Arab countries more progress is required to create an attractive financial environment.

The promise of joint ventures however, is much more attractive when viewed in the context of an Arab common market. Two reasons may be mentioned. First, a unified regional market will stimulate joint ventures to a much greater extent than would separate national markets; and secondly, joint ventures could prove to be a useful mechanism to effect a balanced distribution of benefits among the members of the market. In brief, joint ventures can reinforce and strengthen the various influences which an Arab common market is expected to have on the Arab economies.

Concluding Observation

The preceding analysis has endeavoured, among other things, to identify some of the major issues associated with closer Arab economic co-operation. One major point which has been stressed is that policy co-ordination is an integral part of the concept of integration and that the pursuit of proper policies is an important prerequisite for reaping the benefits of integration. Identification of the potential benefits of integrating national markets cannot be considered in isolation from the type of economic policies followed in the unified markets. This close relationship between policy co-ordination and the benefits of integration raises two corollary points which could only be touched upon in this chapter. The first is that economic co-operation among Arab or other countries is less likely to lead to substantial benefits for the co-operating countries, the less it takes the form of close economic integration which implies, among other things, some degree of policy co-ordination.[54] The second is that when one speaks of policy co-ordination in developing countries one is also referring to developmental policies. Integration and development are part of the overall policy framework which a single country, bent on integrating with other countries, has to consider. From the point of view of the single country, to integrate or not to integrate is a developmental issue with all its projected costs and benefits. Some of the recent analyses of integration among developing countries have raised the issues of co-ordinating developmental strategies as one important prerequisite for a successful integration effort.[55] This is an important and complex issue particularly as concerns the feasibility of policy co-ordination among markedly different national economies especially when prevailing national ideologies are also dissimilar. But it is, none the less, an area which is yet to be fully investigated and researched.

Acknowledgements

The author is grateful to Professor G. Sirhan and Professor E. Ghantus for comments on an earlier draft and to Miss Caroline Mujabbir for research assistance.

Notes

1. Cf. T. Scistovsky, *Economic Theory and Western European Integration* (Unwin University Books, London 1958), p.16.
2. A recent study has differentiated three integration styles: (1) the project approach, i.e. the carrying out of projects jointly among the countries concerned; (2) market integration which seeks to expand the market size of national units into an economy of regional dimensions; and (3) integrated development which emphasises measures to promote interdependence and which deliberately seeks to account for an equitable inter-country distribution of benefits, arising from integration. (See I.C. Orantes and G. Rosenthal, 'Reflections on the Conceptual Framework of Central American Economic Integration', *Cepal Review* (United Nations, first half of 1977), pp. 22–8.)
3. Some of the factors responsible for this failure are discussed below, p. 101 ff.
4. Unless otherwise indicated the war period refers to the Second World War.
5. It may be contended by some that co-operation among sub-groups of Arab countries may be more feasible and effective than overall regional co-operation and that sub-regional integration may lead the way to overall Arab integration. This issue is not considered in this chapter.
6. The signatory countries were then Egypt, Iraq, Jordan, Lebanon, Saudi Arabia, Syria and Northern Yemen – Kuwait joined later. The treaty was amended on 15 December 1954, 25 January 1956, 29 May 1957 and 14 January 1959. These amendments pertained to modifications in the lists of goods covered by the treaty and to clarifications concerning certain of its provisions.
7. Where the local value added was not less than 50 per cent of the total cost of production.
8. The treaty specified that current transfers were to be facilitated subject to existing regulations while free capital transfers were to be permitted provided they were destined for development projects.
9. See B. Dajani, 'Arab Economic Co-operation: Practical and Historical Aspects', *Day of Arab Economic Co-operation,* 22 March 1972 (Kuwait Economic Society), pp. 50, 53 in Arabic.
10. Council decree No. 17 of 8/3/64.
11. In contrast as of mid-1977, 13 Arab countries had been signatories to the treaty on Arab economic unity.
12. See 'The Arab Common Market and the Stages it has Undergone', memorandum submitted by the CAEU to the 20th annual meeting of the Arab Chambers of Commerce, Industry and Agriculture, held in Alexandria (ARE), 17–21 May 1976 (in Arabic).
13. See preceding memorandum of the CAEU and memorandum concerning the accomplishments of the Arab Common Market submitted by the Secretariat of the General Union of the Arab Chambers of Commerce, Industry and

Agriculture to its 21st annual meeting held in Damascus, 14–19 May 1977 (in Arabic).

14. In early 1977 the Arab Monetary Fund was established. It has yet to begin operations.

15. Up to August 1971 member countries of the International Monetary Fund were required to declare a par value for their national currency in terms of gold or the US dollar which itself was fixed in terms of gold. This system broke down on 15 August 1971 when the US authorities were no longer prepared (as was the case before) to convert officially held dollar balances into gold or other reserve assets. In practice a floating rate system has since evolved, with many currencies being linked to the SDR or the US dollar. The Kingston Agreement of January 1976 concerning the new international monetary system recognises the possibility of varying exchange rate policies among member countries of the IMF.

16. For a recent description of the exchange systems of these countries see IMF, *28th Annual Report on Exchange Restrictions* (Washington DC, 1977).

17. In practice the rate of the Yemeni currency has been stabilised since early 1973.

18. In principle, Syria maintains a dual rate system but since 18 July 1973 the rates have been unified.

19. Legislative decree No. 348 of 29 December 1969.

20. The institution was established in 1970.

21. The Union of Arab Banks, *Conference on the Flow of Arab Funds to Arab Credit Institutions and Organs* (Abu Dhabi, March 1977), pp. 33–4 (in Arabic).

22. Specifically, since late 1973-early 1974 when the oil prices were raised five-fold in comparison with the prices prevailing in 1972.

23. Without, however, neglecting the trade aspects of co-operation.

24. Such as the national funds for economic development created by a number of petroleum-exporting countries and the various regional banks which have been set up as a multilateral form of co-operation. For a review of these institutions see Council of Arab Economic Unity, *Arab Projects and Joint Arab-International Projects* (February 1977), in Arabic.

25. In January 1973-June 1975 Arab financial flows (disbursements) to developing countries (Arab and non-Arab) and to multilateral institutions amounted to about US $9 billion (excluding IMF facility). See UNCTAD, *Financial Solidarity for Development* (New York, 1977), p. 13.

26. Part of the underlying motive for the renewed emphasis may of course be related to non-economic factors.

27. See General Union of the Chambers of Commerce, Industry and Agriculture for the Arab Countries, *The Arab Capital Market*, proceedings of a conference held in Damascus, 14–19 May 1977 (in Arabic).

28. Trade data are taken from the first (and as yet the most recent) CAEU *Annual Bulletin for the Arab Countries Foreign Trade Statistics* which included only two years, namely 1970 and 1973. The main advantage of this bulletin is that the data are classified by regions as well as by broad groups of products in accordance with the Standard International Trade Classification (SITC). It does not suffer from certain shortcomings which should be kept in mind. The data for total trade of each country, for example, did not appear to be always reliable. In one instance the addition of the subtotals exceeded the grand total. In other instances the subtotals did not add up to the indicated grand total. It was therefore decided to use the IFS data for total trade figures of each individual country. Further, in certain instances national sources were used either because the CAEU Bulletin did not cover them or the data appeared to be unreliable.

29. Similar ratios apply to earlier years. See ECWA, 'Economic Cooperation

and Integration Efforts in Selected Countries of Western Asia', *Studies on Development Problems in Countries of Western Asia, 1974* (United Nations, 1975), p. 38.

30. As used here manufactures refer to Codes 5-8 in the SITC. Code 5 refers to chemicals, Code 6 to manufactured goods classified by material, Code 7 to machinery and transport equipment and Code 8 to miscellaneous manufactured articles.

31. Admittedly the rise is measured from a relatively small base. It is recalled that effective 1970, all customs barriers had been abolished on inter-ACM goods. However, this in itself may not explain the recorded rise, since administrative hindrances to trade have continued to exist.

32. Kuwait, Lebanon, Libya, Morocco, Saudi Arabia, Jordan and Tunisia. Excluded are Algeria, Democratic Yemen, the Yemen Arab Republic and the Gulf countries of Bahrain, Qatar, Oman and the UAG. For some of them the required data were not available. Their exclusion, however, does not change the picture materially.

33. This method of course is not totally satisfactory. A more adequate rate is one reflecting purchasing power parity.

34. A summary of certain development indicators pertaining to the Arab countries of the Middle East is included in United Nations (ECWA), *Statistical Abstract of the Arab World 1968-1975* (Amman, 1977) and *Development Trends and Prospects in Selected ECWA Countries* 77–1029 (August 1977).

35. Article 14 of the treaty establishing the Arab Common Market specifies that each member may request the exemption of certain products from the agreed measures of liberalisation. It is reported that frequent use was made of this clause though the duration of the exemptions lists was not to go beyond the final stages of liberalisation. See UN (ECWA), 'Economic Co-operation and Integration Efforts in Selected Countries of Asia', *Studies in Development Problems in Countries of Western Asia 1974* (UN, 1975), pp. 36–7.

36. First introduced by Viner, the concept of trade creation is used to indicate a switch from a higher-cost to a lower-cost industry as a consequence of establishing a customs union. Trade diversion has the opposite result. See Jacob Viner, *The Customs Unions Issue* (Carnegie Endowment for International Peace, New York, 1950).

37. See J.E. Meade, *The Theory of Customs Union* (North Holland, Amsterdam, 1955).

38. See R.G. Lipsey, 'The Theory of Customs Union: A General Survey', *Economic Journal* (September 1960) reprinted in Caves and Johnson (eds), *Readings in International Economics,* vol. XI (Richard D. Irwin, 1968).

39. Ibid., pp. 273–4 in *Readings.*

40. Cf. G.M. Meir, *The International Economics of Development* (New York, Harper and Row Publishers, 1968), pp. 201–13.

41. Phosphate production plays an important role in the Jordanian economy. In 1975 phosphates accounted for about 60 per cent of total exports.

42. The greater portion of Lebanese exports comprise manufactures.

43. Tariffs applied for revenue purposes are an accepted and even a necessary means for raising tax revenues particularly in developing countries.

44. At the same time, it would seem that restrictions in the Arab world on labour movements are sometimes motivated by purely non-economic reasons.

45. See, for example, Alfred Maizels, *Growth and Trade* (Cambridge University Press, 1970), pp. 8–10.

46. This should not be taken to imply that developing countries need to follow in the footsteps of the industrial countries. The industrial model they opt for may differ substantially from that experienced by today's industrial

countries. A discussion of this issue, however, is outside the scope of the present study.

47. See B. Balassa, *Economic Development and Integration* (Mexico, Centro Estudios Monetarios Latinamericanos, 1965). The author makes the point that without integration exports of individual developing countries will grow but not at a rate which would be sufficient to reduce international disparities in living standards (p. 62).

48. The optimal size of plants, however, is not necessarily predicated on the existence of large markets.

49. For a study of such issues see UNCTAD, *Current Problems of Economic Integration, the distribution of benefits and costs in integration among developing countries* TD/B/394 (United Nations, 1973). In the trade field, for example, this study points out that the less developed partners may obtain preferential trade treatment by longer transitional periods for opening up their markets to trade or by giving priority to the liberalisation of trade in commodities of special export interest to the less developed partners. In the monetary and payments fields compensation may be provided within the framework of payments arrangements. In the fiscal field, fiscal transfers may be linked, for instance, to productive investments in less developed partners. Measures related to common services would include policies relating to the setting of rates and service fees, location of administrative offices etc. (pp. 15–19).

50. For a discussion of some of these issues see Samir Makdisi, 'The Petroleum-exporting Countries and the Evolving International Monetary System: with Special Reference to the ECWA Region', in Economic Commission for Western Asia, *Studies on Development Problems in Countries of Western Asia, 1975* (United Nations, 1977), pp. 56–61.

51. It is however, primarily an oil-producing economy with no biases for the establishment of traditional industries in contrast with non-traditional ones.

52. See *The Arab Financial Market,* proceedings of a conference held by the Arab Chambers of Commerce, Industry and Agriculture on the development of the Arab financial market, 14–19 May 1977, Damascus (in Arabic).

53. Some writers have emphasised sectoral co-operation as one means of achieving Arab economic unity. See, for example, G.P. Casadio, *The Economic Challenge of the Arabs* (London, Saxon House, 1976), pp. 125–31.

54. We are referring here to benefits which, in principle, would not accrue to the individual countries concerned in the absence of integration.

55. See *Cepal Review,* pp. 21–8.

3 ARAB MIGRATIONS

Abdelwahab Bouhdiba

One of the secrets of the cohesion shown by Arab societies in the past undoubtedly lay in their ability to organise themselves into a relatively homogeneous entity at a cultural, economic and political level. The organisation of the classical Arab world made Arabic an international language and the Islamic *Weltanschauung,* the basis for an ethic with universal pretentions. Membership of the community of the Umma made movement very easy. Despite strong local variations there were at least some common rules governing the organisation of economic life. Migration within the borders of the Dar al Islam, determined by geographical or historical circumstance, was far from difficult. The gradual spread of fixed human settlement is an ancient historical phenomenon within the Arab world; at the same time however it has been an extremely slow process and only in recent decades has it become a mass phenomenon. Even today the Arab is a born traveller, a man forever on the move, in continuous search of structures willing to take him in.

Colonialism's effect was to root populations which had never had a concept of national frontiers within countries divided by more or less artificial boundaries. During the decades which followed her conquest of Algeria, France made every effort to give a clear political and military connotation to the country's borders with Tunisia and Morocco. Paradoxically the extension of the French protectorate to cover Algeria's two neighbours led to a reinforcement of this tendency; similar trends were visible in the Middle East.

This reference to the past enables us to base our analysis on the same premisses which implicitly or explicitly have underlaid the majority of work on Arab immigration published to date. Four distinct patterns should be noted.

1. Emigration, i.e. movement from one geographical zone to another, is by no means a recent phenomenon and is to be found throughout the history of Arab societies. The difference between the past and the present is that whereas previously emigration was confined within the boundaries of the Dar al Islam today this is no longer the case. Over the last half-century emigration outside the Arab

world to Europe, Africa, the Americas and the South Pacific has expanded steadily. It is possible to distinguish three main patterns of migration.

2. Migration within national frontiers. This is a two-sided phenomenon consisting on the one hand of nomadism (which is however on the decrease) and on the other of an ever more intensive exodus from the countryside. In practice the former constitutes nothing more or less than cyclical mobility, a seasonal pattern of settlement, whereas the move to the towns is usually permanent and irreversible, marking a break with previous patterns of life. This form of migration we will term 'internal migration'. It will not however be our major concern in this study. It is not impossible that to a large extent international emigration is nothing more than an extension of the rural exodus; similar causes may in both cases lead to similar results; this hypothesis needs to be verified, however.

3. Migration between the various Arab countries constituting the Dar al Islam. Here changes in residence lead to changes in living standard but with very little effect on migrants' general way of life. Although legal and political boundaries are crossed, the linguistic and ethical frame of reference remains the same. The view of the world prevalent in the host country does not differ radically from that in the country from which the emigrant originates. He is a non-national and yet he is not really a foreigner. This kind of emigration we will call 'inter-Arab' emigration.

4. Emigration to countries which are foreign in the full sense of the word, that is to those countries originally known as the Dar ul h'arb (enemy countries). Here the migrant's situation changes radically, affecting every aspect of his life; the climate, customs, language, the way in which society and work are organised: everything is different. Apart from an infinitesimal number of emigrants who settle in the United States, Canada, Australia and certain countries of Eastern and Western Africa the huge majority go to Europe. In this chapter, the only form of emigration outside the Arab world with which we will deal will be this 'Euro-Arab' migration.

In historical terms the importance for Arab societies assumed over the last few decades by this Euro-Arab migration is a novelty. Our aim in this study will be to attempt an overall view of the question, to clarify the essential features of inter-Arab and Euro-Arab migration whilst at the same time identifying structural or other links between the two phenomena. In particular we will seek to answer the following questions: What is the true nature of the changes which have occurred in recent decades of Euro-Arab migration? Are these changes a temporary result of the balance of power and the pattern of economic relations today existing between the Arab world and Western Europe or should they be considered a structural phenomenon tied to political choices in both north and south concerning the organisation of the internal Arab labour market, the nature and expansion of the European productive system, the international division of labour, population surpluses and shortages, and relative investment levels in Europe and the Arab world?

Our first task will be to indicate the main trends in inter-Arab and Euro-Arab migration and to examine any possible correlations between these. This will enable us to clarify the phenomenon and to advance hypotheses for the future.

Once we have succeeded in identifying the true nature of Arab migration it becomes possible to ask, what is its true significance? Who does this migration benefit? Does it serve the interests of the various countries concerned? Should one speak of disguised exploitation or rather of complementarity? Is it possible for Arab countries to base their strategy on emigration? In what conditions and in what context would this be possible?

Having posed these questions I would like to refer briefly to the difficulties we have met with during our research work. The search for basic data has at times been extremely difficult. So long as we were dealing with Euro-Arab migration we did not find it difficult to collect fairly precise and detailed statistics. The problem of inter-Arab migration is however very new and statistical sources are relatively rare. Work by the ILO and the Arab Labour Organisation enabled us to collect the data series without which our analysis would have been impossible. We then enriched this information with reference to reports by Central Banks and a number of sectorial studies.

As a result we believe that we have reached an acceptable, if far from perfect level of approximation. The degree of precision achieved in our statistics is such as to enable us at least to establish the premisses for argument even if not to give a full answer to the questions we posed earlier.

It is useful to recall the main characteristics of Euro-Arab migration. Arab migration to Europe is a very recent phenomenon. A study by the ILO, *Les Migrations Internationales de 1945 à 1957* (International Migration from 1945 to 1957)[1] concludes that virtually all the migratory flows converging on the European countries in this period consisted of short-distance transfers between neighbouring countries. Migratory flows in frontier regions were of especial importance, limiting emigration to moves 'between neighbouring regions in neighbouring countries'.[2] The report adds that 'short-distance' transfers have often been short-term transfers: daily or weekly frontier crossings, seasonal or officially permanent, in practice short-term movements. The level of net emigration has in most cases been low. Here intra-European migration differs significantly from European migration overseas. The statistics show the relatively unimportant role of the southern countries, Italy excepted, in continental migration over the last twelve years.[3]

In France, for example, out of 603,900 foreign workers who entered the country between 1946 and 1957, 418,400 were Italian, 51,100 German, 47,000 Spanish. The number of Arab immigrants was negligible. It should be noted however that these statistics do not include Algerian emigration; Algeria being considered at this time to be a French 'département'. In 1947, 1948 and 1949 France received 230,000 Algerian immigrants. If one takes account of the return of 153,000 workers to Algeria over the same three years this leaves a net migratory flow of 77,000, that is of nearly 25,000 workers per annum. This was the starting point for a new French policy on immigration.[4] Between 1956 and 1961 there was a reduction in the flow of immigrants due to the Algerian war.[5] After 1961 the flow resumed its previous trend (Table 3.1).

Despite the presence of a large Algerian population and the existence of close relations between France and the countries of the Maghreb it remains true to say that until the beginning of the 1960s Arab emigration to Europe was only on a limited scale. It was only after Algerian independence that emigration from the Maghreb began on a large scale.

It is important to note the way in which Tunisians and Moroccans later also began to make their presence felt on the French labour market. In 1959 1.6 per cent of foreign workers permanently established in France were Tunisian whilst 3 per cent were Moroccan. By 1973 the corresponding figures were 20.3 per cent and 15.8 per cent. In practice there has been a general expansion in the Arab population resident in France.

As far as regards the Maghreb the figures are shown in Table 3.2.[6] It can thus be seen that the French immigrant population originating in the Maghreb has doubled in the last ten years.

In 1971 the foreign population resident in France totalled 3,673,452 persons of whom 1,055,604, that is 28.7 per cent, originated in the Maghreb. By January 1976 there were 4,196,134 resident foreigners, that is 68,000 more than in 1975; 7.7 per cent of the total population thus consisted of foreign residents. These included: 845,694 Algerians of whom 420,000 were economically active; 269,690 Moroccans of whom 168,000 were economically active; 148,805 Tunisians of whom 90,000 were economically active. The number of immigrants from Algeria, Morocco and Tunisia thus totalled 1,264,189 persons of whom 678,000 were economically active.

Table 3.1 Algerian Migration to France, 1956-65

Year	Arrivals	Departures	Net migration
1956	79,000	78,000	1,000
1957	69,000	55,000	14,000
1958	42,000	56,000	−14,000
1959	64,000	48,000	16,000
1960	72,000	54,000	18,000
1961	103,000	70,000	33,000
1962	180,167	155,018	25,149
1963	262,076	211,532	50,544
1964	269,543	225,741	43,802
1965	228,093	237,374	−9,281
Total:	1,368,879	1,190,665	178,214

Source: G. Tapinos, *L'émigration étrangère en France* (Paris, PUF, 1975).

Table 3.2 Maghreb's Workers Resident in France, 1962 and 1972

	Algeria	Morocco	Tunisia	Total
1962	425,000	49,653	34,443	509,096
1972	798,690	218,146	119,646	1,136,482

Source: G. Tapinos, *L'émigration étrangère en France.*

In 1976, out of 3,966,042 foreigners resident in France (refugees excluded) 1,352,577 that is 34.1 per cent originated in the Arab countries (see Table 3.3).

As far as the Maghreb is concerned the main host countries for emigration from the area are still to be found in Western Europe. If one examines the distribution of Moroccans living abroad one discovers that 280,000 are resident in France, 20,000 in the German Federal Republic, 50,000 in Belgium, 40,000 in the Netherlands, 3,000 in Gibraltar and 47,000 in other countries. These figures show that nearly two-thirds of Moroccans living abroad are resident in France.

Table 3.3 State of Origin of Non-refugee Arab Residents in France on 1 January 1976

Algeria	844,320
Saudi Arabia	128
Egypt	2,121
Iraq	652
Jordan	541
Kuwait	56
Lebanon	5,362
Libya	465
Morocco	322,067
Mauritania	5,272
Sudan	220
Syria	3,410
Tunisia	167,463
Total	1,352,077

Source: Ministry of Interior, *Les étrangers en France* (Paris, 1976).

As for Tunisia, it has been estimated that in 1975 out of 240,000 Tunisians living abroad, 35,000 were resident in Libya, 12,000 in Algeria and nearly 190,000 in Western Europe. In the period from 1956 to 1970 18.8 per cent of officially registered unaccompanied emigrant Tunisian workers went to Libya, 10 per cent to the Federal Republic of Germany and 66.5 per cent to France (see Table 3.4). (These figures do not include privately-organised emigration.) Over the last ten years Western Europe has drawn 78 per cent of Tunisian applicants for emigration.

In 1974 nearly 35 per cent of foreigners resident in France originated in the Arab countries (see Table 3.5). Table 3.6 shows the distribution of foreign workers in Western Europe. A number of points should be noted:

1. In 1974 out of a total of 6,397,000 foreign workers engaged in gainful employment in the EEC, 4,700,000 originated in non-member states. Of these, 720,000 came from the Maghreb. These workers were strongly concentrated in France (640,000 persons). Whereas a third of the foreign labour force resident in France comes from the Maghreb, the figure for the Common Market countries as a whole is 11.2 per cent.

2. There is no trend towards a stabilisation of the emigrant population in Western Europe. Rather this has increased continually right up to and including 1975 and 1976, and this despite the energy crisis and the difficulties which certain European countries have experienced in controlling their own national labour markets. None the less, a comparison between the pattern of increase in the period from 1969 to 1974 and the years from 1959 to 1969 does show a significant slowing down in internal migration within the EEC. Whereas in 15 years the number of foreign workers from other countries within the Community has tripled, growing from 566,500 to 1,694,000, the number of workers coming from non-member countries has grown from 500,400 to 4,694,000 and has thus multiplied by a factor of 9.4. The number of workers from the Maghreb has grown from 220,300 to 721,000, a growth factor of 3.3 (see Tables 3.6 and 3.7).

Stating the question in other terms, there has been a constant European demand for foreign labour ever since the last war. The Common Market countries, having discovered the impossibility of satisfying their requirements from within their own frontiers have reacted by adopting an open-door policy on immigration. Whereas in the past migration was limited to frontier regions, it has now been expanded affecting first the countries on the boundaries of the Community and later non-European countries.

The countries which have benefited from this phenomenon have been the countries of Southern Europe: Italy, Greece, Spain, Portugal and Turkey. Later the other Southern Mediterranean countries were also affected. Independence and the consequent break in the ties of domination between Europe and the Maghreb have not hindered emigration; on the contrary the process seems to have been encouraged. There is every reason to suppose that in the coming years emigration will continue to expand.

This situation is due to a number of factors, the comprehension of which is essential to the understanding of the structures of European and Arab economies and societies. The major demographic factor in Europe is the insufficiency of the national labour supply, which is inadequate to meet the requirements of economic growth. If the Netherlands and Austria are excluded, 50 per cent of population growth in Western Europe is due to immigration. In the Mediterranean, Eastern and Northern Europe, on the other hand, the period 1950-70 witnessed a negative correlation between migration and population growth.

Table 3.4 Tunisian Emigration of Workers Unaccompanied by their Families

	1956–60	1961–65	1966–70	Total 1956–70
Emigration for private purposes				
to France	13,600	8,800	2,900	25,300
to Israel	8,900	11,600	9,100	29,600
Subtotal	22,500	20,400	12,000	54,900
Labour migration				
France	300	19,200	51,200	70,700
Libya	–	4,000	16,000	20,000
GFR	–	–	11,000	11,000
Belgium	–	–	400	400
Switzerland	–	300	500	800
Algeria	–	200	100	300
Others	–	100	3,000	3,100
Subtotal	300	23,800	82,200	106,300
Total	22,800	44,200	94,200	161,200

Source: Office des Travailleurs Tunisiens à l'Etranger, de l'Emploi et de la Formation Professionnelle, *La Politique tunisienne en matière d'émigration* (Tunis).

The figures shown in Table 3.8 are here of great significance. In Belgium 27 per cent of population growth is due to migration, in France 55 per cent, in Switzerland 75 per cent. Four-fifths of German population growth is due to migration. In Luxembourg the natural growth of the population has been so slow that 105 per cent of overall growth was due to migration. Everywhere else in Europe the correlation between immigration and natural population growth is a negative one.

Over the last quarter of a century Western Europe has thus balanced its population deficit by relying on an inflow of foreign workers. Immigration has, in other words allowed her to export this deficit. The origins of this trend are to be found in deliberate policy decisions, taken by the countries which were later to form the Common Market in the period immediately following the Second World War.

Table 3.5 Foreign Residents in France

Country of origin	1973 Number	%	1974 Number	%
Algeria	845,694	21.4	871,223	21.8
Portugal	812,007	20.6	840,460	21.0
Italy	572,803	14.5	564,660	14.1
Spain	570,595	14.5	548,600	13.7
Morocco	269,680	6.8	302,255	7.6
Tunisia	148,805	3.8	162,479	4.1
Poland	91,059	2.3	50,896	1.3
Yugoslavia	79,365	2.0	79,445	2.0
Belgium	63,836	1.6	64,315	1.6
Turkey	45,363	1.2	59,178	1.5
Germany	42,717	1.1	44,316	1.1
Other EEC countries	40,461	1.0	44,171	1.1
Others	150,784	3.8	160,728	4.0
Children under the age of 16	140,000	3.5	130,000	3.2
Africans	77,000	1.9	75,000	1.9
Subtotal	3,950,169	100.0	3,997,726	100.0
Refugees	88,860		96,324	
Stateless persons	4,246		4,262	
Overall total	4,043,275		4,089,312	

Source: Ministry of Interior, *Les étrangers en France* (Paris, 1976).

As early as 1945, French decision-makers, economists and financiers rallied to Robert Schuman's view that national reconstruction would depend, in the future, on large-scale immigration. Tapinos has given an excellent summary of the French viewpoint in this period, insisting on the role of foreign immigration as a way of satisfying 'the demographic and economic needs of the country'.[7] As P. Delouvrier and R. Nathan have written: 'Given the hypothesis that the population deficit constitutes a constraint on economic policy and on the development of the French economy the first problem economic policy must face is

Table 3.6 Foreign Workers in Europe

Countries of origin	Belgium 1974	Denmark 1974	GFR 1974	France 1974	Ireland 1974	Italy 1971	Luxembourg 1974	The Netherlands 1974	Great Britain 1971
Belgium		155	10,000	25,000	6	539	7,200	23,410	7,500
Denmark	400		4,000	1,000	25	248	–	180	2,000
Germany	4,500	4,080		25,000	270	7,190	5,800	12,756	71,000
France	15,000	526	50,000		179	4,145	7,100	1,700	16,500
Ireland	200	150	1,000	1,000		300	–	180	452,000
Italy	90,000	477	370,000	230,000	258		10,400	9,000	72,000
Luxembourg	1,400	1	2,000	2,000		32		60	500
The Netherlands	13,500	593	70,000	5,000	98	1,146	600		10,500
Great Britain	5,000	2,515	20,000	11,000	–	4,500	200	3,800	
Total EEC	130,000	8,497	527,000	300,000	836	18,100	31,300	51,086	630,200
Spain	34,000	934	165,000	265,000	109	2,006	1,900	11,341	37,000
Greece	6,000	3,453	225,000	5,000	5	768	–	947	50,000
Portugal	4,000	–	85,000	475,000	13	631	11,800	2,689	10,000
Turkey	10,000	5,730	590,000	25,000	10	317	–	21,925	3,000
Yugoslavia	3,000	4,520	470,000	50,000	7	4,103	600	8,611	4,000
Algeria	3,000	–	2,000	440,000	–	–	–	–	600
Morocco	30,000	1,645	16,000	130,000	–	–	–	9,429	2,000
Tunisia	2,000	–	12,000	70,000	–	–	–	889	200
Others	8,000	11,148	258,000	145,000	830	18,205	1,700	11,071	928,200
Total	100,000	27,430	1,823,000	1,605,000	974	26,030	16,000	66,902	1,035,000
Overall total	230,000	35,927	2,350,000	1,905,000	1,810	44,130	47,300	117,988	1,665,200

Source: EEC, ***Western Europe's Migrant Workers*** (Bruxelles, Minority Rights Group, Report no. 28, 1975).

the population problem.'[8] Certainly no one at this time was thinking in terms of immigration from outside Europe.

Table 3.7 Changes in the Population of Foreign Workers Resident in Europe

Country of origin	1959	1969	1959–69 %	1974	1969–74 %
Belgium	35,000	54,000	+ 54	73,000	+ 36
Denmark	–	–	–	8,000	
Germany	40,100	40,000	0	125,000	+ 212
France	31,300	47,700	+ 52	96,000	+ 101
Ireland	–	–	–	455,000	
Italy	400,000	593,000	+ 48	782,000	+ 32
Luxembourg	4,300	3,500	– 19	6,000	+ 71
Netherlands	55,800	66,100	+ 18	102,000	+ 54
UK	–	–	–	47,000	
Total	566,500	804,300	+ 43	1,694,000	+ 31
Spain	79,600	413,000	+ 419	517,000	+ 25
Greece	7,600	165,000	+ 2,071	290,000	+ 76
Portugal	10,200	200,000	+ 1,861	590,000	+ 195
Turkey	1,100	198,000	+ 17,900	656,000	+ 231
Yugoslavia	7,800	182,000	+ 2,233	545,000	+ 199
Algeria	190,300	244,800	+ 29	446,000	+ 82
Morocco	22,000	83,000	+ 277	190,000	+ 129
Tunisia	8,000	34,000	+ 325	85,000	+ 150
Others	173,800	366,000	+ 111	1,375,000	+ 276
Total	500,400	1,885,800	+ 276	4,694,000	+ 149
Overall total	1,066,900	2,690,100	+ 152	6,388,000	+ 138

Source: EEC, *Western Europe's Migrant Workers.*

Migration was seen as definitive; migrant workers would gradually be assimilated within the local population. INED's prestigious review *Population* published a highly authoritative article by P. Vincent which stated that 'foreigners coming to France must stay in France, giving birth to new Frenchmen who will take the place of the Frenchmen we lack and will continue to lack; these who were never born as a result of the 1915-19 war and the war of 1939'.[9]

From 1947 onwards France adopted a series of annual immigration plans. Tapinos shows clearly how 'immigration is no substitute for natural population growth; none the less the volume of immigration is directly correlated to demographic recovery'.[10]

Table 3.8 Immigration and European Population Growth

Countries	Immigration ('000)			Immigration as a % of population on growth 1950–70
	1950–1960	1960–1970	1950–1970	
Western Europe	+ 3,882	+ 4,882	+ 8,748	+ 51
Austria	– 141	+ 38	– 103	– 17
Belgium	+ 59	+ 152	– 211	+ 27
GFR	+ 2,723	+ 2,057	+ 4,780	+ 81
France	+ 1,080	+ 2,178	+ 3,258	+ 55
Luxembourg	+ 7	+ 15	+ 22	+ 105
The Netherlands	– 142	+ 92	– 50	– 2
Switzerland	+ 296	+ 334	+ 630	+ 72
Mediterranean Europe				
Greece	– 3,475	– 3,826	– 7,301	– 29
Italy	– 196	– 455	– 651	– 36
Malta	– 43	– 38	– 61	– 89
Portugal	– 662	– 1,290	– 1,952	– 90
Spain	– 826	– 551	– 1,377	– 19
Yugoslavia	– 582	– 700	– 1,282	– 26
Eastern Europe	– 2,551	– 1,218	– 3,777	– 21
Northern Europe	– 501	– 197	– 698	– 8

Source: UN, *International Migration Trends, 1950–70* (New York, 1974).

For a more detailed analysis of the development of French immigration policy, we should refer to Tapinos who has given us an extremely complete account. The only point we would like to make here is that despite the efforts of the French authorities, European migration to France was always on an extremely limited scale, barely sufficient to balance the loss of immigrants returning to their countries of origin and Frenchmen emigrating abroad. At the same time however immigration from Algeria developed substantially. The net migration flow from Algeria overtook the flow from Italy on which many decision-makers had placed their hopes, though these hopes seemed for a time to have been met by

Spanish migration.

Although at times there were very significant variations, the situation in the other countries of the Common Market was not fundamentally different from that in France.[11] In Federal Germany immigration was originally conceived of as a purely temporary phenomenon. This view led to hesitations in German policy during the 1960s and the imposition of drastic restrictions on immigration in 1973. In Great Britain the Commonwealth provided a specific 'natural' framework for migration.

In general, European immigration policy has been and continues to be founded to a great extent on the possibility of using various policy measures to facilitate the flow of certain countries' excess labour force to other countries suffering from a labour shortage.

In 1975 a short OECD report stated

> In the climate which characterized the immediate post-war period and the period of reconstruction both ethical and legal principles and the material interest of the international Community concurred in favouring a remedy to the labour shortages which were hindering the rebuilding of the productive apparatus, involving a better use of human resources, that is a transfer of these resources from countries with a surplus to countries with a deficit.[12]

Even the recommendations of the ILO, revised in 1949, were issued so as to favour the pursual of this basic aim.

In practice, as the OECD itself has emphasised, this constituted a complete doctrine of immigration founded on freedom of movement for workers, on the common interests of countries of origin and host countries and on the need to respect the fundamental rights of foreign workers. As far as human and social problems were concerned these were seen 'as inevitable. In any case action to favour the assimilation, training and housing [of immigrants] as well as more general social services should be able at least to reduce if not to eliminate these'.[13] This kind of optimism was bound to come up against obstacles. Events were to show how supposedly minor problems could become desperately important. Immigrant workers were relegated to a second-class status, the discriminatory criteria usually being racial.

Even more seriously the experience of a quarter of a century has shown how immigration has enabled Europe to become a world economic power. Here, at least, the Europeans' original objectives in promoting immigration have been fully achieved. Certainly the countries of origin have drawn certain advantages from emigration which has reduced tensions on national labour markets and which has created a significant inflow of foreign currency. At the same time however the gap between their economies and those of the developed economies has in no way narrowed; they have failed to create the basic conditions for economic take-off. This is true of Greece, Portugal and Turkey just as it is true of Spain. For the countries of the Maghreb where migration began later and which have only recently emerged from the shadows of colonialism this is even more so.

An OECD study group has provided a remarkable analysis of trends in Europe. A continuous and sustained supply of foreign labour power has enabled the European countries to pursue steady economic growth. A policy of full employment has broken through previous manpower ceilings. National labour shortages have been easily filled with a selective and relatively cheap inflow of foreign workers. At the end of the 1960s the expansion of the employment market, continually encouraged by new supplies of foreign labour, was so rapid that Europe went through a period of over-employment.

Domestic demographic constraints, technical constraints, the distribution of wages and social services and other factors have led to a change in the work which immigrants are asked to perform. Immediately following the Second World War they were involved exclusively in national reconstruction work. At the beginning of the 1960s they were still employed mainly in the building industry and in agriculture.

Recruitment of migrant labour was seen as being tied to short-term fluctuations in the economy. Gradually however immigrant workers have begun to move into a wider range of permanent jobs, requiring a greater or lesser degree of specialisation. Their presence has however tended to devalue these jobs, reducing the rate of wage increases. At the same time national labour forces have come to be restricted to the most skilled, highly paid work. Gradually immigration has ceased to be a short-term economic phenomenon and has become a structural one.

Table 3.9 shows the proportion of foreign workers in the total working population. In 1973 foreigners made up 3.4 per cent of the working population of the Netherlands and 6.8 per cent in Belgium. The corresponding figures for Luxembourg and Switzerland were 27.9 per cent and 28.2 per cent. The figures for France and Germany, the two largest countries in the Community, were 9.4 per cent and 9 per cent.

Tables 3.10, 3.11 and 3.12 are even more significant for they show the relative importance of foreign workers in different economic sectors. In Germany, for instance, in certain key sectors foreign workers represent an extremely high proportion of the total workforce. A third of all workers in the rubber, wood-working, food and textile industries are foreigners. The same applies to a quarter of all workers in the metal-working, car, furniture and plastics industries. In France foreign workers are concentrated in the building industry, in public works and in the steel industry (see Table 3.11): 42.3 per cent of Algerian immigrants are concentrated in building and public works, 13.4 per cent in mechanical industries and 8.2 per cent in metal-working (see Table 3.12).

Table 3.9 Ratio of Foreign Workers to Total European Working Population, 1973

Countries	Foreign workers (A)	Total working population (B)	(A)(B) %
GFR	2,500,000	26,500,000	9.4
France	1,930,000	21,400,000	9.0
Switzerland	861,000	3,100,000	28.2
Belgium	265,000	3,900,000	6.8
The Netherlands	160,000	4,700,000	3.4
Luxembourg	43,000	150,000	27.9

Source: *The Economist,* 9 August 1975.

Emigration has enabled the industrialised countries of Europe to resolve the problems deriving from the labour shortages, to accumulate capital and to adopt an open-door policy towards investment. In practice European capital has been invested within Europe. With decolonisation and the fear of nationalisation it has proved easier to import labour than to export capital. Europe has abandoned its colonies. At the same time a kind of 'reverse colonial system' has been adopted, consisting of large-scale imports by the metropolis of docile, unskilled, cheap foreign labour. This has probably acted as a stimulus to domestic investment. At the same time however, in Germany and France at least, it has encouraged the maintenance of technological and productive structures which in the absence of cheap foreign labour would undoubtedly have developed further than they have.

A double labour market has come into being: on the one hand there is a market for nationals who receive clear privileges in terms of real and monetary wages, promotion and social services; on the other a more backward market for immigrant workers where wages are generally lower and job security slight. Table 3.13 gives an idea of existing wages differentials. In all sectors even within individual grades these differentials are very real.

Table 3.10 Sectorial Distribution of German-born and Foreign Workers in the GFR 1972 ('000)

	Foreigners (A)	German Nationals (B)	(A)(B) %
Building	43.9	153.2	22.0
Metal-working	106.2	368.7	28.8
Chemicals	66.6	299.4	18.0
Rubber	3.5	71.1	31.0
Wood	16.1	33.5	32.0
Paper	35.2	119.1	22.0
Steel	39.3	118.3	24.0
Mechanical industries	165.7	601.2	21.0
Transport equipment	136.1	345.5	28.0
Ship-building	11.2	48.4	18.0
Aircraft	2.6	19.4	12.0
Electrical apparatus	187.1	534.4	25.0
Precision instruments	25.6	85.0	23.0
Household goods	144.7	291.0	33.0
Glassware	18.3	50.7	23.0
Furniture	47.2	142.3	24.0
Musical instruments	6.5	37.0	14.0
Paints	32.9	158.7	9.0
Plastics	22.9	101.2	23.0
Footware	22.9	81.2	21.0
Textiles	105.5	252.8	29.0
Clothing	58.6	256.0	18.0
Tobacco	2.0	19.0	9.0
Food industries	75.0	262.1	28.6

Source: J. Sassoon, 'Labour and Capital Movements in the Mediterranean Area', *Lo Spettatore Internationale* (Rome), XI, 1, 1976.

Where there is only a low concentration of foreign workers, differentials are even greater than normal. The lowest average differentials are for unskilled workers, for it is here that the concentration of non-nationals is highest. The highest differential

Table 3.11 Foreign Immigrants Employed in France by Sex and Economic Sector (1 January 1976)

		Agriculture and fishing	Extractive industries	Construction and public works	Other industries	Transport	Commerce	Services	Administration	Total
1 French Muslims born in Algeria	Male	1,160	80	2,660	4,480	520	880	540	2,320	12,640
	Female	60		40	500		120	540	180	1,440
	Total	1,220	80	2,700	4,930	520	1,000	1,030	2,500	14,080
2 Algerians	Male	1,640	2,140	42,760	36,960	3,480	8,820	2,560	2,020	100,380
	Female	60	20	80	660	40	260	520	80	1,720
	Total	1,700	2,160	42,840	37,620	3,520	9,080	3,080	2,100	102,100
1 + 2 French Muslims born in Algeria and Algerians	Male	2,800	2,220	45,420	41,440	4,000	9,700	3,100	4,340	113,020
	Female	120	20	120	1,160	40	380	1,060	260	3,160
	Total	2,920	2,240	45,540	42,600	4,040	10,080	4,160	4,600	116,180
3 EEC nationals	Male	2,240	400	13,680	10,340	1,080	3,300	1,960	2,740	35,740
	Female	340		300	3,420	140	1,340	3,480	420	9,440
	Total	2,580	400	13,980	13,760	1,220	4,640	5,440	3,160	45,180
4 Others	Male	31,000	8,400	103,200	82,220	4,480	17,560	13,140	8,260	268,260
	Female	2,240	20	940	18,540	360	7,260	37,600	2,760	69,720
	Total	33,240	8,420	104,140	100,760	4,840	24,820	50,740	11,020	337,980
2 + 3 + 4 Total foreigners	Male	34,880	10,940	159,640	129,520	9,040	29,680	17,660	13,020	404,380
	Female	2,640	40	1,320	22,600	540	8,860	41,600	3,260	80,880
	Total	37,520	10,980	160,960	152,140	9,580	38,540	59,260	16,280	485,260

Source: Ministry of Interior, *Les étrangers en France* (Paris, 1976).

Table 3.12 Algerian Workers in France by Sector and Qualifications, 1970

	Labourers	Semi-skilled workers	Skilled workers	Foremen	Management and supervisory staff	Salaried workers	Total
Building and public works	83,613	41,442	19,639	111	29	999	145,833
Mechanical industries	11,646	29,226	4,622	70	13	850	46,427
Metal-working	11,185	14,800	2,057	18	12	197	28,269
Chemicals	7,827	7,668	2,108	40	7	519	18,169
Transport	3,362	1,932	844	17	14	2,333	8,502
Textiles	4,518	4,031	2,309	15	3	425	11,301
Building materials	5,911	4,051	999	7	5	152	11,125
Road construction	2,697	2,831	931	3	3	28	6,493
Agriculture	3,033	1,080	485	10	4	487	5,099
Public services	7,055	3,502	1,074	53	38	7,356	19,078
Others	13,010	14,633	2,559	106	62	13,436	43,806
Total	153,967	125,196	38,027	450	190	26,782	344,102

Source: M. Rosanvallon, 'Les aspects économiques de l'émigration algérienne', unpublished degree thesis, Université de Sciences Sociales, Grenoble, June 1974.

(more than 50 per cent) is for salaried staff. Here however there are fewer immigrants affected. The same applies to the second half of the table. The gap between foreigners and Frenchmen is lowest in the mines where immigrant labour is used *en masse.* There is only a slight gap in building, public works and mechanical industry and this is logical. Differentials are highest amongst the 'others' where the concentration of foreign workers is lowest. R. Granier and J.P. Marcian, from whom we have taken our data,[14] conclude, rather too cautiously, 'that the phenomenon of relative under-payment of foreigners exists is certain, even though we unfortunately do not have the statistics necessary to identify the causes [of this situation]'.

Table 3.13 Wage Differentials in France

I. AVERAGE MONTHLY PAY ACCORDING TO GRADE (1973, FRENCH FRANCS)

Qualification	Immigrant workers		Average pay Frenchmen + foreigners
	Average pay	Average differential	
Unskilled workers	835.64	231.78	827.4
Semi-skilled workers	1,018.66	365.20	1,014.4
Skilled workers	1,183.17	387.54	1,237.4
Salaried workers	1,090.15	757.01	1,401.6
Average	997.83	409.82	1,169.3

II. AVERAGE MONTHLY PAY BY SECTOR (1973, FRENCH FRANCS)

Sector	Immigrant workers		Frenchmen + foreigners
	Pay	Differential	
Building and public works	1,041.90	366.57	1,150.40
Mechanical industries	988.24	336.42	1,600.30
Miners	959.23	135.50	1,400.30
Other industries	1,108.98	297.02	1,111.60
Domestic service	865.30	483.79	1,466.20
Others	836.30	636.34	1,792.00
Average	985.06	422.09	1,567.04

Source: R. Granier and J.P. Marcian, 'La rémuneration des travailleurs immigrés en France', *Revue Internationale du Travail,* no. 2, February 1975, pp. 156 ff.

It is of course possible to show, as some authors have succeeded in doing,[15] that structural changes in the situation have been both recurrent and extremely deep. The presence of foreign workers has led to an increased demand for the setting up of new infrastructures; this in turn has called for new investment and has created fresh demand for labour. The OECD has even gone so far as to talk of 'self-feeding immigration'. Given the scale of previous immigration fresh immigration no longer depends on what would have been the needs of the host country's economy had this immigration not taken place. Patterns of immigration and the kinds of work immigrants find tend to perpetuate themselves. 'Emigration is a fairly complex cumulative process which can only be limited or arrested through outside intervention'.[16]

If we are to improve our understanding of this structural phenomenon several factors need to be taken into account. If one examines the gradual adaptation of economies such as those of the Netherlands or of Germany one notes how immigration has made possible 'great flexibility in the adaptation of the national economy and a better balance on local labour markets'.[17] In practice, as has been shown by Reiffers, the high degree of mobility of the foreign labour force is accentuated by the fact that foreign workers' contracts are usually for relatively short terms of employment. The presence of a foreign labour force provides both a safety valve for excess labour and an easily controlled reservoir on which to draw in times of shortage. This makes it possible to adjust production to demand in the use of immigrant workers – last in, first out – and thus to limit companies' social security bills as well as their general expenses. This has enabled Germany and other Common Market countries to 'import' a large proportion of economic growth, or to use the terrible expression of a United Nations report 'to export nearly half of their unemployment'.[18]

Recently the GFR has not only halted immigration; she has succeeded in reversing the process. Despite any incentives they might have had to remain, between September 1973 and March 1975 the number of foreign workers in Germany fell by 475,000, that is by 18 per cent. Various measures were taken: a refusal to renew work contracts, the passing of a law in the Bundestag (on 25 April 1975) forbidding the employment of foreigners without the consent of the Federal labour office. The penalty for non-compliance was set at five years' imprisonment.

The great turning-point was reached in 1975. The European

'lock-out' gathered momentum. One after another the European Common Market countries decided to restrict access to non-EEC labour.[19]

Migration has thus stabilised not only on account of the recession and the reduction in the volume of jobs available on the labour market but also as a result of a drastic change in European immigration policy. The United Nations Report cited earlier notes that 'although there does not seem to have been any concerted action, the main host countries have one after another taken firm measures to halt immigration, and this despite good demand for labour during the period'.[20]

None the less the crisis teaches us that something has changed in the fundamental structure of the European economy, something which requires further analysis. Despite the high levels of unemployment affecting European and (to an even more tragic extent) immigrant workers, there has been no reversal of basic trends. Certainly immigration has slowed down; nevertheless there has been no massive return of foreign workers to their countries of origin. For more than ten years now the employment of foreign labour has become a structural phenomenon within the Western European economy. The devaluing of jobs held by foreigners has made them unattractive to native-born workers. In France as in Germany, as many well-informed observers have noted, European workers refuse to take up posts left vacant by foreigners, and very often prefer to remain unemployed rather than take on a job formerly belonging to a Turk or to an Algerian. In the GFR 'the national labour force has shown itself to be unwilling to take on jobs formerly held by foreigners; it is thus foreigners who are being recruited'.[21]

Whatever the future development of the situation – and always supposing that the European countries do not adapt drastic policies (which in any case they would probably find economically and politically impossible) – it seems as if the presence of a foreign labour force will continue to play an essential role in the functioning of the European economies.

Although the present crisis situation could either worsen or improve in the short term, it is not unlikely that in the longer term there will be a renewed demand for immigrant labour, due to Europe's, and more particularly France and Germany's demographic position which is similar to that immediately following the Second World War. One could even state that this position has worsened and that many Western European countries are suffering from demographic exhaustion. Increased life expectancy and a falling mortality rate have been insufficient to compensate for the falling birth-rate. In many European countries the last few years have witnessed a profound change of trends in population growth. The role of natural population growth in the overall expansion of the population has become less and less important; the role of immigration has on the other hand been growing steadily. In 1973 national population growth in many European countries was very weak or even negative.

GFR	– 0.04%
Belgium	0.18%
France	0.61%
Luxembourg	0.00%
The Netherlands	0.76%

This is a general phenomenon, common to both Eastern and Western Europe. At the same time however, as we shall see, population growth in the sub-Mediterranean countries has been continuing or even accelerating. The European population is stagnant. This is bound to lead to demand for migrant labour from countries with surplus population.

A study by DATAR[22] gives an indication of the size of the problem and of the consequences for the economically active population. The study covers the period from 1970 to 1980. For a number of countries at least, its predictions have already been confirmed. If we suppose that in a decade there is only a 10 per cent increase in the economically active population (that is about 1 per cent per year) and we then subtract the natural increase of population as far as it can be calculated from available data we arrive at a balance of necessary immigration of approximately 6,000,000 persons. Assuming that the Netherlands are capable of supplying their own active population this deficit would consist of 2,200,000 persons in the GFR, 1,900,000 in Great Britain and 750,000 in France (see Table 3.14). This is obviously only speculation. None the less it gives an idea of the scale of immigration required to balance the European population deficit. As we saw in Table 3.8, between 1950 and 1970 the ratio between immigration and natural population increase amounted to 0:81 in the GFR, 0:55 in France and 1:05 in Luxembourg.

The CICRED seminar on 'population research and international migration' which was held in Buenos Aires in March 1974 did not avoid this problem. It is worthwhile quoting the seminar's well-balanced conclusion. The participants observed that nearly everywhere in the world it has been the more developed countries which have 'determined the intensity of international migration, on account both of the unavailability of sufficient local man-power resources to meet their requirements and of the power to control the scale and pattern of migration'.[23] None the less there has been a change of attitude. Growth rates in the host countries are being stabilised. In certain countries there is a zero growth rate. If these trends should become established they are bound, in the medium term, to produce a substantial reduction in international migration.

Table 3.14 Manpower Requirements: Western Europe, 1970-80

Countries	Economically active population	Required increase in economically active population	Natural increase in economically active population	Net migration required
GFR	27,000,000	2,700,000	508,000	2,200,000
Austria	3,200,000	320,000	136,000	180,000
Belgium	3,700,000	370,000	186,000	200,000
Denmark	2,300,000	230,000	28,000	200,000
France	20,000,000	2,200,000	1,454,000	750,000
The Netherlands	4,500,000	450,000	469,000	–
United Kingdom	26,000,000	2,600,000	723,000	1,900,000
Sweden	3,900,000	390,000	19,000	420,000
Switzerland	2,700,000	270,000	127,000	150,000
Total		9,530,000		6,000,000

Source: La Documentation Française, *Regard prospectif sur le bassin méditerranéen* (1973).

The report added that on the other hand 'should there be negative population growth rates for a considerable period of time, the developed countries would be obliged to accept immigration in order to avoid a deterioration in their economies'.[24]

As far as the second hypothesis is concerned it is legitimate to doubt whether the consequences of a zero growth rate would be acceptable. If not, migration would in the future continue. 'In either case, the developed countries need to concern themselves with immigration, as some of them have already done, in a long-term perspective.'[25]

Everything thus leads us to hold to our view that despite the difficulties the Western economies are going through and despite real tensions on European labour markets, the presence of migrant workers in Western societies is now established and will continue to be so for a long time. No longer is immigration a short-term economic development; rather it is structurally tied to the development of the industrialised countries. J. Pierre Dumont summarised the situation very well when he wrote 'it is enough to know that in the nine Community member-states there are more than 11 million immigrants, of whom 6 million, that is a population equivalent to that of Belgium or the Netherlands, are economically active. We can thus say that immigrants constitute the tenth Community partner.'

A long time has passed since immigration acted simply as a shock-absorber or an emergency brake to be used in case of need. In 1973 the industrialised countries discovered their extreme dependence on the energy-producing countries. They have still to discover how they are equally dependent on those countries which produce their man-power.

Should this surprise us? A world market is being created. Why should international flows of labour escape this rule? Surely this is simply one aspect of the international division of labour. Flows of labour are unfortunately in no way different from flows of capital, technology, raw materials and manufactured products and are similarly determined by the present structure of the world economy.

As it expands over the whole of the planet the industrial economy continually creates fresh international migration. Producing on an international scale the European economy cannot see its own finite human resources as a constraint. In short the European economies have been able to maintain their expansion, and will continue to be able to maintain their expansion and their present system of production, exclusively on account of the massive contribution of the foreign labour force.

The problem is to know whether the countries which provide the emigrant labour force will be willing to meet the European countries' requirements, that is, to discover how the emigration problem is seen from their point of view. The problem becomes even more important if one considers that according to certain calculations traditional flows of Arab labour will tend to increase and new flows to come into being. The DATAR study[26] quoted above gives an estimate of surplus labour availability in the Mediterranean countries, shown in Table 3.15.

The report concludes:

There is no risk that the industrialised countries will suffer from a labour shortage. This does not prove that this 'necessary' migration will in fact take place. In practice, it is very likely that companies in the developed countries will invest more and more in the peripheral countries, with an equivalent reduction in investment and thus in requirements for foreign labour, in the industrialised countries.

It nonetheless seems legitimate to say that population supply will be in excess of demand, whatever the scale of investment in the non-industrialised countries and that [Europe will absorb] at least five million foreign workers from the Mediterranean countries.[27]

Table 3.15 Available Surplus Manpower, 1970-1980

	No. of persons	%
Algeria, Morocco, Tunisia	3,000,000	24.0
Egypt, Syria, Libya	4,000,000	32.0
Spain	1,000,000	8.0
Turkey	3,500,000	28.0
Yugoslavia	1,000,000	8.0
Total	12,500,000	100.0

Source: La Documentation Française, ***Regard prospectif sur le bassin Méditerranéen.***

The internal requirements of the Common Market countries correspond to those of the Arab countries, the only countries which interest us in this study.

Certainly it is extremely difficult to acquire even an approximate idea of the characteristics of the Arab labour market. Even the simplest data are lacking. Nevertheless, despite the risk of exposing ourselves to criticism, we will attempt to formulate a number of elementary hypotheses.

First, the population growth common to nearly all the Arab countries increases the potential of their respective labour forces. If the present situation is projected into the future it is clear that a far from negligible supply of labour will be available in the coming decades.

Table 3.16 gives us a general picture of the region, although it includes countries outside the Arab world such as Cyprus, Israel and Turkey. The merit of the figures is their statistical homogeneity and thus their comparability. Given that the data come from the ILO it may be assumed they are reliable. Unfortunately however the use of a

Table 3.16 Employment Projections 1980, 1990

I. NORTHERN AFRICA[a]

		1960	1970	1973	1980	1990	Rates of growth 1960–70	1970–73	1973–80	1980–90
Population ('000)		65,392	86,606	95,200	119,385	163,230	2.9	3.2	3.3	3.2
Active population ('000)		18,882	23,600	25,560	30,965	41,850	2.3	2.6	2.7	3.0
Employment ('000)		17,527	20,880	23,580	28,600	38,700	1.8	3.1	2.8	3.1
Unemployment ('000)		1,355	1,820	1,980	2,365	3,150				
Rate of unemployment %		7.2	7.7	7.7	7.6	7.6				
% of total employment:[b]	S1	63.2	56.6	54.0	44.0	30.0				
	S2	10.1	12.7	14.0	18.0	24.0				
	S3	13.7	14.9	15.0	18.0	21.0				
	S4	13.0	15.8	17.0	20.0	25.0				
GDP ($ US millions 1960 prices)		9,100	15,500	19,100	32,700	70,600	5.5	7.0	8.0	8.0
GDP pro capita ($ US 1960 prices)		140	180	200	275	430	2.6	3.8	4.6	4.0

II. THE MIDDLE EAST[c]

		1960	1970	1973	1980	1990	Rates of growth 1960–70	1970–73	1973–80	1980–90
Population ('000)		58,370	77,109	84,260	104,301	140,283	2.8	3.0	3.1	3.1
Active population ('000)		22,200	27,376	29,310	34,962	45,938	2.1	2.3	2.5	2.8
Employment ('000)		20,850	25,996	28,080	33,600	44,400	2.2	2.6	2.7	2.9
Unemployment ('000)		1,350	1,380	1,230	1,362	1,538				
Rate of unemployment %		6.1	5.0	4.2	3.9	3.3				
% of total employment:[b]	S1	53.0	40.0	36.0	29.0	20.0				
	S2	13.8	18.5	20.0	23.0	26.0				
	S3	16.9	19.8	21.0	23.0	26.0				
	S4	16.3	21.7	23.0	25.0	28.0				
GDP ($ US millions 1960 prices)		13,900	27,300	33,700	57,800	122,500	7.0	7.3	8.0	7.8
GDP pro capita ($ US 1960 prices)		240	355	400	555	875	4.1	4.2	4.8	4.6

a. Algeria, Egypt, Libya, Morocco, Sudan, Tunisia.
b. S1 – Agriculture; S2 – Manufacturing industry; S3 – Services, finance and banking; S4 – Building, commerce and others.
c. Saudi Arabia, Cyprus, United Arab Emirates, Iraq, Jordan, Israel, Kuwait, Qatar, Turkey, The Arab Republic of Yemen, The Democratic Republic of Yemen, Syria.
Source: Yves Sabolo, 'Emploi et chômage, 1960–1990', *Revue Internationale du Travail,* 6 December 1975.

regional average hides the dissimilarities which exist between such different countries as Kuwait and Jordan, Tunisia and Libya. None the less it seems clear that the annual rate of population growth in the whole region will remain at a high level: more than 3 per cent. This will lead to an increase in the economically active population. Thus even a rapid rate of growth in GDP (7-8 per cent) will lead to a per capita increase of only 4-5 per cent. An analysis of the economically active population shows unemployment of 4.0 million in 1980 and 4.6 million in 1990. Between 1973 and 1990 the rate of unemployment in the Middle East should fall from 4.2 per cent to 3.3 per cent. In the Maghreb, on the other hand, unemployment will probably remain stationary at around 7.6 per cent; conditions will in other words continue to be very favourable for emigration.

Table 3.17 Arab Population Growth 1970-75

Country	Population ('000) 1970	1975	Annual growth rate (%)	Population density x km
Algeria	14,330	16,792	3.22	6
Bahrain	215	215	3.14	360
Egypt	33,329	37,543	2.41	35
Gaza	501	594	3.47	–
Iraq	9,356	11,067	3.42	23
Jordan	2,280	2,688	3.35	25
Kuwait	760	1,085	7.38	51
Lebanon	2,469	2,869	3.05	285
Libya	1,938	2,255	3.07	1
Morocco	15,126	17,504	2.96	35
Oman	657	766	3.12	3
Qatar	79	92	3.09	4
Saudi Arabia	7,740	8,966	2.98	4
Sudan	15,695	18,268	3.08	7
Syria	6,247	7,259	3.05	36
Tunisia	5,137	5,747	2.27	33
The United Arab Emirates	190	222	3.16	2
The Arab Republic of Yemen	5,767	6,668	2.94	31
The Democratic Republic of Yemen	1,436	1,667	3.03	5
Total	123,252	142,267	3.3	–

Source: UN, *Population Projections,* medium variant, ESA/P/WP56, October 1975.

Table 3.17 shows that between 1970 and 1975 the total Arab population increased from 123 million to 142 million. This is equivalent to 4 million more Arabs each year. Kuwait's rapid rate of population growth is largely due to inter-Arab migration. It should thus be excluded from our calculations. Between 1975 and 1985 the Arab economically active population will increase by more than 13 million (Table 3.18). The problem is to know whether this additional supply of labour will find employment in the Arab countries.

An analysis of the sectorial distribution of the economically active population makes this appear a somewhat doubtful proposition. The importance of the primary sector is clear (Table 3.19). It is only in certain of the oil-producing countries (Kuwait, Bahrain and to a lesser extent Libya) that less than half of the economically active Arab population are employed in agriculture. The 'secondary sector', that is manufacturing industry, plays only a very limited role (14.1 per cent of employment in Algeria, 19.3 per cent in Tunisia). As in many developing countries the tertiary sector plays a disproportionately important role in all the Arab countries with the exception of the oil-producing states.

It seems likely that the modernisation of the Arab economies and the rural exodus will lead to a considerable proportion of workers currently engaged in the primary sector becoming available for work in the secondary and tertiary sectors. It is clear that if there is insufficient investment in these sectors these workers will be unable to find jobs. Our picture of the overall situation must thus take into account not only overall growth in the economically active population but also transfers from one sector to another.

At the same time it should be borne in mind that not all Arab countries are equally prosperous. In 1974 Kuwait's GNP per capita was 55 times that of North Yemen (Table 3.20). Between 1965 and 1974 the GNP of the UAE expanded at a rate of 10.4 per cent per annum. Oman achieved a growth rate of 19.2 per cent. During the same period however there was a less significant growth in the Lebanon, Algeria, Syria, Morocco, Sudan and Egypt. In the Democratic Republic of Yemen economic activity fell by 4.3 per cent and in Jordan by 2.5 per cent. Certainly present economic conditions are extremely favourable to GNP growth. It is always essential however to consider the way in which this growth is distributed between sectors and countries. It is this, as we shall see, which explains inter-Arab migration.

Quite apart from the population inbalances which emigration helps

Table 3.18 Arab Economically Active Populations 1970-85

Country	Labour force ('000)				Annual growth rate		
	1970	1975	1980	1985	1970–75	1975–80	1980–85
Algeria	3,369	3,894	4,545	5,362	2.94	3.14	3.36
Egypt	9,174	10,357	11,741	13,426	2.46	2.54	2.72
Iraq	2,395	2,770	3,224	3,784	2.95	3.08	3.25
Jordan	564	641	737	857	2.59	2.83	3.06
Kuwait	282	431	637	911	8.85	8.13	7.42
Lebanon and Gaza	864	986	1,112	1,264	2.68	2.43	2.60
Libya	488	550	625	721	2.42	2.59	2.90
Morocco	4,161	4,782	5,543	6,526	2.32	3.00	3.29
Oman, Bahrain, Qatar and United Arab Emirates	290	331	381	441	2.68	2.85	2.97
Saudi Arabia	2,109	2,355	2,649	3,025	2.23	2.38	2.69
Sudan	5,065	5,830	6,760	7,938	2.85	3.00	3.26
Syria	1,574	1,817	2,109	2,466	2.91	3.03	3.18
Tunisia	1,273	1,457	1,685	1,964	2.74	2.95	3.11
The Arab Republic of Yemen	1,689	1,911	2,178	2,512	2.50	2.65	2.89
The Democratic Republic of Yemen	347	388	436	498	2.26	2.36	2.69
Total	33,644	38,500	44,362	51,695			

Source: ILO, *Labour Force Projections,* Parts I and II, Asia and Africa, Geneva, 1975.

to attenuate, it represents in practice an export of services. Emigrants' remittances, 'the emigrants' billions', constitute in practice one of the most important sectors in the economies of labour-exporting countries. In Tunisia, for instance, foreign currency remittances are a far from negligible item in the national balance of payments. Between 1961 and 1974 total remittances increased from 598,000 to 44,000,000 dinars (1 dinar = $2.32), as shown in Table 3.21. In the other Maghreb countries the importance of remittances is even clearer. Table 3.22 shows the scale of the phenomenon.

Table 3.19 Distribution of the Economically Active Arab Population

Country	Year	Primary	Sector Secondary [% of total employment]	Tertiary
Algeria	1966	56.7	14.1	29.2
Egypt	1966	53.3	16.2	30.5
Libya	1964	37.1	19.0	43.9
Morocco	1971	53.1	17.2	29.7
Tunisia	1966	42.6	19.3	38.1
Bahrain	1971	6.7	34.5	58.8
Kuwait	1970	1.7	34.2	64.1
Lebanon	1970	18.9	25.3	55.8
Syria	1971	58.2	16.9	24.9

Source: Calculated from ILO statistics by Rasevic, ***Population, Employment and Development in the Arab Countries,*** Seminar on manpower and employment planning in Arab countries, Beirut, 13-14 May 1975 (doc. E/EC WA/ILO/WG/4/2).

In 1973 emigration provided nearly a quarter of Moroccan and one-fifth of Algerian external revenue. The equivalent figure for Tunisia, a relative newcomer on the European labour market, was only 11.6 per cent.

In short, it is domestic conditions in the countries of origin which explain to a large extent the latter's emigration policy: rapid growth of the population at large and of the economically active population in particular, chronic unemployment and concealed under-employment, low agricultural productivity, fluctuating rates of economic growth. Given the impossibility of finding employment for the available labour force it becomes necessary to export it, the result being a significant improvement in the balance of payments.

Table 3.20 Growth of Population and of GNP in Arab Population

	GNP per capita at market prices ($)			Population ('000)	GNP at market prices ($ million)	Growth rates (%)	
	1974	1971	1970	1974		Population 1965–74	GNP per capita 1965–74
Kuwait	10,030	3,860	3,760	930	9,330	7.8	– 2.3
UAE	11,060	3,150	2,390	548	6,060	17.1	10.4
Qatar	7,240	2,370	1,730	190	1,380	8.5	8.1
Libya	4,440	1,450	1,770	2,352	10,430	4.2	6.5
Lebanon	1,070	660	590	3,065	3,290	2.8	3.7
Bahrain	2,350	640	550	245	580	3.1	21.2
Saudi Arabia	2,830	540	440	8,008	22,670	1.8	9.2
Oman	1,660	450	350	750	1,250	3.1	19.2
Algeria	730	360	300	15,215	11,100	3.3	4.5
Tunisia	650	320	250	5,460	3,560	2.3	5.4
Iraq	1,110	370	320	10,770	12,000	3.3	4.8
Syria	560	290	290	7,177	3,990	3.3	4.2
Jordan	430	260	250	2,620	1,120	3.4	– 2.5
Morocco	430	260	230	16,291	7,070	2.4	2.8
Egypt	280	220	210	36,350	10,220	2.4	1.0
Yemen-PDR	220	120	120	1,632	360	2.9	– 4.3
Sudan	230	120	120	15,227	3,460	2.2	4.3
Yemen-AR	180	90	80	6,379	1,160	2.4	4.2

Source: IBRD, *World Atlas.*

Table 3.21 Emigrants' Foreign Currency Remittances (Tunisian Dinars)

1961	598,000
1962	465,000
1963	2,400,000
1964	2,760,000
1965	3,025,000
1966	4,020,000
1967	5,890,000
1968	7,725,000
1969	13,415,000
1970	15,235,000
1971	22,735,000
1972	29,565,000
1973	33,000,000
1974	44,000,000

Source: Tunisia's Central Bank.

Table 3.22 Financial Transfers by Migrant Workers from France to the Maghreb, 1973

	Algeria	Morocco	Tunisia
Total transfers (million French Francs)	1,687	1,036	446
Transfers per immigrant	3,660 FF	4,000 FF	2,970 FF
Transfers per resident in the country of origin	116 FF	64.50 FF	83 FF
Transfers as a % of total external revenue	20 %	24.7 %	11.6 %

Source: OECD, Centre de dévelopement, *Migrations et transfers de Technologie. Etude de cas* (Paris, 1975).

The Tunisian example is a typical one. Even since 1967, when an office was set up to deal with Tunisian workers abroad, employment and vocational training ('L'Office des Travailleurs Tunisiens a l'étranger, de l'emploi et de la Formation Professionnelle') the Tunisian government has adopted a deliberate concerted policy in favour of emigration. In the Fourth Plan (for the period 1973-6) it was stated explicitly that it is unlikely that during this period a balance could be achieved between demand for labour and supply.

> If the aim is to guarantee a job, even if it is abroad, to anyone who seeks one, emigration will continue to be necessary. The estimated level of emigration during the four year period will thus amount to about 60,000 men. In the present economic situation it seems possible that this or even a higher level will be reached [Plan – duplicated – p. 128].

At this time it was thought that 60 per cent of new requests for work would be satisfied through emigration and 40 per cent through the creation of new jobs within Tunisia. In practice, due to the European recession, difficulties with Tunisia's Libyan neighbours, who have expelled nearly 14,000 Tunisian workers more or less permanently settled in Libya, and the growth rate of the Tunisian economy the proportions have been reversed. None the less, emigration's two main objectives, the reduction of unemployment pressure and the generation of foreign currency income, have to a large extent been achieved.

Despite the persistent tension between France and Algeria and the growth of racial prejudice in France which in 1973 led Algeria to cut off the supply of immigrants, the Algerian and Moroccan situations do not differ fundamentally from the situation in Tunisia.

The Maghreb countries are directly dependent on the European and more especially on the French economies. The privileged relations, the traditional trade flows, the proximity of the two regions and the existence of reliable, rapid means of transport have played a fundamental role. An organic relationship has been established between the European and the Maghreb labour markets – which have proved, at least to some extent, to be complementary. This phenomenon has brought clear advantages to both partners. The host countries have managed to satisfy their demand for labour. The countries of origin have managed to diminish the tension due to the rapid growth of requests for work. At the same time they have received significant sums of foreign currency. What really needs to be emphasised however is how here too migration is no longer a short-term economic trend but rather a structural phenomenon rooted in the financial, economic, social and technological structures of the two regions. We are thus forced to the conclusion that it will not only survive the present crisis of the European economy but will even expand, once this crisis is over.

None the less not all Maghreb emigration goes to Europe. The Maghreb is part of the Arab world. The call of the East is real. Although it has to date assumed only secondary importance it may be expected to gain in importance with the passage of time. An overall analysis of the Euro-Arab region requires an examination of inter-Arab migration.

Arab workers migrate to the other Arab countries for more or less the same reasons as they emigrate to Europe. Paradoxically inter-Arab migration has ancient origins and yet is very recent. Until the colonial period the cultural unity of the Arab world favoured sometimes massive transfers of entire population groups. Colonisation and the setting up of Arab states finally led to the creation of politically and legally well-defined borders in place of the rather vague demarcation lines which decided the territories of the classical Arab kingdoms and dynasties. Since the Second World War however there has been a change in the way in which the economic space has been structured.

Just as the creation of the state of Israel has constituted the major political and territorial development in the region, the discovery of oil has been the most important economic development in the last quarter century of Arab history, a kind of birth certificate for the modern Arab world. What was Kuwait 20 years ago, or Libya? Today the best way of classifying the Arab countries is by their oil wealth. There exist countries whose economy and finances are founded exclusively on oil: Kuwait, the United Arab Emirates, Saudi Arabia, Libya. There are other countries such as Egypt, Jordan, Tunisia and Morocco with little or no oil wealth but with other resources, notably in agriculture. There are countries which are major oil producers but which have a more balanced economy with important agricultural resources, such as Iraq and Algeria. Finally there are countries such as the Yemen which seem to be completely lacking in resources.

It is perfectly understandable that migratory flows should have been established between the oil-producing countries and those countries lacking in oil. This is even more the case if one considers that despite a uniformly high rate of population growth, economic growth rates differ enormously nearly everywhere in the Arab world. It is possible to identify two extreme situations: countries with a major labour surplus and countries with a serious deficit. Table 3.20 gives an idea of trends in population and economic growth. We have already pointed out the exceptional position of countries such as UAE, Kuwait and Qatar whose populations are expanding at the remarkable rate of 17.1, 7.8 and 8.5 per cent per year respectively. This growth is however due to immigration rather than to the natural expansion of the population.

The increase in wealth in the oil-producing countries has led to a general improvement in the living standards of the Arab population. Despite inflation, wages have been very high and in certain sectors have approached European levels. Any international comparison is something of a risk. For the moment it is impossible to make any objective study. The figures for the Arab countries supplied in the 1975 'Annuaire des statistiques du travail' issued by the ILO are fragmentary and of very little use. A comparative study of Tunisians employed in Tunisia and Libya has however given very interesting results.[28]

Table 3.23 Wage Disparities in Libya and Tunisia (June-July 1973) in Tunisian Dinars

Sector		Average monthly wage of Tunisian workers employed in Tunisia	Average monthly wage of Tunisian workers employed in Libya
Industrial workers	Private sector	13.000	42.000
	State sector	18.000	105.000
Animal rearing		22.000	82.000
Plumbing		24.000	111.000
Building		42.000	120.000
Decorator		33.000	100.000

Source: Unpublished study by M. Mtar.

Table 3.23 shows how workers with similar levels of skill employed in the same sector may earn nominal incomes from three to five times higher in Libya than in Tunisia. Skilled workers in craft industries seem to be the most favoured. Emigration thus leads to genuine social promotion. Of course it is necessary to take account of prices which are higher in the host country than in the country of origin. Even so the net result continues to favour the migrant worker.

Although generalisation is not always possible, even higher salary differentials are to be found between Libya and Egypt or Yemen and Saudi Arabia. The differences between Syria, Kuwait and Saudi Arabia are rather smaller. Wage differentials between the Arab countries largely explain the fascination of emigration.

Two fundamental factors – the existence of a surplus population and the oil boom – have led to the emergence on the Arab labour market of host countries, that is nearly all the major oil producers plus the Lebanon, and labour suppliers: the others and again the Lebanon.

Table 3.24, calculated by Abdelmajid Farrag from Cairo University, gives the first more or less complete picture of inter-Arab migration.[29] This table leads us to the following conclusion. Around the years 1972-3 there were at least 900,000 foreign workers in the Arab world, of whom 650,000[30] originated in other Arab countries. In other words roughly 75 per cent of foreign workers in the Arab world were Arabs whereas only 25 per cent were non-Arabs: Pakistanis, Indians, Turks or European technical personnel. There can be no doubting the vitality of the Arab labour market. What is more, we have already seen how by 1974 nearly 720,000 workers from the Maghreb had settled in France. There was thus a certain overall balance between the number of Arab migrants to Europe and the number moving within the Arab world. None the less, if one excludes the relatively large Tunisian colony in Libya, there are only two main flows of Arab migration: Maghreb workers who settle in France and inter-Arab migration in the Middle East. The EEC countries drain the supply of Maghreb workers seeking to emigrate, workers who are often unaware of the job opportunities existing within the Arab world. These could act as a substitute for European emigration should the EEC 'lock-out' continue and local labour markets prove to be lacking in the capacity to satisfy the demand for work. For this to occur, however, political and legal conditions would have to be favourable, and this is not always the case.

Nearly half of inter-Arab migration is to Saudi Arabia which exerts its fascination over the whole region and especially over the Yemen. More than half of all Yemeni workers work in Saudi Arabia, 85 per cent of all Yemeni emigration is in this direction. The second most important countries are the Gulf States: Kuwait, Qatar, Bahrain and the UAE which have absorbed nearly 200,000 immigrants, that is more than 30 per cent of inter-Arab migration. The third most important pole of attraction is Libya which absorbs 16.5 per cent of the total flow.

The countries which provide the largest number of emigrants are Egypt, Syria and Palestine, each of which supply between 90,000 and 100,000 workers to neighbouring countries. Each in other words supplies about 14 per cent of total inter-Arab migration.

If we are to have a complete picture it is necessary to take into account the existence of Arab workers in the territories occupied by

Table 3.24 Inter-Arab Migration

	Year	Yemen	Egypt	Syria	Palestine	Lebanon	Jordan	Oman	Other Arab countries	Total Arab countries	Other countries	Uncertain	Total
Saudi Arabia	1970	200,000 to 250,000	n.a.	40,000	50,000	30,000	?	?	?	(345,000)	?	65,000	(410,000)
Kuwait	1970	6,898	17,714	12,659		8,419	41,299	10,299	24,467	121,755	53,925	—	175,680
Libya	1973	—	60,752	6,162	4,324	8,324	4,324	—	24,215	108,101	20,300	—	128,401
Lebanon	1970	?	4,500	33,800	8,100	—	?	?	?	46,400	?	21,600	68,000
UAE	1968	?	11,100	—	6,640	?	6,640	6,640	4,430	35,450	8,819	?	44,269
Qatar	1970	?	?	?	?	?	?	?	?	(24,000)	16,090	?	(40,090)
Bahrain	1971	2,000	?	?	2,000	?	2,000	5,600	4,000	15,600	6,000	751	22,351
Oman	1973	?	?	?	?	?	?	?	?	(2,000)	3,000	?	(5,000)
Total		(233,898)	94,066	92,621	71,064	46,743	54,263	22,539	57,112	(698,306)	108,134	87,351	(893,791)

Source: M.A.M. Farrag, ***Migration between Arab Countries,*** seminar on manpower and employment planning in Arab countries, Beirut, 13-14 May 1975, and the Libyan Ministry of Interior. Precise data for Iraq are unavailable.

Israel. Following the 1967 war, migration was organised by the Israeli authorities with the setting up of Israeli employment agencies in the occupied territories, where there existed a considerable surplus labour force. The number of immigrant Arab workers employed in Israel rose from 10,000 in 1969 to 70,000 in 1974. This figure represented 21.5 per cent of the total labour force in the occupied territories. In practice the proportion of the Arab labour force working for Israel is much higher: 37 per cent if one takes account of workers recruited unofficially and 50 per cent if one includes the part of the labour force employed 'in situ' to meet the demands of the Israeli market.[31]

The occupying power has used its power in the occupied territories in such a way that 20 per cent of the Arab labour force is employed in agricultural work and 50 per cent in the building industry.

For the various Arab host countries immigration is hardly less essential than for the Common Market countries, even though there are far fewer problems of assimilation.

Table 3.25 shows the importance of migrant workers in the functioning of the economies of the oil-producing countries. Nationals represent a maximum of 78 per cent of the economically active population (in Libya). The equivalent figures for Bahrain and Saudi Arabia are 62.9 per cent and 50 per cent respectively. In the UAE nationals make up 43 per cent of the work force; in Abu Dhabi and Qatar only 17 per cent. In 1968 Abu Dhabi had a population of 46,000 of whom 26,000, that is 56.5 per cent, were immigrants. Today two-thirds of the population are immigrants. For many Arabs the Gulf States represent a kind of 'Far East' complete with pioneers and adventure.

It is interesting to examine the sectors in which these non-nationals are employed. In the desert countries agriculture is relatively unimportant; fishing rather more so. In Kuwait, Saudi Arabia and Qatar this sector has been almost entirely abandoned to non-nationals. In Libya the opposite has happened. As in Europe, building work has been left to foreigners who make up 60 per cent of the sectorial labour force in Kuwait, 64.6 per cent in Libya, 48 per cent in Saudi Arabia, 45.8 per cent in Bahrain, 96 per cent in Abu Dhabi and 82 per cent in Qatar. The extractive sector, although it gives rise to a high level of investment and generates a large turnover, absorbs little labour. The labour force is for the most part highly skilled and, given the level of automation in the oil industry, is composed almost exclusively of technicians. This sector has been largely abandoned to foreigners: Europeans, Palestinians and Egyptians. Manufacturing industry, to the

Table 3.25 Distribution of Foreigners and Nationals by Economic Activity (% of total economically active population)

	Agriculture and fishing	Extractive industries	Manufacturing industry	Building	Electricity and gas	Commerce	Transport	Service and others	Total
Kuwait									
Nationals	19.7	23.3	19.0	6.5	29.4	22.1	19.4	35.6	25.4
Arab non-nationals	52.2	57.1	57.1	53.7	59.3	54.4	49.3	47.4	51.7
Foreigners	28.1	19.6	23.9	39.8	11.3	23.5	31.3	17.0	22.9
Libya									
Nationals	89.5	67.9	64.1	35.4	84.3	90.3	95.6	80.0	78.0
Foreigners	10.5	32.1	35.9	64.6	15.7	9.7	4.4	20.0	22.0
Saudi Arabia									
Nationals	4	50	55	52	80	59	49	39	50
Foreigners	96	50	55	48	20	41	51	61	50
Bahrain									
Nationals	76.0	73.7	32.9	54.2	86.8	63.0	65.4	60.6	62.9
Foreigners	24.0	26.3	67.1	45.8	13.2	37.0	34.6	39.4	37.1
Abu Dhabi									
Nationals	63	19.5		4	–	9	28	16.2	17
Foreigners	37	80.5		96	–	91	72	83.8	83
UAE									
Nationals	93	34		18	–	43	47	36.2	43
Foreigners	7	66		82	–	57	53	63.8	57
Qatar									
Nationals	5	–	13	–	–	19	34	14	17
Foreigners	95	–	87	–	–	81	66	86	83

extent that it exists, has similarly been abandoned to foreigners who make up 81 per cent of the sectorial labour force in Kuwait, 55 per cent in Saudi Arabia, 67.1 per cent in Bahrain. In Libya 35.9 per cent of industrial workers are of foreign origin, that is the highest concentration in any sector with the exception of the building industry.

To an even greater extent than in Europe, foreigners in the oil-producing states play an essential role in the functioning of the economy. What is more, the importance of this foreign labour force is growing. In Libya the number of foreign workers has increased from 90,400 in December 1972 to 140,200 in 1973 and 193,700 in 1974, i.e. from an index of 100 in 1972 to 155 in 1973 and 214 in 1974. During the same period the number of Arab non-nationals increased from 73,400 (100) to 119,400 (152) to 165,800 (226). The number of non-Arab foreigners rose from 17,000 (100) to 20,800 (122) to 27,900 (225) (see Table 3.26).

Table 3.26 Distribution by Nationality of Foreign Workers in Libya

Country of origin	1972	December 1973	1974
Egypt	49.3	60.4	62.3
Tunisia	20.2	18.3	18.5
Jordan	5.0	3.9	3.3
Lebanon	10.4	5.3	4.1
Palestine	6.0	4.0	3.4
Syria	5.6	5.7	6.3
Other Arab countries	3.5	2.4	2.1
Total Arabs (%)	100.0	100.0	100.0
Total Arabs	73.4	119.4	165.8
Non-Arabs	17.0	20.8	27.9
Total ('000)	90.4	140.2	193.7

Source: Farrag, ***Migration between Arab Countries.***

The analysis of the Libyan economically active population shows the essential role of foreign labour in Libyan development. In ten years the Libyan economically active population expanded at an average rate of 4.4 per cent per annum. This rate of expansion was higher than the overall rate of population growth. At the same time however it was much lower than the annual rate of economic growth (8.1 per cent).

An even more acute situation of this kind is to be found in the Gulf countries which constitute genuine 'new countries'.

Table 3.27 The Libyan Economically Active Population

	1964	1972	1975
Male	367,834	464,000	521,000
Female	19,365	31,000	40,000
Total	387,199	495,000	561,000
	(100)	(127)	(144)

Source: Farrag, *Migration between Arab Countries.*

We have already noted the importance of Yemeni immigration to Saudi Arabia. Table 3.24 shows that 44.5 per cent of Arabs working in Kuwait are either Palestinians, Jordanians or Syrians. Table 3.28 provides an estimate of the distribution by countries of origin of migrant workers resident in Libya in 1975. From the data it may be calculated that in 1975 64.5 per cent of foreigners working in Libya were of Egyptian origin, whereas 16 per cent came from Tunisia. This signifies that her two neighbours provided Libya with more than four-fifths of her immigrant labour force.

Table 3.28 Foreign Workers in Libya by Countries of Origin, 1975

Tunisia	30,101
Algeria	505
Morocco	1,315
Mauritania	75
Egypt	122,316
Syria	9,552
Jordan	8,236
Lebanon	7,605
Palestine	7,322
Sudan	1,995
Iraq	238
Yemen	217
Saudi Arabia	54
Total	189,531

Source: Farrag, *Migration between Arab Countries.*

The attraction exerted by Arab countries on candidates for emigration is a function not only of the policies adopted by the governments of the future host countries but also of those adopted by the countries where the migrants originate. It would however be wrong to under-estimate the role of other factors such as distance and regional political tensions.

It must be recognised that difficulties exist and limit the potential for inter-Arab migration. Certainly this migration is to some extent more natural than emigration to Europe. Linguistic and religious similarities and similarities in customs are of great importance. Even so the volume of migration is much lower than it could be; much lower, in fact, than the level to be expected in the coming years with the rapid economic development of the oil-producing states. For the moment these states have been forced to rely on Pakistani, Indian, Cypriot, Turkish and Greek workers.

Political tension and the brutal reactions to which this leads can easily turn foreign workers into so many hostages. This was seen in 1976 with the massive expulsion of Egyptian and Tunisian workers settled in Libya and of Moroccan workers in Algeria. In these conditions is it really surprising that the plan to revitalise the Euphrates Valley through the resettlement of 500,000 Egyptian *Fallahs* is making little progress? To date only a hundred heads of families and their families (396 persons) have agreed to take part in the scheme.[32]

For several years now the Arab Labour Organisation has been paying close attention to Arab immigration policy, the aim being to rationalise the Arab labour market on a sound regional basis. Work in this direction has however been slow. The difficulties which have been met with are objective. Whether or not these difficulties will be removed depends on developments in the Arab world in the coming years.

As far as factors encouraging migration are concerned, official action by Arab governments and the Arab League has been less important than the fascination exerted by the general improvement in living standards in the rich Arab countries. It is however very difficult to measure a phenomenon which for many Arab migrants is both a dream and a reality.

We have attempted to use the United Nations Statistical Yearbook to provide a number of important indices of social development (Table 3.29). The data for the oil-producing countries are not always the most satisfactory. Rather the contrary: as young countries they are often sadly lacking in infrastructures. The role of immigrants will

Table 3.29 Selected Social Indicators

Country	Asphalted roads ('000 miles) 1970–1	Average life expectancy 1972	% of dwellings with running water[a] 1973	Literacy rate 1971	Newspapers sold per 1,000 inhabitants 1971	Telephone lines per 1,000 inhabitants 1972	Population per hospital bed 1972	Radios per 1,000 inhabitants 1972	Television sets per 1,000 inhabitants 1972
Morocco	84	51	64.8	14	16	11	670	95	14
Algeria	38	51	22.7	20	20	13	356	47	10
Tunisia	113	52	63.9	30	16	17	408	74	15
Libya	12	52	–	25	–	20	256	46	1.2
Egypt	33	53	39.5	26	22	11	461	143	17
Sudan	1	48	14.8	10	–	3	1,044	80	4
Iraq	41	52	20.8	14	–	12	525	350	52
Kuwait	13	64	–	53	48	88	207	132	137
Qatar	–	–	–	–	–	131	130	–	–
UAE	–	52	30.9	21	–	71	–	–	–
Syria	13	53	41.9	31	–	–	1,087	374	22
Saudi Arabia	9	42	–	15	7	10	1,140	11	2.3
Jordan	99	–	–	–	15	–	1,287	203	28

a. Urban dwellings only.
Source: UN, *Statistical Yearbook*, 1973.

be to make the creation of these infrastructures a possibility. Even so the means employed seem inadequate for the tasks to be accomplished.

We discover that the country with the longest network of surfaced roads is Tunisia, with three times as many miles as Egypt or Algeria and ten times as many as Libya. Saudi Arabia, on the other hand, with 9,000 miles has ten times less asphalted roads than neighbouring Jordan.

The oil-producing countries suffer from an inadequate supply of running water. The literacy rate varies from 53 per cent in Kuwait to 15 per cent in Saudi Arabia. The highest number of newspapers per 1,000 inhabitants is to be found in Kuwait (48); the lowest in Saudi Arabia. In Kuwait there are 131 telephone lines for every 1,000 inhabitants, in Tunisia 17, in Algeria 13 and in Saudi Arabia only 10. It is Saudi Arabia on the other hand which has the best hospital service (1,140 inhabitants per hospital bed). There are similar inequalities in the distribution of the press, radio and TV.

This is not difficult to understand. We are dealing here with societies undergoing a process of rapid change and internal reorganisation. This is not itself of great interest to our study. The migrants' role is not just to participate in a process which is already underway but to help set the process in motion and to give it new drive. The motivation, the social position and the psychological attitude of the inter-Arab migrant differs significantly from that of the emigrant to Europe. We have seen this on several occasions. The Egyptian in Libya and the Tunisian in Saudi Arabia feel that they are participating in a development project which involves them just as much as the development of their own country. The 'proletarianisation' of migrant labour is far less evident than in Europe.

Whereas the migrant to Europe nearly always belongs to the same social group, inter-Arab migration affects a far broader range of individuals. When we talk about Euro-Arab migration we usually mean emigration by manual workers. As far as doctors, scholars, researchers, university lecturers, engineers and highly skilled technicians are concerned this is regarded as a separate problem: the brain drain.[33]

If we considered migration by manual workers and highly skilled staff within the framework of a single overall analysis we would find this analysis lacking in explanatory power. It should be noted that there are no intermediate groups between the two extremes.

When on the other hand we deal with inter-Arab migration we discover that immigrants come from a wide range of social groups. In certain cases it can be shown that the majority consist of technicians and management staff. This reduces the difficulties involved in the integration of the migrant with the local population, whatever the social status of the former.

Naturalisation procedures have been greatly simplified. An Arab can acquire Qatari nationality in a fortnight. The Arab Community is more than just a slogan. The Arab labour market for non-nationals is in no way identical to the European market for immigrant labour.

If we return to the work done by M. Farrag we discover (in Tables 3.30 and 3.31) that immigrants belong to widely differing social groups. In Qatar for example, 94.1 per cent of all workers who have received higher education are foreigners, but 84.3 per cent of illiterates are also non-nationals. The scale of the Qatar government's efforts to train management and supervisory staff is shown by the fact that already a quarter of the workers who have received a primary education or an elementary technical training are nationals. This situation is fairly similar to the situation in the United Arab Emirates. Nationals play a greater role in the labour force.

Table 3.30 Level of Education of Arab Workers in Qatar and the UAE

Level of education	Qatar		UAE	
	Nationals	Non-nationals	Nationals	Non-nationals
Illiterates	15.7	84.3	49	51
Primary	24.3	75.7	34	66
Secondary and	13.7	86.3	7	93
technical	25.7	74.3		
Higher education	5.9	94.1	7	93
Total	16.9	83.1	43	57

Source: M.A.M. Farrag, 'Migration between Arab Countries'.

None the less 93 per cent of workers who have received a higher education, 82 per cent of those who have had a secondary or technical education, and 66 per cent of those who have benefited only from a primary education are non-nationals. Illiteracy is at a more or less similar level in both the national and the non-national labour force. In this kind of environment the immigrant does not automatically occupy a menial role. This is an additional factor favouring inter-Arab migration.

In Bahrain non-nationals are concentrated almost totally among unqualified workers (where they make up 42.4 per cent of the total)

and highly qualified workers where they make up 60 per cent of the total. The Libyan situation is similar. Non-nationals constitute 24.5 per cent of the unqualified population and 55.9 per cent of management and supervisory staff.

Table 3.31 Arab Workers in Libya and Bahrain by Level of Qualification

Level of qualification	Libya		Bahrain	
	Nationals	Non-nationals	Nationals	Non-nationals
Unskilled	75.5	24.5	57.6	42.4
Skilled and semi-skilled	81.2	18.8	61.5	38.5
Liberal professions	86.2	13.8	80.2	19.8
Technician	79.8	20.2	64.5	35.5
Management and supervisory staff	44.1	55.9	40.0	60.0
Total	16.9	83.1	43.0	57.0

Source: M.A.M. Farrag, *Migration between Arab Countries.*

For many countries, including Egypt, Lebanon and more recently Tunisia, this export of skills has begun to represent a considerable proportion both of Euro-Arab and inter-Arab immigration. For a long time now Egypt has acted as a supplier of competent management and supervisory staff for use in other Arab countries. None the less, with our present level of knowledge we are unable to give any more detailed evaluation of the sectorial distribution of foreign workers. The fact remains that levels of skill and of education amongst inter-Arab migrants differ enormously. We are dealing here with a market with a marked absorptive capacity at all levels, and where recruitment has still to be effectively rationalised, as it has been on the European labour market. This, incidentally, has limited the range of the Euro-Arab dialogue which has suffered from the inequality of the two partners, an inequality which always works in favour of one side.

Given the pattern of Arab development, major investment has been distributed in such a way that demand for manual labour in the Gulf States, Saudi Arabia and even Libya has been relatively limited. The main demand has been for highly qualified management and supervisory staff. Demand for less skilled workers is concentrated in the tertiary sector. If one examines Saudi Arabia for example one sees that the industrialisation process is founded on investment in sophisticated high technology. As Galia Saouma has written: 'The oil rent makes it possible to buy modern techniques; the "turnkey" formula gives access to new technologies and encourages the professional training of technicians "in situ". This formula however, with all it implies in terms of dependency on imported machinery, spare parts and computer systems, hinders the search for a specific development model for the oil-producing countries.'[34] It makes short-term manpower planning practically impossible. The danger is worsened by the oil-producing Arab states' inability to create a basis for genuine development. For the moment there has been no Arab technological revolution. Certainly the Arab world has witnessed enormous technological achievements; these however have been Western achievements on Arab soil. They have been financed with Arab capital but this is not everything. As Ms Saouma has written: 'The purchase of technological know-how has had its costs in terms both of time and men. At the same time however there can be no doubt that this is the price which must be paid [if these countries are] to cease living off the oil-rent and become productive economies.'

In other words, given the structure of the oil-producing economies it is impossible to study the Arab labour market as an independent entity. It needs to be considered together with the European labour market, world flows of capital and technology and its ability to absorb that technology. Individual workers who prefer to migrate to other Arab countries rather than to Europe do so for many reasons. Religious, ethnic and nationalist motivations may well play a determining role in their choice. None the less the shape of the labour market as a whole is determined by economic considerations and primarily by economic considerations having to do with the Western world.

The development of the Arab agricultural sector has been on a very small scale and has limited itself to involving local manpower. The extremely poor results achieved by the grandiose project to transfer between 300,000 and 500,000 Egyptian *Fellahs* is due, we believe – and a deeper enquiry would here be extremely useful – to the fact that a worker accepts migration only if he believes this will improve his economic and social position. Many people have asked whether this improvement is possible without the worker first leaving the agricultural sector. Superficially at least, it would not seem as if they were mistaken. The worker perceives an improvement in his economic and social condition only when he changes his sector of activity.

In an article which is extremely relevant to this problem, M. Birouti has noted the contradiction between the development plans adopted by many Arab countries, which give priority to industrialisation, and the fact that it is the tertiary sector, which does not receive this priority, that none the less generates the most employment. He thus concludes, rightly, that

> this is due to the fact that in the modern sector techniques have been chosen involving a low intensity of labour. In the oil-rich countries, where the abundance of primary products is paired with a labour shortage, the adoption of advanced methods is not only possible but essential. Even in other countries there exist sectors where there is no choice. In heavy industry, the sector which is often granted priority, the use of advanced techniques is usually essential. None the less it seems that the Arab countries have a tendency to give preference to imported technology. This is obviously more advanced than technology available within the Arab world; at the same time however it uses less labour, costs more, is difficult to use and requires great care in maintenance. The methods used are usually taught by foreign consultants or by local engineers, trained abroad. The result is often the creation of islands of modernity in an ocean of backwardness. These create very few new jobs and lead to a significant loss of employment in traditional sectors of the economy.[35]

The development of the tertiary and secondary sectors is closely tied to technology transfers and to non-Arab investment. In 1967 Western Europe invested $1,209 million in the Arab world; the USA invested $1,565 million making a grand total of $2,775 million (see Tables 3.32 and 3.33).

In 1973 the OECD countries invested more than $3,795 million in the Arab world. The United States invested $2,682 million in the Middle East alone (including Israel). This employment-creation investment obviously helps to meet requirements deriving from decisions often taken outside the Arab world.

These figures, although very limited, show how the sums invested in the Arab countries, although large in absolute terms, are very small compared either to capital accumulation in the Western countries or to the oil rent. In 1972 and 1973 for example OECD investment in the Mediterranean countries totalled less than $2 billion. In the same period gross fixed capital formation in the EEC amounted to $368 billion.[36] It is thus impossible to claim that Western investment in the Arab world could become a crucial element in a substitute policy for emigration. We will return shortly to this question of whether investment in migrants' countries of origin could act as a substitute for emigration.

Table 3.32 Investment by Western European Countries in Specified Arab Countries (1967, $ US Million)

Country	Oil	Mining	Industry	Commerce	Others	Total
Syria	15.0	–	–	–	–	15.0
Iraq	141.0	–	1.7	–	–	142.7
Lebanon	19.9	–	8.0	1.5	10.5	39.9
Jordan	2.0	–	0.5	0.5	3.0	6.0
Egypt	15.0	–	1.0	1.0	–	17.0
Libya	90.0	–	11.0	8.2	22.0	131.2
Tunisia	49.5	8.0	49.9	4.0	14.7	126.1
Algeria	557.0	–	22.0	2.0	4.5	585.5
Morocco	30.0	35.0	40.5	9.0	28.0	142.5
Saudi Arabia	–	–	2.0	–	1.5	3.5
Total	919.4	43.0	136.6	26.2	84.2	1,209.4

Source: J. Sassoon, 'Labour and Capital Movements in the Mediterranean Area'.

It should be noted that both European and American investment is heavily concentrated in the oil sector. In 1967 out of total investment of $2,771.1 million nearly 85 per cent, that is $2,344.4 million, was invested in oil. Once again this is a sector which generates very little employment.

American and European investment in the Arab world should be compared with the total availability of petrodollars: $51.7 billion in 1974 and $90.51 billion in 1975.

Given these enormous resources in the hands of the oil-producing states the role of foreign investment obviously differs from country to country, this being due to the lack of homogeneity within the Arab world and to differences in socio-economic structures, and thus in the degree of interest in receiving investment from any source.

In practice the major Arab oil-producing countries act as host countries for Arab labour. At the same time however they invest in labour-supplying countries, even outside the Arab world. In the first nine months of 1975 the oil-producing countries supplied about $3 billion to neighbouring countries.[37] Nearly half of this sum was supplied by Saudi Arabia.[38] This represented a considerable effort.

Table 3.33 American Investment in Specified Arab Countries (1967, $ US Million)

Country	Oil	Mining	Industry	Commerce	Various	Total
Syria	20.0	–	0.2	–	–	20.2
Iraq	44.0	–	–	–	–	44.0
Lebanon	26.0	–	12.0	3.0	9.0	50.0
Jordan	15.0	–	0.5	0.5	2.0	18.0
Egypt	35.0	–	1.0	2.0	3.0	41.0
Libya	440.0	–	3.0	3.0	1.0	447.0
Tunisia	–	–	6.0	1.0	6.0	13.0
Algeria	110.0	–	4.0	1.0	–	115.0
Morocco	5.0	4.0	12.0	2.0	12.0	35.0
Saudi Arabia	770.0	–	5.0	5.0	2.5	782.5
Total	1,465.0	4.0	43.7	17.5	35.5	1,565.7

Source: J. Sassoon, 'Labour and Capital Movements in the Mediterranean Area'.

The policy decisions taken by Arab countries in the field of employment-creation differ considerably. Algerian policy on industrialisation for example aims to provide a lasting solution to the problem of under-development. This country, which acts as a major supplier of migrant labour to France, has a clear point of view on employment. If Algeria has succeeded in halting her migratory flow this is very probably due to her success with the Agrarian Reform and the rapid development of the manufacturing sector. It should not be forgotten that Algeria possesses considerable reserves of oil and natural gas and that these, at least to some extent, put her in a favourable position.

Other countries such as Tunisia, with little or no oil, have been forced to rely on the internal market and domestic savings as essential sources of investment. The alternative was to be crushed by indebtedness. Tunisia thus provides about 80 per cent of the funds necessary for investment in the country. In 1971-2 Egypt financed 71 per cent of public investment from savings in the public sector.[39]

In other words, neither petrodollars nor Western investment have been directed towards where they would have been most useful for development or where local labour is most readily available. For the moment at least there has been no major flow of capital towards Iraq, Egypt, Tunisia or Algeria and less still towards the Yemen.

It is completely normal that capital should move to where it can earn the best return rather than to where it would be most useful. The Arab example leads us to respond with scepticism to all those who have seen Western capital investment in the labour-supplying countries as an alternative to migration. This question was discussed at the CICRED's Buenos Aires seminar. The participants arrived at the following conclusion, fully confirmed, it seems, by our analysis of developments in the Arab world.

> Even if one accepts that a country might succeed in fully or partially substituting capital transfers with imported foreign man-power, in practice it is highly probable that capital will move where investment is most profitable and not necessarily to the developing countries. What is more, although from a purely economic point of view foreign investment could have exactly the same effect on development as emigration, political considerations may also play an important role and render foreign investment undesirable for developing countries. Negotiations on the conditions in which foreign capital could be invested could provide solutions for some countries' problems. Generally however it is impossible for the developing countries to halt emigration while they wait for the arrival of fresh foreign investment. Practice proves once again that the pattern and intensity of the majority of international migration is determined by the policies adopted in the industrialized countries.[40]

Joseph Sassoon has posed exactly the same problem for the Mediterranean world. He too concludes by asking 'what has changed on the European front to bring about a change in the short run in the attitude of European businessmen to investment location in the Mediterranean countries capable of reversing the flow of migrants? In my opinion, very little.'[41]

As far as Euro-Arab relations are concerned it should be borne in mind that a solution depends more on decisions taken at a European and an Arab regional level than on decisions by individual countries. On account of its oil resources, its managers and its cultural affinities, and despite political tensions, a number of factors within the Arab world favour a positive solution. Once more, complete information is unavailable. The Algerian experience, where emigration has been halted, must be followed closely and analysed.

Never has the potential for Arab development been higher than it is today. This does not mean however that in the coming years one should expect a reversal of the present Euro-Arab migratory flow. Our analysis has convinced us that the phenomenon is irreversible and that a general return of migrants to their countries of origin is pure utopia. At the same time however the industrialisation process underway in Algeria, Tunisia, Egypt and Iraq and the development of oil-producing economies based on the expansion of the tertiary sector in the others signify the emergence of a new situation which should cause present relations of dependency to be transformed into complementary relations between equal partners. This 'rectification' of Euro-Arab relations is written in the logic of history.

Clearly the present balance of power is not always visible. Certain countries such as Germany continue to think only of their own interests. Others such as Algeria suffer from impatience and would like to jump stages in the development process. Others still, such as Tunisia, use courage and courtesy as tools to win a stronger role than their real economic weight should theoretically allow.

Other considerations must also be taken into account. The emergence of Arab poles of financial influence and industrial development is likely to attract migratory flows which up till now have always been directed towards Europe. Pakistanis, Indians and even black Africans have been attracted.

Although there is no attempt to create a system in competition with the European system the Arab world is already tending to impose a new kind of not always easy partnership with Europe. In the Arab world the new international division of labour or as some have preferred to call it, the new economic order, is for the first time beginning to be something more than a mere slogan.

If one takes an overall view of emigration, both within the Arab world and between the Arab world and Europe one can see that in both cases we are dealing with a similar phenomenon, even if it takes on different forms. Arab emigration is due to population problems and to the structural difficulties facing the countries where the migrants originate in their efforts to increase their GNP and to improve living standards. The privileged relationship existing between the Maghreb and Europe and more especially France, have drained most of the Maghreb emigration. The oil-producing countries have taken up the majority of migrant workers from the Middle East. Proximity and the existence of transport and telecommunications systems have played an extremely important role.

Flows of migrant workers thus serve to create affinity between the Arab countries and Mediterranean Europe. These affinities are no mere formality. Resting on entire communities who contribute through their work to the growth of the European economic system they are very real. Through their savings and their culture these communities of foreign workers keep cultural relations alive and force the politicians to take account of their aspirations. The general problem of migration remains; it needs however to be posed differently than in the past.

Policies of assimilation have had their day. Problems of adaptation and of participation are problems of integration rather than of assimilation. The host countries must attempt to integrate their foreign labour force rather than trying to assimilate it. This is a precondition if the Euro-Arab dialogue is to have any sense.

New solutions have to be found. If, as we have never ceased to repeat, emigration is no longer a short-term economic phenomenon but rather a structural one, the integration problem can no longer be seen simply from the point of view of the European host countries or of individual workers. The problem of integration is a general problem. The problems of migration, capital flow and technology transfers must be treated at a regional level, as part of the general problem of relations between the countries on the northern and southern shores of the Mediterranean.

The main problem facing European economic growth is how to find the energy to overcome the present crisis and to set off on a new track. The problem of Arab development is radically different; the question is how to create within the Arab world optimal conditions for the satisfaction of the demand for work while at the same time respecting each country's specific economic, social and political requirements; this of course means investment and the exploitation of modern technology.

Once we have finally rid ourselves of outdated ideas, of artificial drives for power, of the thousand and one forms taken on by dependency relations – all of which requires a long, painful and difficult effort – we will finally be able to recognise the basic complementarity existing between the concerns, potentials and requirements of the Arab world and those of Europe. The Mediterranean unites us. Today it is even less of a barrier than in the past. The future belongs to those countries which succeed in joining their efforts. We are far from achieving this. Certainly there has been co-operation on occasions. Triangular co-operation has been tried here and there:

between Saudi Arabia, Tunisia and France, for example in the fields of television and telecommunications. Each partner contributes what he is able to contribute: capital, technology and labour. These timid experiments must be encouraged. None the less what is really lacking is that change in attitudes necessary if there is to be a real impact on the course of events. Is not the role of research to identify new roads for thought and perhaps for action? The most important strategy in the Euro-Arab dialogue must be a strategy of research.

Notes

1. ILO, *Les migrations internationales de 1945 à 1957* (Geneva, 1959).
2. Ibid., p. 167.
3. Ibid., p. 168.
4. G. Tapinos, *L'émigration étrangère en France* (Paris, PUF, 1975), pp. 29 and 51.
5. Ibid., p. 51. See also P. Bourdieu and A. Darbel, *Travail et Travailleurs algériens en France* (Paris, Morton, 1963).
6. Ph. J. Bernard, *Travailleurs étrangers en Europe Occidentale,* in *Proceedings of the Conference* (Paris – Sorbonne, 5-7 June 1974; La Haye, Mouton, 1976), pp. 80–81.
7. Tapinos, *L'émigration étrangère*, p. 14.
8. Ibid., p. 14.
9. P. Vincent, in *Population*, no. 3, 1946.
10. Tapinos, *L'émigration étrangère,* p. 15.
11. Cf. Heinz Werner, 'Migration and Free Movement of Workers in Western Europe' in Ph. J. Bernard, *Travailleurs étrangers,* pp. 63–5.
12. OECD, *L'OCDE et les migrations internationales* (Paris, 1975), p. 7.
13. Ibid., p. 9.
14. 'La rémuneration des travailleurs immigrés en France', *Revue Internationale du Travail*, no. 2 (February 1975), pp. 156 ff.
15. G. Tapinos, *L'économie des migrations internationales* (Paris, A. Colin, 1974), pp. 197 ff.
16. Ibid., p. 14.
17. J.L. Reiffers, *Le rôle de l'immigration des travailleurs dans la croissance de la République Fédérale d'Allemagne de 1958 à 1965* (Geneva, ILO, March 1970), p. 38.
18. ONU, *Etude sur la situation économique de l'Europe en 1975* (New York, 1976), p. 18.
19. For more details see J. Benoit, 'Face à la crise: le verrouillage européen', *Le Droit Social*, no. 5 (May 1976), pp. 6–10.
20. Ibid., p. 19.
21. Bernard, *Travailleurs étrangers,* p. 9. See also B. Kayser, *Le retour conjoncturel des travailleurs migrants* (Paris, OECD, 1972), and the SOPEMI report, 1975.
22. DATAR, La Documentation française, *Regard prospectif sur le bassin méditerranéen,* 1973.
23. United Nations Secretariat, *International Migration Trends, 1950–1970,* in United Nations, *The Population Debate: Dimensions and Perspectives* (Papers

of the World Population Conference, Bucharest, 1974), vol. I, p. 247.

24. Ibid.

25. Ibid., paragraphs 36 and 37 of the Final Report, vol. I, p. 253.

26. DATAR, La Documentation française, *Regard prospectif sur le bassin méditerranéen* (1973).

27. Ibid.

28. Study on the field by M. Mtar, unpublished.

29. M.A.M. Farrag, *Migration between Arab Countries* in *Manpower and Employment in Arab Countries* (Geneva, ILO, 1976).

30. This is the minimum number, which has been ascertained. Other estimates have calculated a figure of 2 million workers. Farrag himself does not hesitate to quote a figure of two and a half million as being extremely probable. We prefer to base our analysis on the minimum figure. This obviously excludes seasonal workers of whom there are at least a million in the Arab world.

31. Report by the director general of the ILO at the 199th session of the ILO board of directors, Geneva, March 1976.

32. Egyptian *Fellah* families established in Iraq (July 1976).

Number of families	: 100
Average age	: 35
Education	: nearly 100% illiteracy
Training	: traditional agriculture
Bachelors	: 12
Married without children	: 12
Married with 1 child	: 12
Married with 2 children	: 23
Married with 3 children	: 24
Married with 4 children	: 7
Married with 5 children	: 5
Married with 6 children	: 3
Married with 7 children	: 1
Total heads of family + family members	: 396

33. This question has been studied in considerable detail: UNITAR and Columbia University have published numerous reports in which the Arab 'brain drain' is examined in considerable depth. Cf. 'Brain Drain and Study Abroad' (1976), 'The Migration and Return of Professionals' (1972) (unpublished papers). See also Walter Adams, *The Brain Drain* (New York, Macmillan, 1968); Elyas Zayne, *Higrat al Admigha al Arabiya* (Beirut, 1972 (arabic)).

34. Galia Saouma, *Le Monde arabe à la recherche de soi-même* (Rome, Istituto Affari Internazionali, 1976), p. 45.

35. 'Le problème de promotion de l'emploi dans les pays arabes', *Revue Internationale du Travail,* vol. 114, no. 3, p. 200.

36. Joseph Sassoon, 'Labour and Capital Movements in the Mediterranean Area', *Lo Spettatore internazionale* (Rome), vol. XI, no. 1, p. 19.

37. *Grants and Loans to Third World* by the Saudi Development Fund and the Afesd Commitments from 1.1.75 to 1.10.75.

38. $36.3 million through the Saudi Development Fund, $1,150 million to other Arab countries and $55 million to other African and Asian countries.

39. Yusuf J. Ahmad, *La capacité d'absorption de L'Economie Egyptienne* (Paris, OECD, 1976), p. 32.

40. Comité International de Coordination des Recherches Nationales en Démographie, *Recherche démographique en liaison avec les migrations internationales,* in United Nations, *The Population Debate,* vol. I, p. 255.

41. Ibid., p. 21.

NOTES ON CONTRIBUTORS

Roberto Aliboni is Professor of International Economics at the University of Naples and Director of Studies at the Istituto Affari Internazionali, Rome. He has published several works on the problems of the Mediterranean countries, and is at present preparing the economic part of the conclusion for the three-year project 'Stability and Development in the Mediterranean'.

Abdelwahab Bouhdiba is Head of the Sociology, Philosophy and Psychology Departments and Director of the Centre d'Etudes et de Recherches Economiques et Sociales at the University of Tunis. In 1972 he was elected member of the United Nations subcommittee for the fight against discrimination and protection of minorities, and was re-elected to this post in 1975 and 1978. He has been on numerous missions on behalf of the Tunisian government, and has published a large number of books and articles on the Arab world.

Zvi Yehuda Hershlag is Director of the David Horowitz Research Institute for the Developing Countries at the University of Tel Aviv. He is co-editor of the journal *Hamisrach Hechadash* (The New East) and President of the Council of the Israeli Institute of International Affairs, Political Doctrine and Problems of Developing Countries. He has published a great number of books and articles on the Middle East, and more recent publications include: *The Implications of Peace in the Middle East* (1973), and *The Economic Structure of the Middle East* (1975). He is currently preparing a book on the philosophy of development or cost-benefits of growth.

Samir A. Makdisi is Chairman of the Department of Economics at the American University of Beirut. He has served as consultant to OPEC and the IMF, the Economic Commission for Western Asia (ECWA) and to the Lebanese government. As well as numerous articles and contributions to books on the Middle East, he has recently published *Financial Policy of Economic Growth, an Assessment of the Lebanese Experience, 1950-1974, with a Look to the Future* (1978), and is currently working on a monograph on Arab economic integration to be published by the International Affairs Institute in Rome.

INDEX

Abu Dhabi 171
Africa, Africans 45, 57, 73, 78, 79, 135, 185
Agence de Promotion des Investissements 49
agriculture 14, 15, 16, 18, 21, 22, 29, 34, 35, 36, 38, 39, 40, 42, 44, 45, 46, 48, 58, 61, 63, 73, 75, 92, 110, 147, 163, 167, 180; employment 161, 171; exports 39, 75
agro-industry 16, 24, 35, 44, 56, 61, 63
Al-Ahram Al-Iqtisadi 68
Al-Baath 78
Albania 73
Alexandria 51, 68
Algeria 26, 28, 29, 30, 33, 41, 44-5, 63, 68, 71, 72, 73, 74, 93, 109, 110, 134, 139, 161, 167, 175, 177, 183, 184, 185; emigration from 137, 138, 145, 163, 166, 184
Algiers 74
alternative costs 57, 61
Arab: Bank for Economic Development in Africa (ABEDIA) 79; Common Market (ACM) 39, 41, 43, 67, 69, 70, 92, 95, 96, 100, 101, 112, 117, 118, 125, 128, 129; Company for Development of Animal Resources 69; Company for Industrial Investments 69; Economic Unity 68; Industrial Conference (Fourth) 52, 68; Industrial Co-ordination Seminar 68; Labour Organisation 136, 175; League 54, 67, 68, 91, 92, 175; Maritime Petroleum Transport Company 69; Mining Company 69; Petroleum Investment Company 69; Petroleum Services Company 69; Pharmaceutical Industry Company 69; Ship-building and Repair Yard Company 69; Union of Cement Factories 71
Arabian Gulf Organisation for Industrial Consulting (AGOIC) 72
Arabic language 134
Arusha agreement 79
Asseily, George 50
Australia 135
Austria 141

Baghdad 51, 52, 68
Bahrain 69, 72, 93, 161, 169, 171, 173, 178
Bairoch, P. 19
balance of payments 17, 48, 53, 57, 64, 81, 114, 117, 163
Banias oil refinery 39
Belgium 139, 141, 147, 155
Birouti, M. 180, 181
Boudhiba, Abdelwahab 10, 11
brain drain 31, 32, 41, 177
building 147, 148, 152, 171, 173; materials 34
bureaucracy 29, 31, 35, 59, 63

Cairo 51
Canada 135
capital 63, 81; costs 20; goods 19, 40, 46, 47, 50, 56, 71, 75, 80, 116, 126; intensity 16, 21, 22, 55, 69, 81; movement 38, 63, 93, 94, 95, 112, 114, 115, 128, 184, 186
Casablanca 47
cement 28, 30, 35, 37, 40, 41, 45, 46, 50, 57, 69, 71, 78, 80, 117
centre-periphery concept 16, 17, 51, 54, 62
cereals 38, 44
chemicals 28, 34, 37, 38, 42, 46, 47, 48, 49, 63, 73, 80, 116; wages 81
China 124
CICRED seminar 155, 184
citrus products 46, 75
Clark-Kuznets model 14
clothing 24, 26, 28, 37, 40, 48, 76, 116
colonialism 134, 147, 167
Comecon 63

commodities 15, 17, 76, 81, 124
common market, concept 114, 127-8, 129
communications 54, 59, 120
comparative advantage 13, 14, 17, 21, 24, 27, 30, 32, 35, 54, 55, 57, 60, 61, 62, 63, 64, 65, 72, 73, 80, 81
competitiveness 13, 18, 20, 23, 26, 35, 39, 44, 58, 63, 75, 106, 108, 110, 111, 120, 127
complementarity 13, 39, 41, 106, 108, 110, 111, 120
construction 37, 45, 54, 59; materials 34, 43, 46, 49, 78
consumer goods 18, 19, 28, 40, 42, 46, 47, 50, 56, 57, 58, 59, 63, 80
consumption 18, 19, 29, 56, 108, 109
cotton 27, 34, 37, 38, 63, 70
Council of Arab Economic Unity (CAEU) 68, 70, 92, 96
currency 93, 94, 147, 163, 166
customs: duties 92; union 108, 109, 114, 126-7
Cyprus, Cypriots 67, 158, 175

Damascus 78
Dams 38, 57
Dar al Islam 134, 135
Dar ul h'arb 135
DATAR 155, 157
Delouvrier, P. 142
demand 16, 22, 37, 55, 61, 62, 65, 67, 80, 81
desalination 61, 78
desert settlement 78
detergents 40, 46
developed countries 19, 63, 108
developing countries 14, 19, 22, 63, 108, 114, 129
Doha (Qatar) 72
Dumont, J. Pierre 157

East Bank 40
economic co-operation, Arab 50, 52, 55, 58, 65, 73-80, 90-130
economic integration, Arab 13, 15, 18, 41, 50, 52, 54, 58, 60, 61, 62, 63-73, 76, 79, 80, 90, 106, 108, 109, 110, 111, 112, 113, 115-29, 186
economic policy, Arab 111-13, 114, 129
economies of scale 13, 14, 17, 32, 47, 52, 54, 55, 60, 62, 64, 65, 72, 73, 80, 81, 115, 117
Economist, The 76
education and training 22, 31, 42, 43, 44, 54, 70, 178, 179, 180
Egypt 13, 26, 27, 28, 29, 30, 33-6, 39, 41, 43, 53, 54, 63, 66, 71, 72, 74, 76, 78, 92, 94, 96, 100, 107, 109, 110, 113, 118, 124, 161, 167, 169, 177, 179, 180, 183, 184, 185; and emigration 169, 171, 174, 175, 177, 179, 180; bureaucracy 35, 59; wages in 81, 168
electrical industry 30, 34, 44, 48
electricity 35, 37, 38, 40, 43, 46, 48, 110
electronics 39, 42
employment 17, 22, 26, 34, 37, 46, 51, 53, 54, 59, 60, 147, 181, 183; industrial 16, 26, 107, 110
energy 19, 27, 38, 45, 48, 54, 59, 81
Engel curve 29
engineering 34, 38, 43, 48, 49, 50, 69, 70, 73
England 14, 27
entrepreneurship 15, 29, 30, 37, 38, 62
Euphrates 38, 175
European Economic Community (EEC) 39, 45, 50, 63, 64, 66, 68, 73-6, 77, 79, 181; and immigration 137-71 *passim*; Common Agricultural Policy (CAP) 73
exchange policies 93-4, 112, 114
exports 16, 17, 20, 21, 23, 24, 26, 29, 38, 42, 46, 47, 49, 50, 53, 57, 58, 62, 65, 66, 70, 96, 100, 101, 116, 121, 124, 125, 126; promotion 23, 45, 47, 55, 57, 58, 62, 116
extractive industries 14, 19, 37, 171

factor endowments 11, 13, 15, 17, 20, 21, 22, 24, 41, 53, 55, 60, 61, 62, 63, 65, 73, 81
Farrag, Abdelmajid 169, 178
feasibility 43, 56, 63, 72
fertilisers 24, 35, 41, 42, 46, 47, 48, 58, 61, 69, 70, 71, 78
financial resources 81, 94-5, 121
finished products 38, 47, 50, 65
fishing 69, 171

food industry 15, 24, 26, 28, 34, 37, 38, 40, 41, 42, 44, 46, 47, 48, 49, 58, 148
footwear 26, 30, 40, 48
France 15, 17, 27, 49, 50, 74, 75, 134, 155, 187; and immigration 137-54 *passim*, 166, 169, 183
free trade area 92, 113, 114, 125-6, 127
free zones 24, 38, 78
fuel 19, 37, 50
furniture 26, 28, 48, 49, 148

gas 28, 30, 37, 42, 44, 45, 46, 48, 53, 183; liquefaction 28, 44, 61, 78
Germany, West 17, 24; and immigration 139, 141, 146, 147, 148, 153, 154, 155, 185
Ghana 79
Gibraltar 139
global LDCs context 55-6, 62
global Mediterranean policy (GMP) 75
grain 58
Granier, R. 152
grapes 44
Great Britain 17, 18, 39, 146, 155
Greece, Greeks 9, 74, 140, 147, 175
growth, economic 14, 16, 17, 29, 31, 33, 37, 40, 41, 42, 44, 45, 47, 49, 55, 57, 60, 61, 161, 167, 173
Gulf states 28, 109, 113, 169, 171, 174, 179

handicrafts 24, 26, 29, 30, 61
Hansen, Bent 55
heavy industry 28, 37, 42, 44, 45, 49, 50, 56, 57, 63, 181
Heckscher-Ohlin theory 20
Herschlag, Zvi Y. 10
hides and skins 37, 44
Hirschman, A. O. 15, 59
Hoffman, W.G. 18
Hong Kong 17
hydrocarbons 44, 57

IDA 40, 46
illiteracy 35, 177, 178
imports 29, 38, 47, 50, 96, 100, 101, 124, 125, 126; substitution 17, 21, 23, 24, 26, 32, 47, 49, 53, 56, 57, 58, 61, 62, 65, 66, 67, 71, 72, 116, 127
income 22; per capita 14, 17, 18, 45, 53, 57, 106, 107; tax 113
Indians 169, 175, 185
Industrial Development Bank 41
Industrial Development Centre for Arab States (IDCAS) 54, 68, 69
industrialisation 13-82, 116, 117, 127, 181, 183, 185; philosophy and strategy 14-24, 51-63
industry 18, 21, 22, 26, 33, 34, 38, 40, 41, 42, 52, 61
INED 144
inflation 33, 40, 57, 112, 168
infrastructure 21, 22, 37, 39, 41, 59, 62, 63, 175, 177
innovation 15, 20
inter-Arab trade 95-101
interest rate 112, 114
intermediate goods 46, 47, 92
International Labour Organisation (ILO) 136, 146, 158, 168
International Monetary Fund (IMF) 36
investment, domestic and foreign 16, 17, 19, 20, 21, 22, 24, 29, 30, 34, 35, 37, 38, 41, 49, 51, 53, 55, 59, 60, 61, 63, 70, 94, 117, 128, 148, 181, 182, 183, 184; goods 40, 47, 56; trends 60
invisibles 93, 94
inward and outward oriented strategy 55, 58
Iran 67
Iraq 13, 26, 28, 29, 30, 33, 41-4, 54, 68, 71, 72, 81, 92, 94, 96, 100, 109, 110, 118, 167, 184, 185
iron and steel 19, 24, 27, 28, 30, 35, 40, 44, 47, 48, 49, 50, 57, 61, 63, 69, 72, 73, 78, 80, 148
irrigation 78
Islamic Development Bank (IDB) 79
Israel 26, 29, 33, 40, 67, 73, 74, 76, 77, 78, 81, 167, 171, 181
Israeli-Arab context 54-5
Istituto Affari Internazionali 9
Italy 44, 49, 75, 137, 140, 145

Japan 17, 71, 124
Johnson, Harry G. 20
joint ventures 24, 65, 68, 120, 128-9
Jordan 13, 26, 28, 29, 32, 33, 39-41, 54, 66, 74, 92, 93, 96, 100, 109, 112, 118, 121, 160, 161, 174, 177

Kaunda, Kenneth 79
Kemal Ataturk 82
know-how 43, 67, 78, 81
Koreans 11
Kuwait 26, 28, 40, 54, 66, 67, 69, 72, 78, 93, 94, 101, 117, 118, 121, 160, 161, 167, 168, 169, 171, 173, 174, 177; Fund for Arab Economic Development (KFAED) 79

Labour 19, 20, 55, 60, 81, 114, 115, 157; division 20, 60, 62, 81, 185; migration 41, 136-87 *passim*
land reclamation 63
leather 28, 30, 37, 46, 48
Lebanon 26, 28, 29, 50-1, 54, 74, 93, 101, 106, 107, 109, 110, 113, 118, 121, 161, 169, 179
Leontieff, Wassily 51, 55
less developed countries (LDCs) 15, 16, 17, 18, 19, 20, 21, 23, 24, 28, 51, 52, 55-6, 58, 62, 64, 72, 73, 79, 80, 109
levels of development 106-8
liberalisation 18, 19, 30, 36, 37, 39, 49
Libya 26, 29, 40, 54, 69, 73, 93; and immigration 139, 160-79 *passim*
licensing 92, 100, 113
light industry 32, 44, 45, 46, 48
linkages 15, 18, 34, 59, 71, 72, 81
Lipsey, R.G. 108
Liquefied Petroleum Gas (LPG) 71
List, Friedrich 15
location of industry 22, 28, 32, 61-2, 72, 81
Luxembourg 141, 147, 155

machinery and equipment 29, 38, 43, 117, 118
Maghreb countries 45, 50, 73, 74, 75, 137, 138, 140, 147, 160, 163, 166, 167, 169, 185
Maguid, Abdel 77
Makdisi, Samir 10
Malta 74
management 18, 29, 30, 35, 44, 45, 49, 73, 110, 178, 179
manufacturing 10, 16, 17, 19, 26, 28, 29, 32, 36, 37, 41, 42, 45, 46, 48, 49; exports 17, 20, 100, 101, 116, 117, 118, 120, 127, 128, 183
Marcian, J.P. 152
market, marketing 18, 20, 22, 23, 32, 45, 57, 58, 59, 65, 70, 73, 81
Mashreq countries 39, 73, 74
Mauritania 73
Mead, J.E. 108
mechanical industry 30, 37, 44, 48, 148, 152
Mediterranean 9, 13, 51, 73, 75, 141, 184, 186
metal industries 34, 37, 38, 40, 46, 49, 81, 148
Middle East: conflict 52, 74, 75, 76, 78; investment in 181
migration, Arab 11, 48, 134-87
military industry 33, 35, 39, 53, 67
minerals 19, 20, 26, 29, 30, 48
mining 14, 26, 37, 40, 41, 45, 46, 47, 48, 49
monetary policy 112
Morocco 26, 28, 29, 33, 45-8, 71, 72, 73, 74, 76, 93, 101, 109, 110; and immigration 134-9, 161-7 *passim*
motor vehicles 30, 35, 43, 46, 47, 57, 80, 148
Muhammad Ali 53, 82
multinationals 15, 19, 24, 43, 57
Myrdal, Gunnar 15, 16

Nathan, R. 142
national income 39, 81
nationalisation 35, 38
nationalism, Arab 65-6
naturalisation 178
Netherlands 139, 141, 147, 153, 155
nomadism 135
north-south relations 52
nuclear energy 61, 78

Obaid, Ibrahim A. 76, 77
October (1973) War 29, 37, 38, 40, 78, 79
Office Cherifien des Phosphates (OCP) 47
oil 13, 19, 28, 29, 34, 35, 41, 42, 44, 45, 47, 48, 49, 52, 53, 63, 65, 66, 67, 68, 69, 73, 76, 78, 79, 109, 110, 117, 120, 121, 125, 167, 181, 182, 183, 184; crude 28, 35, 38, 47, 53, 65; equipment 50; gas 53; prices 15, 17, 78; refined 28, 34, 39, 41, 47, 48, 53
olive oil 42, 48, 50

Oman 72, 93, 161
Organisation for Economic Co-operation and Development (OECD) 17, 68, 146, 147, 153, 181
Organisation of Arab Petroleum Exporting Countries (OAPEC) 54, 70, 73, 78
Organisation of Petroleum Exporting Countries (OPEC) 15, 28, 42, 64, 73, 78, 79; Special Fund 79

Pakistanis 11, 169, 175, 185
Palestine, Palestinians 169, 171, 174
Pan-Arabic Congress 67
paper 28, 37, 40, 46, 48, 69, 117
peace mentality 77, 78
Perroux, François 16
petrochemicals 24, 28, 35, 42, 44, 45, 61, 63, 71, 73, 78, 111
pharmaceuticals 38, 40, 41, 42, 48, 70, 78
phosphates 32, 38, 40, 41, 42, 45, 46, 47, 48, 58, 65, 76
planning 18, 21, 38, 39, 40, 43, 47, 49, 60, 62, 63, 72, 111
plastics 42, 71, 148
political harmonisation 115
population 15, 18, 24, 33, 36, 41, 48, 57, 141, 142, 144, 145, 155, 156, 160, 161, 167, 168, 185; growth 60, 167-8, 173; INED review 144
ports 59, 69
Portugal 9, 140, 147
power 30, 37, 38, 63
Prebisch, Raoul 14, 16
prices 15, 18, 55, 59, 75, 76, 78, 108
priorities 22, 62
production 15, 17, 22, 31, 35, 53, 56, 59, 70, 108; goods 19, 56, 58
productivity 14, 19, 29, 30, 31, 32, 35, 37, 44, 57, 59, 65, 81, 163
profits 21, 38, 63, 94
protectionism 35, 49, 62

Qatar 72, 93, 94, 167, 169, 171, 178
quality of life 18
quotas 92

Rabat 47
raw materials 29, 35, 36, 38, 47, 55, 75, 81; processing 14, 17, 38, 43, 61, 63
refineries 61, 73, 78
Reiffers, J.L. 153
research and development (R & D) 18, 32, 44, 78
Reshaping the International Order (RIO) 17
residual production factor (R) 31, 32
resource use 115, 117
Romania 39
Rosenstein-Rodan, P. N. 16
Rostow, W. W. 15
rubber 42, 148
rural-urban migration 51, 135, 161

Sabbagh, Nabil 68
Saouma, Galia 180
Sassoon, Joseph 184
Saudi Arabia 11, 26, 29, 40, 54, 66, 68, 69, 93, 109, 167, 168, 169, 173, 174, 177, 183, 187; Development Fund (SDF) 79; Research and Development Corporation 39
Schuman, Robert 142
Schumpeter, J. A. 15
self-reliance/self-sufficiency 15, 58, 62, 71, 80
semi-finished goods 38, 47, 50
services 18, 40, 46, 49
shanty towns 51, 60
Sinai 78
Singapore 17
Skikda 45
small-scale industry 26, 30, 40, 41, 42, 47, 55, 59
Smith, Adam 15
socialism 19, 33, 36, 37, 41, 42, 43, 63
solar energy 61, 78
Somalia 73
Spain 9, 73, 137, 140, 146, 147
Special Arab Fund for Africa (SAFA) 79
storage 45, 59
structure: Arab economies 108-11; industry 29, 53
Sudan 13, 26, 29, 70, 72, 73, 106, 107, 110, 124, 161
Suez 34, 78
sugar 42, 70
Sutcliffe, R.B. 26
Suweira 43
Switzerland 141, 147
Syria 13, 26, 28, 29, 30, 32, 33,

Syria—*cont.*
36-9, 41, 43, 54, 63, 66, 71, 72, 73, 74, 92, 94, 96, 100, 107, 109, 110, 112, 118, 121, 124, 161; and emigration 169, 174; Supreme Planning Council 38

Tapinos, G. 142, 145
targets, development 13, 14, 18, 21, 53, 54, 56, 58, 62, 70
tariffs 23, 26, 41, 58, 66, 74, 75, 92, 108, 112, 113, 125, 126, 127
technology 15, 17, 18, 22, 32, 43, 57, 59, 61, 65, 69, 75, 80, 81, 110, 180, 181, 186
telecommunications 177, 185, 187
textiles 24, 27, 28, 34, 37, 38, 40, 42, 46, 47, 48, 49, 63, 69, 70, 73, 76, 116, 117, 148; wages 81
'the 77' 64
Tinbergen, J. 20
tobacco 37, 42, 48
tourism 40
tractors and trucks 43, 58, 71
trade and transit treaty 92
trade: creation and diversion 17, 108, 109, 116; inter-Arab 95-101; trends 59, 60
transfer payments 39, 93, 113, 114
transport 19, 27, 38, 47, 54, 59, 67, 120; equipment 117, 118
Treaty of Arab Economic Unity 92
Tunisia 26, 28, 29, 33, 48-50, 73, 74, 93, 101, 109, 110, 118, 134, 160, 161, 167, 168, 177, 179, 183, 184, 185, 187; emigration from 138, 139, 163, 165-6, 174, 175
Turkey, Turks 67, 74, 140, 147, 158, 169, 175

Umma community 134
underemployment 51, 163
underutilised capacity 16, 27, 31, 35, 36, 47, 70, 116
unemployment 16, 31, 154, 160, 163, 166
United Arab Emirates (UAE) 72, 93, 112, 161, 167, 169, 171, 178
United Nations (UN) 26, 64, 68, 153, 154; Conference on Trade and Development (UNCTAD) 64; Statistical Year Book 175
USA 15, 17, 24, 70, 71, 73, 76, 77, 124, 135, 181, 182
USSR 39, 76, 124

value-added 14, 16, 22, 23, 39, 40, 46, 53
vegetable oils and fats 38, 42, 46
Vernon, Raymond 20
Vincent, P. 144
Viner, Jacob 108
Volkswagen 43

wages 20, 35, 81, 147, 148, 149, 152, 168
war of 1967 29, 171
water 37, 61, 177
West Bank 40
Western Europe 121, 124, 181, 182; migrant workers in 138-57
wood 26, 28, 49, 81, 148
World Bank 37

Yaoundè agreement 79
Yemen, North and South 93, 94, 107, 109, 110, 161, 167, 168, 169, 174, 184